"Chuck Eigen is a wide-spectrum therapist with both personal and global interests. From his experience, he introduces us to ten experts of diverse methods who share intimately from their own lives about their work. The result is an informative, exciting, and inspiring book. Through each chapter, this book brings into the twenty-first century ancient wisdom for all. This brilliant book will bring our human race closer."

—*Arnold Mindell, creator of Process-Oriented Psychology, author of* DreamBody, The Shaman's Body, *and many other well-known titles*

"Like the many facets of a crystal, this book brings together a variety of perspectives from individual practitioners in the healing professions. What is unique here, however, are the contributors' personal and professional sharings that bring together and help heal in even a small manner the terrible split in the Western world view between psyche and soma, mind and body, spirit and matter. These sharings are broad and inclusive in their understanding and practice of psychotherapy and human relationships. Chuck Eigen's editorial vision—that all people have within themselves both inner resources and psyche/body wisdom—has been achieved. The reader will not be disappointed."

—*Fred Gustafson, D.Min., Jungian Analyst, author of* The Black Madonna *and* Dancing Between Two Worlds: Jung and the Native American Soul; *editor of* The Moonlit Path: Reflections on the Dark Feminine

"Chuck Eigen's selection of authors, methods, and techniques is inspiring and powerful. His book is a great compilation of approaches acknowledging integration of different aspects of the personality with the endless resources of the body dimension. A tour de force of proven methods in the field."

—*Maria Florentina Sassoli y Ezcurdia, Counselor, Primera Escuela Argentina de Psicologia Humanistica, Counseling Focusing Coordinator for Argentina, Certified Hakomi Therapist*

D1637402

"This book is an intriguing juxtaposition of chapters on a wide variety of approaches to mind/body healing, each written by prominent teachers of their respective approach. In addition to describing the approach, the writers are invited to include their personal journeys, which makes for engaging reading."

—*Richard C. Schwartz, Ph.D., creator of Internal Family Systems Therapy, author of* The Mosaic Mind, The Internal Family Systems Therapy Model, *and* You Are the One You've Been Waiting For

"This new book by Chuck Eigen feels like a winner to me. He has chosen for his authors significant figures in the consciousness world representing a diversity of theory and methodology. He has asked them to be more personal in their presentation so the reader could feel in a more personal way what this particular approach has meant to them in their lives. The result is a series of chapters that are fascinating to read and that bring to the reader a more direct and intense experience of the various approaches. I enjoyed the material and came away feeling that I had really been connected to a deeper experience and understanding of the work of so many of my colleagues. Chuck had a particular kind of vision, which he implemented in bringing this book together, and it most certainly has worked far beyond the usual anthologies."

—*Hal Stone, Ph.D., creator of Voice Dialogue, author of* Embracing Heaven and Earth, Embracing Our Selves: The Voice Dialogue Manual, Partnering: A New Kind of Relationship, *and several other well-known titles*

"*Inner Dialogue in Daily Life* is an important book for our time that uncovers the rich terrain of the psyche. The ease with which each chapter unravels its complexity brings the reader to a deeper level of self-awareness through a multidimensional understanding of its nature. *Inner Dialogue in Daily Life* is a brilliantly composed book that I recommend to anyone who has an interest in more fully participating in his or her life."

—*Kalpana (Rose) M. Kumar, M.D., CEO and Medical Director, The Ommani Center for Integrative Medicine, author of* Becoming Real: Harnessing the Power of Menopause for Health and Success

"Chuck Eigen has found a fascinating assortment from hundreds of psychotherapies that exist today. *Inner Dialogue in Daily Life* elaborates psychotherapies that enrich our inner lives and it speaks from the personal experiences of its finely selected authors. Readers will cross into the delicate and enlightening moments of the authors' experiences to discover what those therapies are all about."

—*Akira Ikemi, Ph.D., Professor, Kansai University Graduate School of Professional Clinical Psychology*

"Chuck Eigen takes us on a journey with some of the great innovators in the field of experiential psychology. To read this book is to find the red thread that unifies these ten different approaches to psychotherapy, including, in the words of Eigen, the emphasis on the relationship with the inner life as well as the outer life.

Following the medical model, therapists have often distanced themselves from their clients, creating a barrier that is often damaging to the therapeutic relationship. Like a fresh breath of air, in this book we not only find approaches that give way to the contrary, we also get a good glimpse of the authors themselves, and how their lives have been touched by the therapy they practice.

This book is an extremely useful and needed reference for all of us in this field, and I imagine it can be equally useful for people trying to decide what therapy to go for, or whom to work with, since, as Eigen points out, the therapist's state of mind and presence is her or his most exquisite remedy. The reader will have a much broader picture of his life and his possibilities after reading this compilation of essays."

—*Rosa Belendez, M.D., Certified Hakomi Trainer, Mexico City*

"This book demonstrates the competence of self-reflection, a skill necessary for every therapist. I want students to read it to gain insight into the ways that therapists have developed reflective practices."

—*Nadya A. Fouad, Ph.D., ABPP, University Distinguished Professor and Chair, Department of Educational Psychology, University of Wisconsin*

"This book targets three distinct readerships with equal effectiveness. If you are an experienced journeyman of the inner realms, but have not thought much of the philosophical underpinnings, this book will offer food for thought and inspiration. If you are widely read in the areas of psychology and spirituality, this book helps synthesize the places of intercept between Eastern and Western thought and between therapy and meditation. And if you have lived your life primarily in the social and cultural realms of practicality, this book may open doors to an interest in other aspects of self yet to be discovered. I felt as though I had been given the essential outline to the evolution of experiential psychology as it has developed in the twenty-first century."

—*Gael Ohlgren Rosewood, Faculty, The Rolf Institute and Continuum Movement*

"*Inner Dialogue in Daily Life*, edited by Charles H. Eigen, is an important book, which allows the reader to sample the rich, creative, and diverse approaches within the vast field of psychotherapy. Each chapter represents various points of view and approaches to psychotherapy. This book offers wisdom for cultivating personal insight, development and change. This book is a compelling read for all of us who wish to deepen our experience with our world and ourselves."

—*Robert Balaban, M.D., former Medical Faculty, Harvard University and the University of Wisconsin*

"This book is fascinating, inspiring, and real. It offers a wise perspective to healing which includes the human spirit—a perspective that modern medicine often lacks. The stories in this book are profoundly human. Reading it is like sitting at the elbow of wise people who have 'figured something out,' and they're letting you in on how they did it. Reading about the writers' journeys gave me a lot of hope for discovery through life—that you never stop learning, and that wisdom can grow."

—*Lisa Marr, M.D., Section Chief, Palliative Medicine, Division of Geriatrics and Palliative Medicine, Department of Internal Medicine, University of New Mexico*

INNER DIALOGUE IN DAILY LIFE

of related interest

The Ethical Space of Mindfulness in Clinical Practice
An Exploratory Essay
Donald McCown
Foreword by Kenneth Gergen
ISBN 978 1 84905 850 6
eISBN 978 0 85700 510 6

The Writer's Key
Creative Solutions for Life
Gillie Bolton
ISBN 978 1 84905 475 1
eISBN 978 0 85700 854 1
Writing for Therapy or Personal Development series

Transformation through Journal Writing
The Art of Self-Reflection for the Helping Professions
Jane Wood
ISBN 978 1 84905 347 1
eISBN 978 0 85700 690 5

Soul and Spirit in Dance Movement Psychotherapy
A Transpersonal Approach
Jill Hayes
Foreword by Daria Halprin
ISBN 978 1 84905 308 2
eISBN 978 0 85700 649 3

Mindfulness and the Arts Therapies
Theory and Practice
Edited by Laury Rappaport
ISBN 978 1 84905 909 1
eISBN 978 0 85700 688 2

Spirit and Psyche
A New Paradigm for Psychology, Psychoanalysis and Psychotherapy
Victor L. Schermer
Foreword by Kenneth Porter
ISBN 978 1 85302 926 4
eISBN 978 1 84642 365 9

INNER DIALOGUE IN DAILY LIFE

Contemporary Approaches to Personal and Professional Development in Psychotherapy

Edited by Charles Eigen

Jessica Kingsley *Publishers*
London and Philadelphia

"This we have now is not imagination" on p.55 from Rumi 1995 translated by Coleman Barks is reproduced by permission of Coleman Barks and Reid Boates Literary Agency "The guest house" on p.79 from Rumi 1995 translated by Coleman Barks is reproduced by permission of Coleman Barks and Reid Boates Literary Agency "Out beyond ideas of wrong-doing and right-doing" on p.187 from Rumi 1995 translated by Coleman Barks is reproduced by permission of Coleman Barks and Reid Boates Literary Agency "Of being woven" on p.203 from Rumi 2004 translated by Coleman Barks with John Moyne is reproduced by permission of Coleman Barks and Reid Boates Literary Agency

First published in 2014
by Jessica Kingsley Publishers
73 Collier Street
London N1 9BE, UK
and
400 Market Street, Suite 400
Philadelphia, PA 19106, USA

www.jkp.com

Copyright © Charles Eigen 2014

Library of Congress Cataloging in Publication Data
A CIP catalog record for this book is available from the Library of Congress

British Library Cataloguing in Publication Data
A CIP catalogue record for this book is available from the British Library

ISBN 978 1 84905 983 1
eISBN 978 0 85700 896 1

Printed and bound in Great Britain

For Mary

"But the effect of her being on those around her was incalculably diffusive: for the growing good of the world is partly dependent on unhistoric acts; and that things are not so ill with you and me as they might have been, is half owing to the number who lived faithfully a hidden life, and rest in unvisited tombs."

—*George Eliot,* Middlemarch

CONTENTS

ACKNOWLEDGMENTS

It takes many people to make a book, even more so when the book is made by many writers. I'd like to thank each of the writers in this book, who have embraced this project with enthusiasm, and have so generously shared from their lives. I also want to thank everyone who has supported this project, including those, whom I do not know, who have been of assistance to each writer; this book wouldn't have been possible without their help. Thanks also to my patients and members of my consultation groups, whose questions influenced this book.

Several people have generously offered comments about the manuscript, and support for the project. Thank you to Robert Balaban, M.D.; Rosa Belendez; Sylvia Brinton Perera, Ph.D.; Joan Choderow, Ph.D.; Emily Conrad; Donna Eigen; Nadya Fouad, Ph.D.; Nicholas French; Eugene Gendlin, Ph.D.; Fred Gustafson, D.Min.; Ro Hanus; Akira Ikemi, Ph.D.; Kalpana Rose Kumar, M.D.; Ron Kurtz; Louisa Loveridge-Gallas; Lisa Tomon Marr, M.D.; Georgia Marvin; Boris Matthews, Ph.D.; Arnold Mindell, Ph.D.; Gael Ohgren Rosewood; Jon Progoff; Maria Florentina Sassoli y Ezcurdia; Richard Schwartz, Ph.D.; Warren Sibilla, Ph.D.; and Hal Stone, Ph.D.

Special thanks to Scott Edelstein Literary Agency. Scott has been an invaluable guide through the unfamiliar world of publishing.

I want to thank Coleman Barks for generously allowing me to include his beautiful translations of Rumi poems, and for his good wishes.

Thank you to all my friends who listened to my concerns and excitement over the course of this journey called a book. Thanks to David and Gabrielle Laden, my hiking companions. Thanks to my colleagues at Trillium Care Group. The "car group," Jan Campanelli, Suzan McVicker, and Terry Ortiz. Thanks to Jay Earley for your thoughts on publishing. Thanks to the "dream group," Andrea Bowes, Susan Dellutri, Shakoor Lee, and John Giehlow. Thanks to the "elder Group," Peter Johnson, Andy Moss, Judson Chubuck, Steve Nelson-Raney, and Doug Walters. Thanks to men of the "I group," Mark McCormick, Jim Clark, David Rosenberg, Randy Long, Andy High, Flint Bridge, Paul Soczinski, Larry Sullivan, Jim Morrison, Steve Carini, and Tom Truel. And thanks to the "Madison group," Suz McVicker, Richard Wilberg, Don and Susan Mendenhall, Jean Scott-Honig and Harvey Honig.

I want to thank my family who shared their love and enthusiasm with me, Sonya and Abu Yusuf (and their children, Ameena, Yusuf, Jamila, Sakinah, and Maryam Yusuf), and Maria and Jim Myers (and their children, Jana and Steven Myers); my siblings for their enthusiastic encouragement, Barry and Chris Eigen, Bev Belfer and Ed Anhalt, Donna Eigen, and Daryl and Lucy Jeevani Eigen, and to my nephews and nieces.

I am most thankful to my wife, Mary Bernau-Eigen for her patient support, her wise counsel, her love.

INTRODUCTION

Charles Eigen

The chapters in this book describe ten contemporary approaches to psychotherapy and personal growth that are oriented toward healing, and also the development of an individual's potential. Several of the chapters were written by writers who were selected by the founder of the approach featured in that chapter. Those founders include Mr. Ron Kurtz, and Drs. Eugene Gendlin, Arnold Mindell, Richard C. Schwartz, and Hal and Sidra Stone. Individuals whom I chose wrote the other chapters.

I asked the authors to use their own life examples to elucidate their chapters, and this accounts for the highly personal style. The chapters are introductions to these methods, and reflect how the writers live and work with their respective approaches; as such, they won't indicate the breadth of work by the innovator they represent. Many of the innovators have developed several different dimensions in their work. For example, Gendlin (1986) has applied his Focusing to dreams as well as to the creative thinking process,[1] and Jung had several distinct phases in his work, including his explorations of alchemy, archetypes, typology, and dreams. In

---

1   See www.Focusing.org for information on Thinking at the Edge.

addition, many of these methods have been applied to different aspects of society.

Several of the chapters use the term multiplicity, suggesting the myriad aspects of personality, a normal characteristic of our psychological make-up. Since multiplicity, as a term applicable to a psychological discipline, might be a new concept for some readers, I will give that some focus later in this introduction. It is also, admittedly, an area of particular interest to me.

The methods in this book have a number of features in common. Among them is an emphasis on relationship with the inner life as well as the outer life. Relationship implies dialogue, and inner dialogue is the thread that runs throughout this book. Dialogue, however, is not only verbal; words, in fact, can get in the way of a deeper encounter. Dialogues with another person, or with one's own self, can be expressed in the image, sensation, movement, sound, and intimation that reveal themselves non-verbally. Some of the deepest encounters are deeper than words, deeper than emotions. As William Wordsworth (1807) wrote, in his "Ode: Intimations of Immortality from Recollections of Early Childhood":

> Thanks to the human heart by which we live,
>   Thanks to its tenderness, its joys, and fears,
> To me the meanest flower that blows can give
> Thoughts that do often lie too deep for tears.

When relating to the inner world, it is easy to find a host of thoughts and feelings; and the personification of these, commonly referred to as "parts," or as Jung called them, "autonomous aspects of the psyche." We see that we are more—and less—than whom we thought we were. However, while our parts—that is to say, our thoughts and feelings—may be troubled, the main problem is usually our identification of our conscious ego self with our parts and our interpretation of what is happening. This can be seen when a shift in perspective happens that allows us to exchange one point of view for another.

The methods in this book offer possibilities for shifting our perspectives, and thus clarifying our identities. The possibility of changing one's perspective is the promise of psychotherapy and conflict resolution, as well as spirituality. Shifting your perspective is changing your mind, and the future of humanity depends on it. In this sense, each of these methods can be seen as a prayer for peace.

Many of these methods share an appreciation of certain perspectives from Eastern meditative traditions, notably Buddhism, especially in the clinical application of the quality or state of mind called mindfulness.[2] These methods also recognize the importance of the body as an area that deserves attention in the realm of psychotherapy, as well as in the interest of wellbeing. They affirm the importance of relating to the body, in the recognition that inner dialogue is not only verbal.

Additionally, these methods hold that within each person are resources of inner wisdom that are often untapped, and other supportive qualities that can help individuals to become increasingly reliant upon their own resources, rather than remaining dependent upon the skills of a therapist or other outer authority.

The idea for this book grew out of my own journey in search of healing, which unexpectedly opened up into a path of wonder. In the process, I worked with most of the methods that are written about in this book. This hasn't been a journey with clear steps known at the beginning, like a course of study for an academic degree. Rather, it's been more like a meandering river, with new surprises and challenges around every bend. Many times, I doubted my direction, asking myself: "Shouldn't I be staying with just one approach?" Now, at this point in my journey, I can see that this wandering path has had two outcomes: one is that it has given me a broader, and perhaps deeper, understanding of the world of inner dialogue; the other is this book. I let my interest guide me, and found the truth in the words of an unknown poet: "Trust the current that knows its own way."

Another source of inspiration for this book has been the consult groups for therapists that I've led. My references in those groups to some of these methods would lead to questions about the differences between the approaches. Accordingly, much of the introduction is written with the therapist in mind. I started out to

---

2   Jon Kabat-Zinn defines mindfulness as "paying attention in a particular way: on purpose, in the present moment, and non-judgmentally" (Kabat-Zinn 1994).

write about all the methods, and then saw that it would be better to have individuals, who more exclusively represent each approach, write the chapter about that work. Those chapters are written for a wider audience.

Every person who seeks psychotherapy has a problem with relationship of some kind. The relationship in question might be with other people, or with any of the other aspects of life, including work, society, religion, one's own body, thoughts, beliefs, reactions, memories, and so on. The challenge of relationship is not limited to the practice of psychotherapy, however; relationship is the challenge of daily life. The challenge might be to handle better some difficult situation or circumstance, or the challenge might be to live our lives with more wisdom, joy, and compassion. In any case, the challenge is to relate, in the most skillful way possible, to what life brings our way. Vimala Thakar (2005) states, "Life is relationships, and the act of living implies the act of being related" (p.15). She asks, "And what is the test of relationship? The test of relationship is that we do not lose our inner freedom" (p.25). Respect for the individual's inherent inner freedom also aligns these methods with many of the wisdom traditions.

Beyond psychotherapy is daily life, and while the goals of psychotherapy might be attainable, the challenges of life continually present themselves anew, moment by moment, since it is only in each moment that life can be met. Nor can we rest on our laurels for having successfully met life fully in this moment; the next moment does not wait, and the challenge of living is lifelong. Jungian analyst Adolph Guggenbuhl-Craig says that modern man "…must wrestle with dark uncanny forces in himself and in others. It is only through ever-repeated confrontations with the shadow that he can fulfill his task. He cannot, like the biblical Isaac, spend just one night wrestling with the angel to win his blessing. His struggle for the blessing must last a lifetime" (Guggenbuhl-Craig 1971, p.155).

These methods demonstrate that the quality of a relationship depends a great deal on the quality of a person's presence. We know that our emotional and mental states affect how others relate to us, but we often lose sight of the fact that our own state also affects how and what we perceive, as well as what we think. This is a fact that every married couple knows or needs to learn, but it's also true in every relationship, including the therapeutic one.

Some of the methods in this book highlight the dynamics between the sub-personalities or parts of an individual, and help clients achieve a more harmonious inner, and thus, outer world, by resolving conflicts within and among their parts. They emphasize the relationship between the person (the Self or Aware Ego)[3] with the parts of which the person is aware. With all of these methods, the therapist learns that therapy works best when the therapist is most present, and free of the reactivity, urgency, and effort that are the calling card of parts.

Inner dialogue rests on the premise that we can enter into dialogue with ourselves. But who is talking? This question takes us past psychology into the mystical traditions. Generally speaking, we think of ourselves as a single "I," which could be represented as a single letter "I" within a circle.

In P.D. Ouspensky's book, *The Psychology of Man's Possible Evolution* (1956), there is an image depicting the actual situation, from the viewpoint of the author's tradition. This time, the circle is filled with numerous little "I"s.

The perspective of Ouspensky's tradition predates the view of the psychologies featured in this book. A similar perspective is expressed by the poet Walt Whitman, who declared, "Do I contradict myself? Very well then I contradict myself, I am large, I contain multitudes" (Whitman 1855). Today, the idea of multiplicity is part of our everyday language. You could ask a friend to go to dinner, for example, and he might reply, "I'd like to, but part of me just wants to eat in."

P.D. Ouspensky says of the parts: "Each of these 'I's represents at every given moment a very small part of our 'brain,' 'mind,' or 'intelligence,' but each of them means itself to represent the whole. When man says 'I,' it sounds as if he meant the whole of himself, but really even when he himself thinks that he means it, it is only a passing thought, a passing mood, or passing desire. In an hour's

---

3   "Self" is a term used in Internal Family Systems Therapy. Voice Dialogue uses the term "Aware Ego."

time he may completely forget it, and with the same conviction express an opposite opinion, opposite view, opposite interests. The worst of it is that man does not remember it. In most cases he believes in the last 'I' which expressed itself, as long as it lasts: that is, as long as another 'I'—sometimes quite unconnected with the preceding one—does not express its opinion or its desire louder than the first" (Ouspensky 1956, p.11).

Nevertheless, it seems as if we are who we think we are, and that's the problem. We tend to identify with our feelings, thoughts, and reactions. When we are angry, for instance, we might say, "I am angry," and in that statement become defined by that reaction. In doing so, we may lose sight of the other facets and resources of our being.

While the recognition of psychological multiplicity sheds light on our experience, the situation would be seemingly hopeless if there were no unifying presence, a central me that can relate to the rest of who we are—in other words, a healthy and flexible ego capable of relating to what is outside its own image and parameters and open to the intelligence that surpasses the intellect.

On the one hand, a strong ego is able to remember itself and to be self-possessed in the presence of other forces from within that threaten to possess the personality. On the other hand, a healthy (i.e. mature) ego also has the capacity to forget itself, by (temporarily) letting go of the story of itself, by letting go of thought, in an impersonal identification with awareness.

It might be a mistake to assume that the parts of an individual's personality are always there, even though inactive. From the Buddhist perspective (and probably that of quantum physics), the parts, as well as the ego, and everything else, are temporary patterns that arise according to certain causes and conditions. Working therapeutically with the parts (our clients' or our own), in the relative truth of the world of feeling, requires that we act as though they were real, in and of themselves. This is no different from relating to another person with respect and empathy for how they are feeling, regardless of our analysis.

The parts perspective, especially as taught in Internal Family Systems (IFS) Therapy and Voice Dialogue, can help to free us from identifying with our reactions, and from defining other persons by theirs. If a client has a part that is resistive to the therapist's suggestions for example, there's a good reason for it, at least from the point of view of the resisting part. The answer is not to try to get rid of that part, or to discount or ignore it, but to learn what the concerns of that part are. Through respect and patience, the therapist earns the trust of this and other parts that are trying to protect the client in some way, so that all parts can be offered healing and integration. Resistance, then, is not a problem, but an expression of the guidance of the client's internal system, which knows, within itself, the right way forward. The therapist is freed from needing to know the solutions for the client, but can, instead, partner with the client to discover what is needed and, in the process, help the client to earn the trust of her parts.

For this to work, the therapist needs to be "in self," and relatively free from the influence of her parts, however well intended they may be. Parts elicit parts, and the energy of the self-presence of the therapist simultaneously reassures the parts and helps evoke the self of the client. Therapy then becomes good medicine for both the client and the therapist. The therapist learns that the effective practice of her art involves practicing her own presence. Here, psychotherapy takes another page from spiritual practice, when it becomes clear that one's own state of consciousness is each person's primary responsibility. This is more than controlling one's own mind; it is having the capacity to be present to one's own mind, so that one can be free of the mind's tendency to pull one into the world of its own making.

The methods in this book share the recognition that within all people are resources of inner wisdom; as the poet Robert Browning says in "Paracelus":

> Truth is within ourselves; it takes no rise
> From outward things, whate'er you may believe.
> There is an inmost centre in us all,
> Where truth abides in fullness; and around,
> Wall upon wall, the gross flesh hems it in,
> This perfect, clear perception—which is truth.

> *(Browning 1917)*

We commonly experience the wisdom that results from a shift in perspective. We may become attached to our point of view or married to our conscious attitude. Then a shift in perspective comes along that helps us to change our mind. Jung understood that our conscious attitude requires continual course correction, and that correction is provided, to a significant extent, by our dreams. The practice of inner dialogue in its many forms, verbal as well as non-verbal (a process Carl Jung (1935) termed active imagination), can also provide us with the wisdom of another view. A deeper understanding comes from relating to what stirs, or is frozen, within us. For example, a person may realize, through dialogue with a part, that he is overworked, and that it is imperative to take some time off. This knowledge may be experienced as wise in its accuracy and simplicity, yet seems obvious, once it is recognized.

Of course, there are different levels of wisdom within the individual. Inner wisdom can speak, at times, with the profundity of a sage. One can only wonder at the origins of this wisdom. Could it be that it is the voice of guides in the spiritual realm, or is it coming from within the person, from the storehouse of wisdom acquired through millions of years of human experience, personified by Jung as the "two-million-year-old man" (Jung 1936 in McGuire and Hull 1977, p.88)? Marie-Louise von Franz writes about the creator of our dreams: "One could call it the inventor, organizer, and source of dream images. Jung called this center the 'Self' and described it as the totality of the whole psyche, in order to distinguish it from the 'ego,' which constitutes only a small part of the total psyche" (1964, p.161).

"…the Self can be defined as an inner guiding factor that is different from the conscious personality… How far it develops depends on whether or not the ego is willing to listen to the messages of the Self" (von Franz 1964, p.161).

von Franz continues, "Throughout the ages men have been intuitively aware of the existence of such an inner center. The Greeks called it man's inner Daimon; in Egypt it was expressed by the concept of the Ba-Soul; and the Romans worshipped it as the 'genius' native to each individual" (1964, p.161).

And as Ira Progoff (1979) has said: "There is an interior knowing, that we really know what our life should be, but the problem is, how do we get access to the knowledge that we deeply have?" Now, people are discovering an inner wisdom in the course of their daily lives, often through the assistance of the methods described in this book.

All of the methods in this book have a common basis, and yet each reflects a different view, like different facets of the same jewel. Said in another way, while the innovators of each approach have discovered something new, what they have discovered has an essential commonality, and continuity throughout time, like explorers who all find the same vast river, at different places; it looks very different in the various places where they discover it. It is the river of our inner process. This book aims to give a sense of the different approaches, and how they each contribute to a fuller appreciation of the great river of our inner lives, and of life itself.

REFERENCES

Browning, R., 1917. "Paracelus." In D.H.S. Nicholson and A.H.E. Lee (eds) *The Oxford Book of English Mystical Verse.* Oxford: The Clarendon Press.

Gendlin, E.T., 1986. *Let Your Body Interpret Your Dreams.* Wilmette, IL: Chiron Publications.

Guggenbuhl-Craig, A., 1971. *Power in the Helping Professions.* Dallas, TX: Spring Publications.

Jung, C.G., 1935. "The Tavistock Lectures: On the Theory and Practice of Analytical Psychology." In G. Adler and R.F.C. Hull (eds), 1977. *Collected Works of C.G. Jung, Volume 18: The Symbolic Life: Miscellaneous Writings.* Princeton, NJ: Princeton University Press.

Kabat-Zinn, J., 1994. *Wherever You Go, There You Are: Mindfulness Meditation in Everyday Life.* New York: Hyperion Books.

McGuire, W. and Hull, R.F.C. (eds), 1977. *C.G. Jung Speaking Interviews and Encounters.* Princeton, NJ: Princeton University Press.

Ouspensky, P.D., 1956. *The Psychology of Man's Possible Evolution.* New York: Bantam Books.

Progoff, I., 1979. *Roads Taken and Not Taken* [recorded lecture]. Dialogue House, New York.

Thakar, V., 2005. *Insights Into the Bhagavad Gita.* Delhi: Motilal Banarsidass Publishers.

von Franz, M.L., 1964. "The Process of Individuation." In C.G. Jung (ed.) *Man and His Symbols*. Garden City, NY: Doubleday and Co.

Whitman, W., 1855. "Song of Myself." In *Leaves of Grass*.

Wordsworth, W., 1807. "Ode: Intimations of Immortality from Recollections of Early Childhood." In A.T. Quiller-Couch (ed.), 1919. *The Oxford Book of English Verse*. Oxford: The Clarendon Press.

CHAPTER ONE

INNER DIALOGUE AND THE PSYCHOLOGY OF CARL JUNG

Harvey Honig, Ph.D.

On September 20, 2009, a picture of one of the most unusual books published in our time graced the cover of the *New York Times Sunday Magazine* (Corbett 2009). The cover story was devoted to an event that was significant in the world of publishing; but even more significant in revealing a seminal chapter in the life and work of Carl Jung. This cover story announced the publication of *The Red Book* (Jung and Shandasani 2009), a most singular event in the world of inner dialogue.

For those not acquainted with this book, it is a very beautiful rendering of Jung's inner process during a critical and difficult period of his life. During this period of crisis after his break with Freud, he spent a great deal of time dialoguing with inner figures who seemed to come from beyond his personal world, figures that were numinous and revelatory. He painstakingly transcribed these dialogues in a beautiful script and illustrated them with some very striking images, and the effect on this viewer and many others I have talked with, including people having no particular connection with Jung, is similar to that which occurs upon viewing a sacred manuscript.

The journey this book narrates and illustrates was both a perilous journey for Jung and a very rich expedition into the deep inner world of the personal and collective psyche. It was significant in Jung's personal individuation, in the development of his own psychology; and, as particularly relevant for this chapter, in the development of his process of active imagination.

The internal exploratory process that Jung chronicles in this book is the direct or indirect forerunner of most of the inner dialogue processes in use today. It is not that Jung invented inner dialogue; similar processes have existed throughout the history of humanity, going back to shamanic journeys. Jung tapped into a process that simply emerged from his deeper Self. This was not an intellectual creation; it emerged from Jung's need to integrate inner and outer psychic forces that were so powerful that they threatened to overwhelm him. As a pioneer in this exploration of what McGlashan (1967) has called "the savage and beautiful country," Jung had no clear map.

The description of the inner world in quotes above is the title of a book by Alan McGlashan which Stanley Kubrick cites as one of the sources for his movie *2001, A Space Odyssey* (Agel 1970). McGlashan was very much influenced by the ideas of Jung, and was a close friend of Laurens van der Post. He had a very active outer life, including two battles as a WWI pilot with the Red Baron. He was an active participant in the world of healing and in the events of his time until his death at the age of 99. However, it was the inner world of the mind that was most fascinating to him, and which in his view offered the new frontier for exploration.

Kubrick's reference to this book makes it clear that he viewed his movie as primarily being about that perilous inner journey which McGlashan views as the remaining frontier to be explored in our time. The same kind of courage required to face the dangers of space exploration portrayed in that journey was required of Jung in this inner journey. And, as portrayed in the enigmatic images of a new birth at the end of that movie, the inner journey of exploration of a new universe gave birth to new manifestations of Jung's larger Self. It also gave birth to an outline of much of the subsequent development of his psychology, and a new form of interacting with the unconscious, which Jung called active imagination.

I am not making the claim in this chapter that the subsequent forms of inner dialogue, portrayed in this book, all trace their lineage to Jung. There are some that are direct descendants or offshoots, and there are some that are parallel or independent discoveries or adaptations of this process. Also, all of these approaches, including Jung's, are located in a historical lineage of dialogical methods utilized in various intellectual and healing traditions throughout history. Nevertheless, the process which Jung reveals in the pages of *The Red Book* is the earliest use of this kind of internal dialogue specifically developed for that kind of psychological exploration and growth, and is, therefore, extremely significant in the history of inner dialogue.

When these inner dialogues began, Jung's outer life had gone through a dramatic shift. His break with Freud had caused him a great deal of turmoil, and his position in the world of depth psychology at that time had also undergone a seismic shift. From a period in which he occupied a very central position in the international psychoanalytic movement, he came to be viewed by many in that movement as an apostate because of his break with Freud. Jung's quotidian outer life of teaching, analytic work, and family responsibilities was the anchor that kept him grounded as he began devoting significant time each evening to these inner exploratory journeys in an effort to clarify who he was and what was true for him. It was from these journeys that the outlines emerged not only of the process he was to call active imagination, but also the central themes of his psychology, which he had named analytical psychology.

What, then, is active imagination? For Jung the process involved moving into a state of relaxation or suspension of conscious focus, and allowing figures and images from the unconscious to emerge and dialogue with him. He wrote down the dialogues and carefully and artfully portrayed the images which emerged in an attempt to honor and give sacred space to these inner figures. As he listened to these inner figures, he sought a balanced state in which his ego was aware and involved in the process, but the primary direction and content of the dialogue came from the unconscious. Much of the material came as a great surprise to his ego consciousness, and appeared to come from beyond his personal ego and beyond his personal unconscious.

He continued this process of inner dialogue for many years, and found that it provided the direction and awareness from the unconscious that helped him to resolve his personal crisis. It allowed him to integrate more of what he called his number-two personality. This aspect, which up until this time had been less consciously developed in his life, was more connected with the objective psyche, the more collective aspect of the psyche. Jung felt that this aspect was more connected with the world of his mother, but we could also associate it with the more right-brained world that Jill Bolte Taylor describes in her book *My Stroke of Insight* (Taylor 2006).

This connection helped him to understand that many of these contents that had been flooding in from the unconscious were influenced by collective events of this time. Initially, the dialogues threatened to overwhelm Jung, but after he made this connection with the collective nature of his images, he was able to relax and let the dialogues unfold. For Jung, this was not so much a technique that he discovered as it was a way of relating to his personal and the collective unconscious. It was a relationship between ego and Self, in which he allowed ego consciousness to be present, but guided by the wisdom of the unconscious.

Subsequent developments and elaborations of this process of inner dialogue in Jungian psychology include processes which use dialogue with dream figures, painting, movement, or any creative process to further the interaction between the ego and the unconscious. One of the most widely utilized of these processes is the sand tray, in which the individuals using this process create tableaux in a rectangular container of sand with a variety of figures designed to lend themselves to expressing dream images or allowing the unconscious to speak in other ways, such as expressing significant family dynamics. Active imagination has been expanded in many creative ways, and contemporary Jungians and non-Jungians continue to find creative uses for it.

One of the most striking examples of this was recently given by two Chinese Jungians (Chenghou and Heyong 2010) who described their use of sand tray creations in responding to traumatized children and adults after the great earthquake that occurred a few years ago. They found this technique to be very powerful in the prevention and treatment of post-traumatic stress disorder in children and families. They provide a very interesting account of their ongoing work in the *Jung Journal* (Chenghou and Heyong 2010).

All of these forms of active imagination provide ways for the individuals utilizing them to be in charge of their own process, to engage directly with their own unconscious and individuation. They all are variations on Jung's original dialogues, and provide ways for the ego and unconscious to carry the dialogue further.

An example of the value of this process is taken from an analysand who had suffered from severe depression as an adolescent. She was a creative and intelligent young woman who had shut down her exuberant inner child in response to her mother's anger. After her adolescence, she also shut down the sad inner child to focus on surviving a very challenging professional training program. This adaptation had allowed her to become a successful professional, operating at a high level of competence. However, she had lost much of the spontaneity and creativity of her early life.

Through the process of dialogue with figures from her dreams, she was able to contact first the sad little girl, then the exuberant little girl that had been shut down in the course of her life. This was initially frightening, as the release of the sad little girl brought fears of the return of her depression, but the unconscious was cooperative in allowing her to access her inner figures at a pace that she could handle. This has been instrumental in allowing her to integrate these figures from her early life into her current life.

Other examples from my practice include people who have painted significant figures from their dreams and, in the process, came to know much more about these figures and their role in their lives. The quality of the painting or drawing is not important, only that it allows free play of the unconscious with the participation of the ego.

There is much more that could be said about the inner journey which Jung describes in *The Red Book*, and chapters and books have been and will be written about this part of Jung's journey, but the focus of this chapter is primarily on the significance of this inner dialogue in the development of active imagination and in the development of his psychology.

Jung had already developed some of the major elements of his psychology before the period of *The Red Book*. He shared with Freud the view of the importance of dreams and of the unconscious, which is what drew him to Freud and his circle. He also felt that Freud had mapped out the process of ego development and the defensive structures of the personal unconscious. However, he became increasingly restive as he felt constricted by some elements of Freudian psychology, which he felt were influenced more by cultural and political influences of that time rather than by any empirical evidence of timeless structures.

One of the central differences that emerged was Freud's need to reduce every human drive to its biological source. Jung's experience was that some of the drives that had developed over the course of human evolution, such as creativity and religion, had their own teleological and evolutionary thrust, and could not be explained totally by their biological origins.

It was not easy for Jung to acknowledge these differences and follow the truth of his own discoveries and convictions. He and Freud had been very close, even sharing their dreams with one another as they traveled together on the trip to Clark University in the United States. Freud had invested a great deal of psychic energy in his mentoring of Jung, and saw him as a figure that could lead and guide the psychoanalytic movement to great success. Jung knew that his expression of his own convictions would be experienced as a betrayal. The difficulty this separation created for each of them is expressed in their letters to each other during this period, recorded in *The Freud/Jung Letters*. (There is a complete edition of these letters available under the above title, but there is a briefer version of this interchange edited and summarized by McGlashan in his introduction to the abridged edition (McGuire *et al.* 1994). McGlashan viewed their split as a necessary one, freeing each of them to fully develop his own ideas, without the inevitable conflict of two creative minds in tension.)

One of the other major developments of Jung's psychology emerged from his attempt to understand why the significant differences in perception of these underlying realities had occurred in the three major branches of depth psychology at that time; those of Freud, Adler, and his own. Jung's observation of the way these theoretical differences developed led him to the idea that there are fundamental differences in the way people perceive, evaluate, and understand reality. This observation led him to formulate the hypothesis that there were fundamental differences in typology between Freud, himself, and Adler that led them to the different description of reality expressed in their different theories about psychology. In the form of their psychologies, they are expressing the natural differences in perception and judgment that are expressed in the timeless parable of the five blind men and the elephant.

Jung developed these fundamental differences in his early major work *Psychological Types* (Jung 1971a). This book brought into the public domain terms such as introversion and extraversion, which describe the two basic orientations toward reality, as well as the four major functions through which we process reality. We perceive reality through the lenses of intuition and sensation, and we evaluate these perceptions through the functions of thinking and feeling. Thus, this book formed the basis for understanding that there is a dialectical relationship between ways of perceiving and ways of evaluating reality. The typologies are not a static classification, but a description of the way people understand and communicate about reality. Katherine Cook Briggs and Isabel Briggs Meyers further worked with these ideas to develop the Meyers Briggs typology inventory, perhaps the most widely used measurement of personality in the world (Meyers with Meyers 1995).

All of Jung's ideas about psychology derived from his own experience, either his personal experience or the experience of his patients. They were not developed on the basis of theoretical neatness, but out of the need to make sense of his experience and the experience of others. His theories kept evolving and changing as new challenges or experiences came into his life, and in that sense they were a constant dialogue with reality. What many view as the mystical nature of his ideas is in reality his firm conviction that he needed to include all of experience, not merely that experience which can be measured and quantified.

In that sense he can be compared to Richard Alpert, a psychologist who taught at Harvard and became known with Timothy Leary for his experiments with LSD. As Richard Alpert, he wrote a culturally significant book called *Be Here Now* (Alpert 1971). After his own experience with archetypal, collective, and spiritual aspects of reality in the course of his experimentation, he was led to India to explore these dimensions further. These experiences opened other dimensions of reality to him, and Alpert could no longer be content with the typical psychological career. He could no longer limit his consciousness to those aspects of reality that lend themselves to quantification and control, and he became a spiritual teacher and guide, taking on the name given to him by his guru, the name Ram Dass.

Ram Dass was fond of a story of Mulla Nasrudin that is quite relevant to this idea (Shah 1973). He told a story of a man who was walking home at night when he encountered another man on his hands and knees under a lamppost, who seemed to be searching for something. He stopped and asked what the man on his hands and knees was searching for. The reply was that he had lost his wallet. After helping him search unsuccessfully for a time, the first man asked the other where he had lost the wallet. He replied that he had lost it in the alley nearby. Astonished, the first man asked why he was looking there. His answer was that he was looking there because the light was better.[1] For Ram Dass, this was a telling metaphor for most of the psychological research of his time, which focused on that which can be measured, rather than the most important questions.

---

1   This Ram Dass story can be found in the original in Sufi teaching stories or as quoted in his address to the American Psychological Association.

For both Ram Dass and Jung, the sole focus on the material and the measurable leads us to lose sight of where the real treasure is. For Ram Dass, this led him to abandon his scientific career. Jung was led to continue the psychological and scientific enterprise, but to expand his search to focus on the issues that were the most meaningful to him and other humans. His method for going beyond the subjective and remaining empirical was to look for prior explorations of these larger questions and check his own conclusions against those of earlier explorers. He found these kinds of explorations in mythology, in alchemy, and in religion. He also constantly checked and verified his own experiences against those of his patients. It is because of this experiential element that many people are drawn to Jung's ideas. His ideas help them to make sense of their personal experience, and for that reason they seem intuitively true.

Jung's experience in the course of his life led organically to a view of nature and the natural world as energized by polarities, as dialectical in their very nature. Early in life he had the revelation that within himself he was dealing with two personalities; his number-one personality, which more closely related to the everyday world of persona and ego, and his number-two personality, which he related to the more primal, natural, unconscious world that came to him through his mother.

These two sides of his personality led him to value the unconscious, Lunar, right-brain, interconnected nature of reality as well as the more logical and discrete aspects which are typically more measurable and attractive to people who want to measure and control reality. His connection with his number-two personality also naturally led him to value the missing feminine and ecological consciousness before this became popular in psychology and the larger world.

The number-one aspect of his personality dominated the early part of Jung's career, and during that period he developed ideas that utilized aspects of measurement and control. He developed one of the very early psychological tests, the word association experiment (Jung 1910), which measured reaction times to key words as a measure of complex activity (i.e. words that connected with unconscious triggers of reactivity). He also developed the measurements of galvanic skin response to determine reactivity in the test subject (Jung 1919): this ultimately formed the basis for the invention of the lie detector. Jung used his test to ferret out a thief at the hospital. However, he also realized that his test measured reactivity, rather than actual guilt or innocence, and he immediately realized the limitations of his own invention and did not pursue that use.

Early in his career, Jung realized that therapy was a dialectical process between analyst and analysand, in which the unfolding individuation process changed both parties. Jung was also one of the first to see the process as guided primarily by the analysand's own path of individuation, rather than a process in which the therapist is in charge and is responsible for fixing the problem. In that sense, Jung's therapy was the first client-centered therapy, but in Jung's view the real guide was the Self of the analysand. The process was directed by the unconscious as well as the more conscious awareness of both the analyst and the analysand. He was one of the first to focus on the strengths of the analysand, especially in terms of the potential or undeveloped aspects emerging in the individuation process. Even the neuroses and conflicts had a positive aspect for Jung, when they motivated the individuals suffering them to find a more healthy balance of the psyche.

Jung viewed this as true in his own life. He realized that his encounter with his unconscious during his period of crisis was really a deep encounter with his number-two personality; the Lunar, interconnected aspect. In this sense, it was an attempt by the Self to move Jung to a more balanced and integrated relationship between his number-one and number-two personalities. Another positive outcome of this crisis was that it profoundly shifted his focus from more conventional aspects of psychiatry to the more collective, archetypal, and interconnected aspects of reality. In clinical terms, the shift was in the understanding of the role and importance of adaptation. Gradually, Jung recognized that adapting to the external environment, although obviously necessary, was not sufficient. As he engaged the figures and experiences emerging from the unconscious (especially between 1912 and 1920), he recognized that it was just as important to adapt to the inner world that the unconscious cast up. He would never be the same person, and his psychology was also profoundly enlarged and deepened (Jung 1990; Stevens 1994).

My own encounter with Jung occurred at a time of a profound shift in my own life, a time in which what had once seemed solid and timeless had become porous and undependable. I had grown up in a rural mid-western part of Canada, and later Kansas, in the family of a conservative Lutheran minister. In this milieu, the only reality for the rural folks who surrounded me was the sensate, material reality encountered in farming. For my father and my family, the only true measure of reality was the Bible and the Lutheran confessions. Anything else was not important. My acceptance of these realities had led me to a very pragmatic focus on religion, and to pursuing a career as a Lutheran minister.

At the end of my seminary training, I embarked on a dual career of pastor to a small congregation in Wellington, Ohio, and the pursuit of a master's degree in pastoral counseling from nearby Oberlin School of Theology. By this time, my two original measures of reality had begun to prove inadequate. My experience of reality had expanded to the point that I had long ago begun to question the answers and formulations that described the nature of reality in my childhood. This process was only accelerated at Oberlin, and exacerbated a personal conflict of opposites between the reality of my role as Lutheran minister and my role as intellectual pursuer of truth.

It was at this point that I encountered the world of Jung. Up to this point in my life, Jung had been totally unknown to me, as had the whole realm of the unconscious. Oberlin offered a course called introduction to Jung, which was taught by a minister named Otis Maxfield, who had spent some time at the Jung Institute in Zurich. He shared the radical (to me at that time) notion that we all dream, and that dreams have meaning. For the first time since childhood, I became aware of my dreams, and began to try to understand them. I began reading Jung, and between the new awareness brought by my dreams, Jung, reading the theology of Paul Tillich, and the more open views of my professors at Oberlin, my reality was expanding rapidly enough to make my head spin.

It was not only Jung's ideas that made sense to me, but in his approach to working with the unconscious and inner dialogue, he gave me a method that I could use to find an inner gyroscope to keep me oriented. He also gave me an example of someone who pursued truth wherever it led, of someone who honored his own process of individuation, even when it led to inconvenient and difficult decisions.

This inner compass which I found in my dreams and this example of following one's own path of individuation then led me, after a period of intense inner conflict, to leave the path of ministry and move to Chicago to enter analysis with June Singer, who was the Jungian analyst who lived closest to me at the time. The process of analysis provided a method wherein I could hold the tension of opposites, until the unconscious provided me with a new synthesis. I had experienced lifelong periods of depression, and was often quite anxious. I was also going through the dissolution of a marriage to someone whom I had met in my earlier world, who could not companion me in this new world. Throughout this period of change and growth, analysis provided me with the skills I needed to survive incredible change, and the awareness that change and growth are the basic elements of reality. During this period I also began a graduate program in clinical psychology at Loyola University, which again necessitated integrating two very different approaches to psychology. In the clinical dimension of my training, these worlds were not so far apart, as my Jungian understanding allowed me the flexibility to utilize whatever approach was being taught in the clinical setting. However, in the research and academic aspects, it was my experience that Jung was either ignored or distorted.

Even in the clinical world, I found that Jung was often ignored. There was little mention of his pioneering work in developing the modern form of psychotherapy and in the history of psychological testing. We were taught to use the Rorschach and the Thematic

Apperception Test (TAT),[2] which were both developed by people who had studied with Jung, but there was no recognition of the role he played in providing the framework for those developments. It seemed that modern testing wanted to move away from any role of intuition, and to reduce even the projective tests to systematic, measurable, operationally defined operations.

However, throughout this process, the anchor of my own analytic work provided the inner focus, which allowed me to successfully negotiate both worlds. It was during my analysis that Jungian psychology, which I had understood academically, took on a more personal and deeper dimension, which had more power to transform my straw into gold.

I became much more aware of my persona, which had been the most rewarded aspect of my personality as a child growing up in a minister's family, and during my brief career as a minister. The persona is that aspect of ourselves that we show to the world, the mask composed of our roles and the adaptive self we assume in order to survive. It comes from the Latin word for mask, and relates to the roles in the classic world of drama. In Jung's view, there was nothing wrong with the persona; it is a necessary part of our interface with the world. However, for Jung it was also very important to be aware of our persona and the difference between that and our real Self (Jung *et al.* 1965). The persona is also related to the shadow, in that too much identification with the persona leads to a corresponding development of shadow.

In my family, there was very little awareness of any part of ourselves separate from our persona. The most important thing for us was not to bring shame by doing anything inappropriate for a minister's child. There was also very little acceptance of or awareness of our shadows, which were correspondingly huge and hidden. It was my time at Oberlin and my time in analysis that helped me to get in touch with deeper and more real aspects of my true Self.

During my time of transition from minister to graduate student, I rebelled against that persona and took on the persona of a

---

2   A set of photographs compiled by Henry Murray and used as projective test.

freethinking child of the late sixties and early seventies. However, in that early period of my graduate work and analysis, I was still acting out of the persona. It was in reality just another form of adaptation to the outer world. I also became aware of a corresponding shadow, and to what an extent the new aspects of my rebel persona were really my acting out of my anger with my father and all the patriarchal and rigid structures that had dominated so much of my earlier life. However, I also became aware of the gold in that shadow in the energy and the wholeness that were potentially there as I integrated that anger rather than simply acting it out.

My individual journey was reflected in the turmoil of that time, and led me to a study of a particular example of someone who lived out that tension of opposites. My dissertation (Honig, 1979) was a study of Camilla Hall, who had joined the Symbionese Liberation Army (SLA), the group that had kidnapped Patti Hearst. The leaders and members were examples of some of the best and the worst of the radical movement of that time, and often that interplay of best and worst was expressed within the personalities of the individual members.

Camilla was the daughter of a Lutheran minister, a man I had a chance to interview. Camilla's parents were, in contrast to mine, very open, liberal, and politically aware. They were a very normal and healthy family in every sense except one; Camilla was the sole surviving child in this family. Her three siblings had all died tragic deaths from illness while they were embarking on very promising lives. As the only surviving child of George and Lenore Hall, Camilla seemed to combine many of the best qualities of her parents. She was an intelligent idealist like her father, and an artist like her mother.

After college, Camilla worked briefly as a caseworker with unmarried mothers for about a year before she found herself compelled to expand her horizons and her creativity by moving to California and attempting to make a living as an artist outside of Los Angeles. She then moved to the San Francisco area, where her idealism was engaged when she met one of the members of the SLA. At least, that was her conscious view of her reasons for joining the organization. Her fairly brief life as a revolutionary came to an end in Los Angeles when the SWAT team that had surrounded the house where the majority of the group had gone underground killed her. She was shot through the forehead after emerging with another woman member from the house. Shortly after they were killed, the SWAT team used incendiary devices to immolate the rest of the group.

What motivated this young idealist to engage in an enterprise that had such a tragic end? Were her apparently very loving parents to blame for her choices? To all who knew them, they seemed to be ideal parents who had raised children who had appeared to be psychologically healthy. I interviewed George Hall about a year after Camilla's death, and her death was clearly an extremely painful event for both of her parents. It raised many questions for them about God, life, and themselves. Camilla had kept in touch with them, but had shared nothing of her shadow life as a revolutionary. Her death was in itself an incredible shock, to say nothing of the revelations that followed about her secret life.

All of the forces that go into the outcome of a life like Camilla's are very complex (some of them are detailed more in my thesis; see Honig 1979) but, to put it briefly, it was my conclusion that Camilla lived out the unlived shadow of her parents' unconscious anger over the deaths of their children. Her parents certainly went through the normal questioning of the divine order, and perhaps even experienced anger at the unfairness of their losses. However, they were not the kinds of people who could fully rage at the unfairness of life, or question the fundamental rightness of the divine order.

I also believe that Camilla was not fully aware of her own angry shadow. Because her own survivor guilt pushed her anger even further away, she lived out her unintegrated shadow through the SLA. Her own unconscious anger over the unfairness of life merged with the collective anger of the SLA over the unfairness of the political realities of that time, with tragic results for all involved.

Camilla's life and death were, for me, a powerful reminder of the power of the unconscious, and vividly illustrated what happens when people get caught in archetypal collective forces powerful enough to overwhelm the ego. Many scholars who studied the leaders and members of the revolutionary movements of that era arrived at the conclusion that the majority of members of these groups represented two extreme polarities among the young people of that time. They were some of the best and brightest young people of our time, young leaders who were living out the ideals of their parents and living them out in uncompromising ways; but they were also young men and women who were stuck in a form of adolescent rebellion, acting out their parental complexes. In between was a whole continuum of people who acted out of various combinations of both motivations.

Also, this was a time when the personal psychological dynamic of these individuals was powerfully caught in the collective split between the archetypal polarities of Puer and Senex. In the Jungian framework, the Puer is the eternal boy, the idealist who cannot compromise with reality, while the Senex is the rigid old man, who reacts to any threat to existing psychic structures by defending rigidly against change. This is an eternal conflict, but it was particularly active as a dynamic during this period, within the historical context of the late sixties and early seventies.

One of the major differences between the more integrated leaders and members, and those simply acting out a split, was the presence of what Internal Family Systems adherents would call self-leadership, and Jungians would call the archetype of the Self. When ego or sub-aspects of the personality primarily dominated the actions of these individuals, these revolutionaries tended to be caught in the Puer aspect. When the Self was more present, there was a more genuine vision, and an attempt to move our country closer to its stated ideals.

It was helpful to me, in my own journey, to become more conscious of these forces playing out in my life, and thus to avoid being totally caught up in these personal and collective shadow energies. I also was able to connect with my own larger Self, the more integrated and integrating aspect that helped sustain me when my own earlier ideals were no longer tenable. Connection with the larger Self provided me with the equanimity and security I needed when facing that inevitable awareness that even Jungians acted unconsciously, and that not every aspect of Jungian psychology perfectly mirrored or contained reality.

One of the important ideas to emerge for Jung from his dialogue with his unconscious during that critical period was the awareness of the importance of the right relationship between the ego and the Self. Jung's view of this relationship was more nuanced than that expressed by those who viewed ego development as crucial, and those who see the goal of life as the elimination of the ego (Jung and Shamdasani 2009; Jung 1971b). In this sense, his view is similar to Ken Wilber's of the necessity of ego development as a prior requirement for the phase of moving beyond ego into Self (Wilber 2011).

For Jung this dialectical relationship is necessary throughout life, although he would agree that the development of the ego is more important in the early stages of life, and the development of Self a necessary requirement for the second half of life. What Jung means by this is that in the dialogue between ego and Self, whether in active imagination, in working with dreams, or in life decisions, it is important for the ego to be present and to hold its place in the dialogue with the Self. However, the real guidance in every case, and the ultimate source of guidance, is the Self. This distinction was an important awareness that helped me to find a more balanced relationship between ego and Self during my own midlife development period.

In my family of origin, ego was something to be radically stamped out. I desperately needed to develop and claim the ego, but without the larger archetypal container of the Self, I, too, could have lived out the archetypal journey of Icarus. It was my analytic work that allowed me to discover that even when I learned to distrust and question every authority and to believe only what could be empirically demonstrated, at the level of the unconscious there is an organizing principle of the Self that knows more than my ego does, and transcends the limitations of my ego-dominated reality. My ego needed to be strengthened and enlarged; encompassing more of reality, but it could never encompass and understand all of reality. Therefore, my ego needed to engage the Self, but allow the Self to guide and direct the process.

This is what Jung discovered in his original dialogue with the unconscious. The guiding principle for all forms of active imagination, no matter what particular technique is used, is that while the ego needs to be engaged in the process, the Self should be in the leadership position. This process guides what Jung called individuation, the eternal dialectical process between ego and Self. In the unfolding process of individuation, the encounter with the shadow, which tends to be part of the initial analytic journey, takes us deeper into the unconscious. The next part of the individuation process tends to be the encounter with the anima/animus, the archetypal soul opposites within each one of us.

For Jung, one's images of the anima/animus tended to be dominated by one's own culturally mediated experience, and, thus, particular gender contents were associated with the anima or animus. In reality, each of these describes a polarity within each one of us that varies according to our conscious, ego position. If, as a man, my ego personality tends to be that of an idealistic airhead, my anima, my missing other half, will be a practical, grounded woman. If, as a woman, my primary adaptation has been one of aggressive competitiveness, my animus would perhaps be a more nurturing, relational masculine image. It is, as in Taoism, an eternal interplay of yin/yang energies.

I have attempted to provide some examples, from my own life and the larger world, of how these concepts operate, and their relevance in providing self-understanding for many people. This is not by any means a complete outline of Jungian ideas. The list of references will provide sources for a more complete exposition of Jungian psychology. In this chapter, I am limiting my focus to concepts that are central to the process of analysis and individuation.

Many people view Jung's ideas as intellectual and obscure; and, in truth, many of his writings are quite complex. However, the concepts from Jung's psychology that I have presented here are readily comprehensible to almost anyone capable of understanding basic relational concepts. I recently presented these concepts of persona/ego/shadow/anima/animus to clients in an ongoing therapy group in a fairly small western city. Almost every one of the fifteen people in these two groups was able to understand and apply these concepts in concrete and meaningful ways to elucidate and clarify dynamics and relationships they were currently struggling to work through. In truth, these concepts are part of psychological discourse for many people today, although they are often vaguely understood.

For example, many people view these concepts as descriptions of fixed entities, rather than as dialogical descriptions of relationships. This is particularly important in the case of the relationship between ego and anima/animus. The dynamic of this relationship is universal, as is the need to connect with and integrate unlived parts of ourselves. These unconscious opposites, the anima/animus, are projected on lovers we meet, but the contents of these images vary in relationship to our conscious ego. In other words, images of the anima and animus have no fixed content, but provide the image to complete the conscious ego. Therefore, if a man's conscious ego is predominantly one of a feeling/nurturing person, his anima image may be more of a thinking/logical person.

Shadow and anima/animus carry these rejected and unlived parts of ourselves, and contain our missing wholeness. This is why connecting with them is so essential in the process of individuation, and why they play such a central role in our archetypal stories, such as *Dr Jekyll and Mr Hyde*, and myths and fairy tales like Psyche and Eros, and Beauty and the Beast. Robert Johnson is a Jungian analyst who has written clear, brief expositions of the concept of anima and animus and how they relate to our lives and relationships, especially our primary love relationships, in three of his books—*We, She, and He* (1983, 1989a, 1989b).

The successful reintegration of the projected aspects of anima or animus allows the next stage of the individuation journey to occur, the inner marriage. This allows us to move from codependent relationships, in which we long for the perfect other to complete us or to heal our original psychic wounds. These original wounds continue to affect our relationships, thereby preventing us from moving into adult, interdependent ones. We are no longer living the myth of Eros, longing for the other half to complete us, for the "gods" encountered through the individuation process have granted us completeness. This process is symbolically described in the myth of Psyche and Eros.

Whether or not the outer collective recognizes the validity of same-sex marriages, the unconscious certainly validates the inner marriage in gay people as much as in straight ones. Recently a lesbian client was describing her own journey of individuation, in which her process took her from symptom-focused psychotherapy, to more depth-oriented psychotherapy and then to analysis. She was relating it to the change in her relationships, as she moved from either fearing intimacy or longing for completion, to a sense of marriage with her own animus. This inner marriage allowed her to move beyond the childhood longing for someone to take care of her, and into truly being able to love her partner. The process of integration and inner marriage operated just as much with the two of them as with a straight couple. Now, she and her partner could help each other grow into completion, as they learned to move beyond looking for love in order to complete Self and into loving from a complete Self. Naturally, she was aware that this process was not complete, but would be completing itself for the rest of her life in all of her relationships. Her example illustrates the point that the anima/animus polarity is not dependent on gender, but is related to the process of the recovery of the unconscious other.

At this point I would like to move from the relevance of Jungian concepts for individual development to the concept of the collective unconscious, and the relevance of Jungian concepts for the collective world of our time.

One of the reasons I studied the life of Camilla Hall was because I believed that her life helped to shed light on the collective forces that were playing out during the late 1960s. From a Jungian perspective, in our national politics we were playing out the projection of shadow, the tension between Puer and Senex, and the long, collective struggle for the masculine and feminine energies to find balance.

For many years prior to the Vietnam war, Russia and the United States were involved in the mutual projection of shadow that we called the Cold War. Each power viewed the other as hostile and aggressive, and seriously overestimated the potential threat of the other. In the civil rights struggles, there was a similar projection onto the black minority of aggressive and sexual impulses, as well as qualities of laziness and lack of control. As Sam Keen (2004) has pointed out in his own writing on this subject, any caricature of a minority carries a projection of the shadow of the majority culture. This is the reason that stereotypes of minority cultures are so similar as to be almost interchangeable, whether it involves projections by whites onto blacks in this country, or projections by Swiss onto Italian migrant workers, projections of the French onto Algerians, or Germans onto Turks. One could go on endlessly, and we could diagnose what is missing in the unconscious of the majority culture by what is projected onto the minority culture. These projections are dangerous not only to the minority culture in that they create fear and the need to control. (The more repressed the culture is, and the more identified with the persona, the more this fear is played out in the need to punish and control the minorities that carry these shadow projections.)

Such projections also are dangerous as they infect the psyches of the minority. In the same way that a child in a family who carries the family shadow and is the family scapegoat can take on that role, similarly, scapegoating can be psychically damaging to a minority culture. However, the process is also damaging to the majority culture, as the qualities of our own shadow that we deny and project on the other are actually needed for our own wholeness. For instance, in the United States we are continuing to project our collective shadow onto the latest immigrant population. We do so in successive waves—onto the Irish or the Italians, or onto blacks, onto Arabs, or onto the current scapegoat of illegal immigrants.

In all of these cases, the intensity of the fear has very little to do with the actual threat. This is why it is so difficult to use logic or statistical evidence to convince the people who are frightened. For instance, the statistical evidence that the four large southwest cities with the greatest migrant population have the lowest levels of violent crime has little effect on people who are frightened by change and the influx of people who carry their own frightening impulses. Every negative incident involving illegal immigrants becomes multiplied by the level of fear, until it becomes much more real to these people than any amount of scientific or sociological data. This shadow projection then also tends to generalize to legal immigrants and to all people who look similar, and the current shadow carriers tend to blend and overlap.

During the Vietnam era, and all of the Cold War era, the projection of the shadow was both created and sustained by the level of fear. The more we were afraid of the threat of nuclear annihilation which we ourselves had once released on the world, the more we needed to project our own aggression and need to dominate and control, to the point that we were the greatest threat to our own survival, as expressed in the anti-communist motto used in the US during the Cold War: "better dead than Red." This interplay was satirized to great effect in the movie *Dr. Strangelove* (Naylor and Kubrick 1964)—a satire of the macho cowboy mentality that needs to dominate and control. This movie also illustrates the interplay between projection of shadow and projection of negative anima.[3]

Norman Mailer (1988) wrote a book called *Why Are We in Vietnam?* that was an account of a group of Texans that go up to Alaska to hunt grizzly bears. Many people were puzzled by the theme of this book, and how it applied to Vietnam. In the psychological landscape of that time, it made perfect sense to me. This was a period when white men in power were threatened by the loss of their power to blacks, to women, and even to their children, who were challenging their right to run the world. The men in power needed to prove their continued power in the traditional way that men needed to prove themselves: by going to war and asserting their dominance.

The conflict over the Vietnam War was not only a political conflict, although that is the way most people framed it. From my perspective of Jungian archetypal psychology, it was a conflict between Senex and Puer, as played out dramatically in the 1968

---

3   The negative anima is a term used for the negative aspect of the archetype that becomes more powerful when it is repressed. For instance, in this case the cult of hyper-masculinity, which is fostered in a cowboy mentality, is a result of the fear and repression of the feminine. This ultimately results in distorting the feminine so it becomes something to be feared or controlled. A similar process occurs to cause the negative aspect of the animus to emerge for women.

Democratic National Convention. It was a conflict between those who were aware of our own shadow and wanted to heal it, and those who continued to unconsciously project it. The latter group wanted to dominate and control the projected shadow through the mechanism of war and empire-building. It was a conflict between those who welcomed the emergence of the feminine and were able to embrace the new relationship of the masculine and feminine, and those who were threatened by the emergence of the feminine and needed to go out and prove their manhood.

These conflicts are still being played out, with disastrous effects on ourselves and on the world. There are still Texans on a bear hunt—Senex figures who remain threatened by the shadow and by the emergence of the feminine, who need to dominate and control. Obviously, in Mailer's (1988) book and in this framework, we are not talking literally about Texas, but the primary architects of the current war grew up with that cowboy mentality. This was the mentality of the frontier, in which hardened men systematically laid waste to the inhabitants and the animals in their need to dominate and control. There was very little presence of the feminine in that realm, in either women or men. It was a mentality that allowed survival in a tough world, but was highly destructive to people, animals, and the land. Life was nasty, brutish, and short. As is the case of many survival adaptations, the qualities that allowed us to survive in crisis now threaten our survival—only now it is not just individual survival that is at stake, but our collective survival.

It is paradoxical that the most powerful nation in the world militarily is so afraid that any assault is experienced as a threat to survival. It is the same paradox expressed in the people who live in gated communities who are frightened at any incident that could threaten their security. Some men who accumulate incredible wealth and power are still afraid of not having enough and of being powerless. Because these fears are so irrational and so disconnected from the reality of the situation, they become impervious to logic and factual data. Often the irrational fears that drive such persons are rooted in childhood fears and conditioning rather than present reality. This irrationality is also revealed in the frequent contradictions and total illogic of the men who pursued the war in the beginning, and the many men who vote against their own interests for these men in power. This pattern is described in detail in the book *What's the Matter with Kansas?* (Frank 2004). This book exemplifies the coping pattern of identifying with the aggressor, which many men and some women have adopted. It is their way of coping with loss of economic and social power. They identify with the "power" projected onto the men in charge at the cost of their own wellbeing.

These are examples of the way Jungian concepts can help us to understand the archetypal forces at play in our world today, and the impact of the collective unconscious on our body politic. I could elaborate with other current examples of these, such as the mutual projections of shadow in fundamentalists of all stripes.

Whether these fundamentalists are the political and religious fundamentalists in our country, or the religious fundamentalists in the Muslim world or the world of Israel, the archetypal forces and mechanisms make them mirror images of one another, even as they attempt to control and eliminate their shadow—the shadow of the fear of change, of modernity, and of loss of masculine power and dominance. I could cite the irrational nature of our burgeoning prison system, in which we have attempted to control and dominate the shadow by imprisoning it. This creates the same drastic drain on our national resources as is required in the individual who rigidly represses his or her shadow out of irrational fear. I could cite the irrational nature of our ecological crisis, in which our need to both dominate and control nature is threatening our survival. Again, this need to dominate and control seems so strong that it overpowers basic drives men have always had to provide for the survival of their children and families and of the species. This drive toward dominance is so powerful and irrational that, for many of these patriarchal men, it leads to a strong denial that the threat to their families and their children could be real. An example is the need to deny the reality of global warming when it conflicts with the profit motive.

The movie *Avatar* by James Cameron (2009) recently illustrated this archetypal drama and its inevitable conclusion in a most dramatic and striking portrayal of this collective conflict. This movie had a powerful impact on many people and on our collective consciousness, because it dealt with these archetypal themes. We see clearly in this movie the projection of the shadow and of the need to eliminate all those who stand in the way of the drive to dominate and control, which is displayed in men who are separated from their feminine nature. One of the criticisms of the movie was that it seemed to deal somewhat in stereotypes; however, as in the *Star Wars* (Lucas 1977) trilogy, when we are dealing with characters that embody archetypal forces, they can take on a larger-than-life quality. I also believe that the tremendous popularity and impact of *Avatar* came from the fact that the archetypal struggles portrayed in it are so close to the central conflict of our time.

In the movie, the forces of love and balance win against the forces of control and domination, and there is a true inner marriage that transcends the limitations of the body. *Avatar* and the three *Matrix* films (Wachowski and Wachowski 1999) deal with similar archetypal themes, and may or may not be directly influenced by the work of Carl Jung. I do know this influence is true for the movies *2001, A Space Odyssey* (Kubrick 1968) and *Star Wars* (Lucas 1977). Often, these collective themes emerge from the unconscious in great artists, or at least in artists that pick up on the central archetypal themes of our time. As in the case of inner dialogue, they may be directly or partly influenced by the ideas of Jung, or they may be directly in touch with these archetypal ideas on their own.

Whether or not Jung's influence is noted in these particular works of art, his understanding of and interaction with the collective unconscious and the world of archetypes has brought this way of thinking into our cultural domain, and has provided a symbolic and semantic vocabulary to deal with these ideas. These ideas and concepts continue to have an influence on our consciousness today.

At the same time, this dialogue goes both ways, and the body of Jungian work continues to be developed by its interaction with the world. Jungian theory and thought are influenced by the latest developments in physics, in neuropsychology and brain research, and by other current developments in psychology. Jung himself was influenced by his interactions with the ideas and great thinkers of his time, such as in his interactions with Richard Wilhelm, who helped bring Eastern thought into his purview. His conversations with Einstein and Pauli helped him to know and understand ideas of relativity and quantum physics. Jung's ideas were constantly evolving and changing to match his experience and the impact of current thinking and science. He was keenly interested in the political, scientific, literary, and theological knowledge of his time, as well as in popular culture.

It appears to me that for most Jungian analysts, the focus is too narrowly on the world of analysis and the analytic enterprise. This work of individual analysis is extremely important, and the novelist Herman Hesse and the great Italian director Federico Fellini are examples of people who have been influenced by their experience of being in Jungian analysis, and who have brought this influence to the larger culture through their artistic works.

However, it is possible that the greatest impact of Jungian ideas may be outside of and beyond the sphere of personal analysis—perhaps strongly influencing our collective cultural need to individuate. This impact may sometimes be unacknowledged, as were many of his contributions to the general practice of psychotherapy. It may be indirect, as in the influence of his ideas on the general culture. However, in many cases Jung's impact is direct and acknowledged. For instance, George Lucas acknowledged that the impact of Joseph Campbell's book *The Hero with a Thousand Faces* (Campbell 1972) was seminal for his ideas in *Star Wars* (Lucas 1977).

I also believe that an important element of this dialogue comes from people who are outside the world of Jungian analysis, who are beginning to move these ideas into the world in their own way. One of these relevant voices is that of Debbie Ford, who in her shadow workshops and her book and DVD, *The Shadow Effect*, is attempting to do exactly what I have suggested—apply this concept of the shadow to popular culture (Chopra *et al.* 2010). She has now teamed with Deepak Chopra as they to attempt to spread these ideas through the resources of the popular media, and there are many workshops and showings of this DVD across our country.

In it they acknowledge that the unintegrated shadow is so destructive and so powerful in our time that we must make every effort to help heal this split in our world before it leads to further cultural splitting and mutual destruction. Their efforts are focused more on the need for individuals to do shadow work, and on providing experiential methods and exercises for this work than on analyzing the impact on the world cultural and political situation, but they do cite examples of the operation of the shadow in the collective culture.

I personally welcome the efforts of people like Debbie Ford and Deepak Chopra, and any other people who have not been formally trained in Jungian analysis, but have found these ideas to be powerful and useful in their own lives, and want to share them with the larger culture.

It is not Jung the person that we celebrate and acknowledge— we are moving beyond the time of the hero and the guru. Jung himself encouraged us in his book *Modern Man in Search of a Soul* (1933) to do in our own lives what Jesus did in his, rather than mindlessly imitating him. Jung was not a perfect human being to be copied, but a self-acknowledged wounded healer, who, out of the effort to heal his own wounds, has left us a rich legacy of ideas and techniques to be applied to the world of our time by anyone who has been helped and influenced by these ideas. Some of these developments will happen within the Jungian world, if it is not too engaged in holding the treasure tightly in an attempt to preserve some kind of pure ideal. More of these developments will happen in the continued dialogue between the world and these ideas, and will continue to evolve into something totally new.

It is significant that the most recent emergence of Jung in our culture, which marks a kind of reemergence, is the Jung of *The Red Book* (Jung and Shamdasani 2009). In it Jung is not recording the emergence of some kind of hero, of some idealized human being; but of a great mind and visionary who explored the frontiers of the collective unconscious through inner dialogue, and embarked on a strange and terrible journey of exploration through inner dialogue. This dangerous but fruitful journey brought back not only healing for himself in his personal crisis, but tools for inner dialogue which are proving fruitful in many forms and branches for healing many people. He also brought back awareness of the collective psyche and its archetypal forms and power, which led him to develop and refine many ideas, which were central to his psychological and inner work. Over time, and in dialogue with his colleagues and the world of ideas of his time, he developed these ideas into a psychology that is useful to our collective body in our collective process of individuation.

One of the reasons Jung was able to explore the farthest reaches of the objective psyche was that he remained grounded in daily reality. Concurrently with his work in *The Red Book* (Jung and Shamdasani 2009), Jung was seeing patients, being a father and husband to his family, and was working on his psychology of consciousness that he published during this period as *Psychological Types* (Jung 1971a).

This collective process of individuation requires healing the many psychic splits and integrating the polarized opposites of our time. These ideas and tools are too valuable and necessary for our world to be somehow protected and kept pure. They need to be part of an ongoing process of dialogue with the world.

The work of Jung has had and will continue to have much to offer in this process of dialogue. However, many contemporary approaches to inner dialogue also have a great deal to offer to Jungians. In my experience, Jungians have been more open in recent decades to dialogue with other forms of analysis, but less open to what these other forms of inner dialogue have to offer, even when, as in process work, they have emerged directly from the work of Jung.

I consider myself very fortunate to have experienced at various levels of depth several of these approaches. I was involved in the basic Hakomi training for two years, studied process work in some depth, and have had some exposure to Internal Family Systems, Progoff Intensive Journal, Focusing, and Gestalt. All of these experiences have added to my Jungian training in developing aspects of awareness that were less developed in classical Jungian training. For example, through the methods of working directly with body states and with various states of consciousness, I have gained more awareness of the interactive process as manifested in the immediate behavioral responses in the consulting room. The river of consciousness flows through many streams, and while it is important to have a thorough grounding in one's approach, it seems to me to be very much in the spirit of Jung to be open to the way consciousness continues to emerge and interact in all of these streams. Perhaps this book may help to make this ongoing dialogue more possible.

REFERENCES

Agel, J. (ed.), 1970. *The Making of Kubrick's 2001.* New York: Signet.

Alpert, R., 1971. *Be Here Now.* San Cristobal, NM: Lama Foundation.

Chenghou, C., and Heyong, S., 2010. "'Garden of the heart-soul' in the earthquake area of China: Creativity and transformation." *Jung Journal: Culture & Psyche 4, 2,* 5–15.

Chopra, D., Ford, D., and Williamson, M., 2010. *The Shadow Effect: Illuminating the Hidden Power of Your True Self.* New York: HarperOne. Also in DVD format, 2009: Hay House.

Corbett, S., 2009. "The holy grail of the unconscious." *The New York Times Sunday Magazine,* 20 September.

Frank, T., 2004. *What's the Matter with Kansas? How Conservatives Won the Heart of America.* New York: Metropolitan.

Honig, H., 1979. "A Psychological Study of Camilla Hall." Dissertation, Loyola University.

Johnson, R.A., 1983. *We: Understanding the Psychology of Romantic Love.* New York: HarperCollins.

Johnson, R.A., 1989a. *She: Understanding Feminine Psychology.* New York: Perennial Library.

Johnson, R.A., 1989b. *He: Understanding Masculine Psychology.* New York: Perennial Library.

Jung, C.G., 1910. "The Association Method by Carl G. Jung." *The American Journal of Psychology 31,* 219–269.

Jung, C.G., 1919. *Studies in Word Association: Studies Carried Out at the Psychiatric Clinic of the University of Zurich under the Direction of C.G. Jung MD, LLD.* M.D. Eder (trans.). New York: Moffat, Yard and Company.

Jung, C.G., 1933. *Modern Man in Search of a Soul.* San Diego, CA: Harcourt Brace & World, Inc.

Jung, C.G., 1971a. *Psychological Types.* Princeton, NJ: Princeton University Press.

Jung, C.G., 1971b. "The Relations between the Ego and the Unconscious." In J. Campbell (ed.) *The Portable Jung.* New York: Viking.

Jung, C.G., 1990. *Analytical Psychology: Its Theory and Practice (The Tavistock Lectures).* London: Ark Paperbacks.

Jung, C.G. and Shamdasani, S., 2009. *The Red Book: Liber Novus.* New York: W.W. Norton & Co.

Jung, C.G.; Jaffe, A. (ed.); Winston, R. and Winston, C. (trans.), 1965. *Memories, Dreams, Reflections.* New York, NY: Random House.

Keen, S., 2004. *Faces of the Enemy: Reflections of the Hostile Imagination.* San Francisco, CA: Harper and Row.

Kubrick, S. (dir.), 1968. *2001, A Space Odyssey.* Metro-Goldwyn-Mayer.

Mailer, N., 1988. *Why Are We in Vietnam?* Oxford: Oxford University Press.

McGlashan, A., 1967. *The Savage and Beautiful Country.* Boston, MA: Houghton Mifflin.

McGuire, W. (ed.); Manheim R. and Hull, R.F.C. (trans); McGlashan, A. (abridged), 1994. *The Freud/Jung Letters: The Correspondence Between Sigmund Freud and C.G. Jung.* Princeton, NJ: Princeton University Press.

Meyers, I.B. with Meyers, P.B., 1995. *Gifts Differing.* Palo Alto, CA: Consulting Psychologists Press.

Naylor, D. and Kubrick, S. (dirs), 1964. *Dr. Strangelove.* Sony Pictures Home Entertainment.

Shah, I., 1973. *The Exploits of the Incomparable Mulla Nasrudin.* London: Picador.

Singer, J., 1994. *Boundaries of the Soul: The Practice of Jung's Psychology* (Revised Edition). New York: Random House.

Stevens, A., 1994. *Jung. A Very Short Introduction.* Oxford: Oxford University Press.

Taylor, J.B., 2006. *My Stroke of Insight: A Brain Scientist's Personal Journey.* New York: Viking.

Wachowski, A. and Wachowski, L. (dirs), 1999. *The Matrix.* Warner Bros.

Wilber, K., 2011. *A Brief History of Everything* (Revised Edition). Boston, MA: Shambala.

CHAPTER TWO

RIVER OF KNOWING
A Journey with Focusing
Joan Klagsbrun, Ph.D.

This we have now is not imagination
This is not grief or joy
Not a judging state of elation or sadness
Those come and go
This is the presence that doesn't

(Rumi 1995)

FINDING FOCUSING

It was my 30th birthday party. I remember all my friends gathered around me, celebrating, when suddenly I burst into tears. I felt an almost overwhelming sense of despair that I had been pretending wasn't there. It was something I had been vaguely aware of for months—my life was no longer working. I wasn't looking forward to a new decade, and I felt there was little to celebrate from the old one. The painful image that came to me was of a clay pot that had been fired into the wrong shape. I was stuck in an unhappy marriage, one that I had entered into soon after graduating from college. And my work as a new psychotherapist, something I had been looking forward to for a long time, didn't feel right either. I had been trained in a pathology-oriented model that just didn't fit who I was. To top in all off, my mother had just been diagnosed with advanced ovarian cancer, and her prognosis wasn't encouraging. I felt alone and trapped.

Out of desperation rather than inspiration, I decided to spend a month at Naropa Institute in Boulder, Colorado. They were offering a program that included the study and practice of meditation, poetry, and an intriguing new system called Focusing taught by a philosopher named Eugene Gendlin.

I had taken a look at his philosophy book called *Experiencing and the Creation of Meaning* (Gendlin 1962), and was captivated by this innovative and iconoclastic professor from the University of Chicago. He professed a concept that fascinated me: "feeling without symbolization is blind; symbolization without feeling is empty" (p.5). Now I sat in the front row as he led us through an intriguing process of paying inward attention to the center of the body. I intuitively understood that Gendlin was asking us to sense into the "lived body"—a personal repository of experience and memory—more than the actual physical body. The objective was, as he explained it, to get a sense of what we were "invisibly carrying." He explained that there were specific physical resonances that we experienced when we thought about a situation, and these palpably felt feelings could lead us to new understandings. He guided us in dialoguing with a kind of inner felt sense so that small new steps of change could emerge. These steps released the tension inside, and opened doorways to pursue new behaviors. Most importantly for me, the process brought a welcome sense of calm, relief, and clarity.

I liked the idea of what seemed to be a private conversation with myself, and I later learned more about this application of Gendlin's assertion that we can, as humans, tap into the vast complexity of body knowing and dialogue within this implicit realm. I discovered within myself a calm interior space where I could reflect on my problems and issues with a refreshing kind of intimacy, while maintaining enough distance to keep me from becoming overwhelmed. The experience was both exciting and revelatory. I also remember feeling a surprising sense of relief to be cataloguing these issues.

Gendlin guided us to check with our bodies for the problems that stood in the way of our feeling OK. I was amazed at how many there were in my mind, but I found only a few major ones were causing discomfort inside my body. Those few, however, were disruptive enough to evoke a familiar sense of being weighed down by insurmountable issues. But when Gendlin said, "Please just greet each of these problems, but don't fall into them—keep a little distance and just imagine you are stacking them up next to you on an imaginary bench." I felt myself smiling. "They'll break the bench," I thought—they were simply too massive. But I found to my surprise I could do as he asked—one by one, name them, feel how they felt in my body (one was tight, another constricting my throat, a third pressing down on my solar plexus), and then set them aside. When the main ones had been placed on the bench, I felt lighter, as if I had sent them away for a moment and had some respite from the weight of them. I later learned that these moves of Focusing, that facilitate getting the "right distance" from pressing issues, allow a person to be neither overwhelmed nor cut off entirely from an issue.

Then he had us choose one concern to work on. I chose my mother's illness. "This issue has many parts," he said, "but what does the *whole* of it feel like? See if there is a word or image that would capture how it all is for you."

> Getting the feel of the whole situation and finding the evocative words or images that capture that whole are important aspects of the Focusing process.

Tears started to stream down my cheeks. "Sad," I thought, but then I listened more closely inside. "Sad" didn't really capture it. The word devastated came to me. Yes, that came closest to matching the whole, complicated, murky feeling inside. Strangely, in the midst of acknowledging this feeling of devastation, I noticed that my body seemed to relax, and my breathing deepened. "Now see if you can keep this word or image company, and wait to see if it has something to tell you."

I waited and listened, and to my surprise, the devastated feeling had a lot to say. It told me I needed to stop being squashed inside, and to let myself cry, to talk to friends more about how lost I felt. And then another message came to me—I needed to share how scared and devastated I felt, and to clearly communicate these feelings to my mother, instead of playing the role of the strong daughter. With that action step came a great sigh.

Action steps often come organically out of the felt sense.

I knew that confiding in her would help me, and I also realized that perhaps she would actually be relieved to have me speak honestly to her. Perhaps we could find a way to be more real instead of ignoring the elephant in the room, as we had been doing.

I felt incredulous that listening to my inner self could feel good. Nothing was different—my mother still had cancer—but my relationship to the situation had truly shifted. And the process of shifting it had, in some way, released me. I knew right away that I wanted to bring this Focusing process more into my everyday life, and to share it with my clients in therapy.

When I opened my eyes, Gene Gendlin was nodding and smiling his warm smile, looking directly at me. He seemed to know that I had had an important experience. During the week I had several more chances to do Focusing, and to hear about the philosophy from which it evolved. I slowly came to understand Gendlin's brilliance in naming this dimension of experience, a dimension that was neither thought nor feelings but what he called *felt meanings* that emerged from a bodily felt experience.

"If only you were on the east coast," I said to him at the end of that life-changing week. "I would really like to study with you. I can sense that this way of working fits who I am—it's kind of like gestalt therapy for introverts." He chuckled. I knew then that this approach would both profoundly change my relationship to myself, as well as the way I worked as a therapist. He shared that in fact he was leaving Chicago for a two-year sabbatical in New York, and he would be glad to supervise me whenever I could get there from Boston.

I took him up on the offer. Every other Friday I would drive down from Boston to see him and, coincidentally, since my parents lived in New York, I would often visit my mother fresh from an hour spent working with Gene.

My mother and I had been close, but we didn't have an easy relationship. I had felt her at times to be judgmental and controlling, and I think she, in turn, experienced me as somewhat distant and resistant to her authority. Now that she was becoming more ill, however, I felt keenly motivated to become more intimate, as did she. Her illness had softened her, and it had made me more vulnerable. We needed to be close, to talk more frankly.

I told her about my experience with Focusing and how devastated I felt about the thought of losing her. She surprised me by accepting how I felt without any judgment. I stopped pretending to be brave, and cried more in her presence. She offered me the mothering I needed. I was even able to tell her about my desire to leave my marriage, and she surprised me by being understanding. One day, I got up the courage to ask if she would be willing to try some Focusing, since it had been so helpful to me.

"Why not," she laughed, rather uncharacteristically. "What do I have to lose?"

It was a cold, brisk March day. We sat on the porch bundled under a blanket. I suggested that she close her eyes and take a few breaths, and bring her attention down into the center of her body and notice what wanted her awareness there. She waited a long time, but I could tell by the pensive and engaged expression on her face that she was sorting a lot before she spoke.

"Well," she said, "what I find is less fear about dying than I would have guessed. I actually feel a lot of gratitude for the 60 years I have had. I am remembering some highlights of my life. I think my favorite days were the days you and your sister were born." Her voice became more somber. "Now I can feel a real hard knot in my stomach. Something in their feels like a ball of fists, all knotted up."

There was a long uncomfortable silence. I tentatively asked her to say more about the knotted-up feeling, though I was worried I might have crossed the line and she would stop the process. Then, much to my surprise, she began. "It's the chemo treatments. Something doesn't feel right about continuing them." She paused for a moment. "They make me so sick, week after week and month after month, and since the doctors are giving me little hope of getting well, I'd like to stop."

She paused, closed her eyes again, and said, "I have the image of a ship at sea, with no more fuel, adrift on a grey sea." She continued, "Enough is enough." She opened her eyes and turned to me. "But what is knotted up there is that I feel I ought to go on for all of you. I feel you are counting on me to keep getting the chemo, and that I'll let you all down if I stop. The truth is that I would like to live whatever time I have without these punishing treatments." She seemed as if her words had surprised even her. "I didn't quite have the words for it before now."

We sat together crying. "Are you OK with this?" she asked after a while.

"Mother, we want you to be around as long as you can, but it sounds as if you have had enough," I said. "If that's what you really want, of course we'll support you."

We hugged, and she seemed lighter and stronger when she looked me in the eye and said, "Well, dear, being the captain of my ship as I sail out does seem to be a lot more my style!"

My mother stopped the chemo the next week, with the full support of our family. I will always be grateful we had found a way to speak honestly and deeply to each other at the end of her life. At one point, a couple of days later, she turned to me smiling and said, "Just so you know, the ball of knots is gone." I was gratified she had gotten to choose how she died as well as how she lived.

FOCUSING FOR SELF-CARE

I have now been practicing and teaching Focusing for 35 years. It has become, for me, a deeply comforting way to connect with myself, and to hear from those elusive inner places that I can palpably feel but can't yet put into words. Focusing has changed how I deal with difficult issues, and with uncomfortable and unresolved feelings that I can sense in my body. Rather than analyze my issues or try to change my feelings, Focusing has led me to a greater acceptance of what is. It has offered me a practice in which I can gently sense into my own truth, neither overwhelmed by it, nor needing to distance myself from it. It has been an effective way to release and uncramp my body and mind. It has given me, as well as many of my clients and students, the ability to keep company with those parts that are blocked and with the many inner critical voices. Being with these aspects of myself in a gentle, respectful way helps me to hear their point of view and makes for more overall harmony and less judgment.

There have been many times in my life when I have reached an impasse, times when I have been unsure of which direction to take. Focusing has provided me with a reliable tool for making wholehearted decisions, and for clarifying vague and unresolved feelings. By listening to what is implicit, what is not yet clear, what is right below words and concepts, I can touch into something that feels like a trustworthy body knowing.

I use Focusing almost every day when I am alone to clarify moments of uncertainty by asking my body: "What feels *wrong* here?" or "What would making that decision *feel* like?" or "What am I *hungry* for?" And then, with curiosity, I silently await my body's response—perhaps a vague pressure in my chest or possibly a swirling sort of ache in my lower abdomen or some other unique inner sense—and then I begin listening to the sensation's story of what got it so pressured or swirling. Very often within a few minutes of attentive listening and gentle asking—is there more?—I get a surprising but crucial insight into the roots of my unsettling experience, as well as a way forward that exactly fits my needs.

FOCUSING PARTNERSHIP

Sometimes, however, Focusing as a solitary practice does not seem to be enough. My process is often enriched by the presence of another person who skillfully listens to my inner explorations, who reflects my words and accompanies me as the issues unfold. The role of the partner is not to give advice, or analyze, or ask intrusive questions, but simply to provide a gentle, accepting presence. Thus I have a Focusing partnership with another trained focuser with whom I exchange Focusing sessions every week over the telephone. Our time together is evenly divided so we each, in turn, focus and listen for a half hour or so. Over the years that we have been with each other, we have found immense comfort and pleasure as we each find our own authentic direction, take new steps, or discover unfolding dimensions in our relationships. It is as if my partner holds the frame of my self-dialogue, enabling me to dip into murky issues safely, without drowning or having to avoid the problem altogether.

This Focusing partnership allows the practice to be used in a wide variety of circumstances, and with many different kinds of people. A partner can be anyone who is trained not to ask questions or give advice, but who has learned how to be fully present and to accompany the focuser during their turn. Focusing partners follow a prescribed way to listen inside and become aware of something that the body feels about a particular situation. There is an assumption with Focusing that words can come right from these bodily felt feelings, if one pauses and keeps attending there. When words or images come, they seem to bring insight, a new perspective, as well as a physiological sense of relief. A felt shift or a bodily release of tension often comes with the new clarity.

As an illustration, let me tell you of an incident on which I first self-focused and then later exchanged Focusing with my partner. Each process was profoundly helpful, but the one with my partner provided me with an illuminating breakthrough. I went on vacation expecting to feel lighter as I stepped off the plane into a new, beautiful environment. But to my surprise, it was as if I had brought all my old emotional baggage along—and when I sensed inside, it felt like I was bearing staggering weights, like two sacks of sand draped across my shoulders, pushing me toward the ground. I began to list what created all that heaviness: there was palpable regret that felt like a lump in my gut about a decision I had made to take on more teaching; there was wincing embarrassment about a writing deadline I had missed; I felt awful shame about disappointing a friend who had been ill; there was frustration about my bouts of insomnia that seemed to be becoming chronic; and one or two other issues involving relationships and money. What came to me was that everything I thought and felt was weighing me down. And yet paradoxically, just separating the issues and noting each one in turn seemed to release me from the weight of the previously undifferentiated mass. I was trying not to fall into these issues, but sit next to them, which is part of the Focusing approach. I took the time to notice what the right experiential distance needed to be for each one.

When issues feel overwhelming, I need more space or distance so that I can get a whiff of them without being too close. At other times, issues need to come in closer, so I can really feel them in my body instead of merely abstractly knowing that they are there. At this moment, however, I knew my issues were too close and overwhelming. I needed to give myself more space away from them. As I sat with the packages of misery at safe distances away, I asked my body what the whole thing needed. What came to me was a tingling, airy throbbing in my heart area that said, "Leave the packages right here for now. Go and enjoy hiking for a couple of days. Then come back and work on whatever is still there." A rush of relaxation coursed through my whole body.

Forty-eight hours later, feeling more resilient and energized, I came back to the list of problems that I had arrived with. I sat quietly, inviting my attention to move from the outside environment to my invisible insides.

What came there were fewer items than before. The regret about taking on the extra class disappeared. I could feel some relief, and noticed that the shame about letting down my friend was also considerably less. Time and distance had softened these issues, and, when I checked, they were no longer weighing on me in the same way. But the embarrassment of missing a deadline still felt heavy and brought back old, bad feelings about myself, and a critical inner voice that called me a failure. "How is all of this for you?" I asked my body. Almost instantly I got an inner sense of noisy static from a radio whose volume I couldn't turn down. I asked several gentle questions of the static, but it would not or could not seem to respond. I felt stuck.

I needed my Focusing partner for company and support. Luckily she picked up the phone on the second ring and said she was free to spend some minutes Focusing with me.

With my partner on the other end of the phone, I began with the question to my body, "What is between me and feeling fine about this issue?"

I responded, "Static that will not be turned down!"

My partner invited me to ask if the static would be willing to move out temporarily of my body, and it said it was willing to be placed on an imaginary bench. It transformed into an image that was like a despairing, foggy feeling, like a dark cloud. I asked Foggy Despair to speak to me.

"It's been so long—so much effort. And nothing ever changes. I kind of want to give up—I just won't be able to deal with this," it said. My partner softly asked, "So would it be OK for Foggy Despair to give up?"

Foggy Despair seemed surprised that it actually had that option. "Well, there is some rightness to that," it ventured. "Maybe not to give up on the whole endeavor," it continued, "but something has to change." I began to see that pushing and driving simply weren't working, and maybe there was a new way to deal with my writing block and my embarrassment about missing the deadline.

The heaviness inside felt some relief at this unexpected turn.

My partner reminded me to ask Foggy Despair what it needed. I imagined myself sitting next to my despair on the park bench. There was no immediate answer for a few minutes, but I kept my awareness on the felt sense of this feeling of giving up. Finally, what came was: "I need company," it said. "I don't want to be alone."

"I can't do this alone," I thought. A big breath came with that step forward. It was easier now staying with that lightening feeling, and I smiled to myself, I asked about which people might be willing to support me. One name came clearly, and I could sense the synchronicity of the choice. I felt a huge sense of relief. The session had been just 25 minutes in chronological time, but there had been a radical change in how my body was carrying the whole issue. Now I was ready to become a listener to my Focusing partner as she took her turn.

A BRIEF HISTORY OF FOCUSING

Focusing has an interesting history because it was first described not by a psychotherapist or counselor, but by a philosopher, Eugene Gendlin. He had escaped from Germany with his family and immigrated to the United States as a teenager. He received his doctorate from the University of Chicago in 1958. In his dissertation, he outlined his philosophy of the implicit in which he endeavored to "dip into the larger realm at the edge of thinking" (Preston 2008, p.351). However, because Gendlin didn't want to be solely an academic philosopher, he was intent on applying his philosophy to a living practice. He studied client-centered psychotherapy with Carl Rogers, and in the late 1960s the two of them collaborated in designing a series of research studies (Gendlin 1969, 1981). These studies set out to articulate some key concepts from Gendlin's philosophy of the implicit. Both men were eager to find out why some clients were successful in psychotherapy, while many were not. They tape-recorded several hundred psychotherapy sessions, searching for information that would reveal what behaviors or insights distinguished successful patients from those that were not.

One profound finding emerged from their studies. They discovered that there was one distinct characteristic of clients who got better in therapy that was not shared by those who didn't make so much progress. The successful clients were able to find and consult their inner felt meaning about a situation. They would typically pause and wait, sitting with what was still unclear in their inner felt experience. As Gendlin described it, they attended to the implicit bodily sense that they had of their problems, which, at first, seemed murky and more than they could easily put in words. However, when they paused and got a sense of what their bodies were experiencing, specific tensions inside could be distinctly felt. Some were able to describe in detail those inner sensations, often labeling them with a word or an image.

Focusing was the name Gendlin gave to this process. It was, he said, a "deliberate procedure for attending to the bodily sense of one's problems" (Gendlin and Tavris 1970, p.57). He called this new approach Focusing because it was like looking through the lens of a camera at a fuzzy view. But when the observer turns the lens this way and that, the issue finally comes into focus, becoming clear and identifiable.

Many subsequent research studies have confirmed that a client's ability to focus is predictive of successful psychotherapy. Gendlin has four times received awards from the American Psychological Association for his groundbreaking work.

Back in the 1960s, Gendlin, excited by these research study results (Gendlin 1969), asked whether Focusing could be taught. He devised a protocol of Focusing instructions so that clients could learn how to focus, and thereby increase the efficacy of their psychotherapy sessions. His book, *Focusing*, which was first published in 1981 and reprinted in 2007, has been translated into 20 languages.

Within a few years of the publication of *Focusing*, many people found that Focusing was relevant for many other endeavors besides psychotherapy. Today, Focusing is utilized in business, the arts, education, bodywork, theology, childcare, spirituality, and medicine. In the realm of counseling, it has been found to helpful in many settings such as pastoral, vocational, and rehabilitative care. Recently, Focusing has been introduced as a community self-help tool in psychosocial wellness programs for victims of war in Afghanistan and Gaza, and in developing countries such as Pakistan, Ecuador and El Salvador.

Focusing now has a presence in 43 countries and most states in the United States. The non-profit Focusing Institute helps to coordinate the growth of the method worldwide.

FOCUSING AND PSYCHOTHERAPY

I have been personally changed by my practice of Focusing, and Focusing (both the philosophy and the practice) has also changed how I work as a therapist. By welcoming the bodily dimension of felt meaning to my own life, I more naturally want to listen for the dimension in clients. I am more alert to their felt sense experiences. I work to nourish and expand their bodily knowing, and I trust that level of knowing. Thus, I no longer feel I always have to be the expert with the right interpretation. I have developed more trust in my clients' abilities to discover their unique paths and to find their own forward movement. Gendlin puts it this way in his *Focusing-Oriented Psychotherapy*: "A step has its own growth direction. One cannot legislate the direction" (Gendlin 1996, p.21).

Focusing joins well with many types of psychotherapies, such as psychoanalysis, mindfulness-based therapies, and cognitive behavioral therapies. By helping clients pay attention to the not-yet-conceptualized aspects of their feelings or issues, therapeutic progress can be accelerated, and blockages can often be worked through. When Focusing is integrated into therapy, a successful outcome is more likely. And, the practice of Focusing also improves life quality. As Gendlin has said: "Focusing will enable you to find and change where your life is stuck, cramped, hemmed in, slowed down. And it will enable you to change—to live from a deeper place than just your thoughts and feelings" (Gendlin 1981, p.21).

Two client experiences with Focusing

Sally began our session ranting about her cousin's terrible behavior toward her own father, who was Sally's uncle. "He is turning 80 in a few months, and she won't come to see him." (The uncle lives in Sally's town.) Sally went on for a while talking about all the outrageous behavior of her cousin. I asked, "Can we notice how you are inside as you speak about this? How it is for you to feel so outraged? How is it for you that she ignores her dad? What is it like for you to witness this?"

Sally took a couple of breaths, slowed down and put her hand on her chest, and with her eyes closed finally entered into her own feelings of sadness. All around her heart area she found what seemed to be shards of glass cutting into tender tissue. The pain was palpable. Sally cried and freshly remembered the deaths of her parents when she was in her early twenties, and she wept at her longing to have gotten more time with them. She spent time talking about how different life would have been had they not died and left her so vulnerable. With some encouragement from me, she was able to sit alongside the pain with compassion for its suffering. I found myself asking her if there was a kind of gentle company this pain needed. Within several minutes, Sally reported, "The pain is not so sharp now. It's more…tender…softly aching…it feels better to be with it instead of running away from it like I have done for a long time."

I could feel Sally's relief that she was treating herself the way she described treating her child when he was sick, home from school and needing extra nurturance. "I am feeling more tender toward myself," she acknowledged. And then without a conscious link, she said: "And I don't feel so intensely angry with my cousin."

After a reflective pause she looked up and said, much to my surprise. "I want to stop trying to control her behavior. My meddling is making tension between my uncle and me. He can't help it that his daughter is ignoring him."

> In Focusing a pause is crucial. One waits for words to emerge directly from a felt sense.

Then, as Sally seemed stuck as to how to deal with her cousin in a new way, I wondered out loud what this whole situation might need.

> A very powerful question in Focusing can be what does it need? And often by waiting, something comes that can be surprising, as it doesn't emerge from the logical thinking domain.

Sally paused to check inside and then a smile came to her face. "I actually love my uncle seemingly more than his own daughter does. I can't control *her*, but I can choose how *I* celebrate him… I just thought of a great way to show my appreciation and love. There are about 80 days before he turns 80, I think I will leave something in his mailbox—a brownie and a poem or some little thing to show my appreciation each day for 80 days."

You can imagine how pleased I was that the session ended on such a different note than it began. Sally left feeling freer and more positive, and as importantly, she left with a new experience of connecting with her deepest self. In this session, Sally had done the work of getting right to the place where something new could happen and where authentic steps of forward living naturally arose. It reminded me of what Gendlin says in *Focusing-Oriented Psychotherapy* (1996, p.46): "Every experience and event contains implicit further movement. To find it, one must sense its unclear edge" (which is more intricate than one's words can convey). "Every experience can be carried forward." Sally was able to find genuine movement from raging about her cousin's behavior to finding a fresh response to the situation that felt positive for her.

Harry came into his session complaining that his boss was constantly hounding him for more work than he felt he could deliver. At home his wife constantly asked him to do more errands, fix things in the house, talk more, everything more. "It's really so unfair," he said, "I feel like the whole world is sucking me dry." This phrase really got my attention. There was so much feeling in his words.

> In Focusing we listen for provocative words, images and metaphors that signal the emergence of this level of experience.

I repeated to him: "You feel like the whole world is sucking you dry." I added, "I imagine you're feeling how unfair it is that everyone around you asks so much of you."

> Reflection in Focusing is both a matter of staying on track and making sure that the listener can hear the meaning of the words he has uttered. As Gendlin (1996, p.46) wrote: "To reflect is thus a rare and powerful way to let clients enter into their own experience. It is a way of being as close as possible to someone without imposing something on them."

He nodded, sitting with it for a while. Then he said, "It's a kind of a heavy thick feeling that weighs on me…like a lead apron, you know, the ones they use when you get an x-ray. I can feel it compressing the breathing in my chest."

That image was also pretty vivid for me. "It's like the asthma attacks I had when I was a kid. No, it's even worse than that. With this, I can't take anything and there's no relief. I feel like the life is being squeezed out of me."

I took in what he said and said it back with the same emphasis he used. "Something is squeezing the life out of you." He frowned, then nodded, staying very present and attentive. "I want to say, 'No! Get off me!'" he said, "but something stops me."

"So there is something that wants to say 'No!' and a part that stops and holds you back from saying no." His head dropped onto his chest, and he nodded.

"So, what is the 'no' part like?" I asked. "Can you say it again for me, the way you might feel you want to say it?"

Harry looked up at the ceiling, and shouted "No!" and even demonstrated his own no gesture with his arm raised above his head, as if he was warding off a blow. He did that a few times, and then with a half-smile he said, "Hey, this feels good."

I could see his breathing settle. "So something in you really wants to call out no and makes this gesture?" (I mimicked him.)

"Yeah," he said, "but then I hold back."

We then spent a few minutes with the feeling of wanting to hold back.

"I have the image of a crab scuttling away under a rock," he said. "It's afraid, and wants to avoid a confrontation." He took some time to "step into" the crab's point of view, what it felt like to be always looking for a place to hide. Then I asked him if we could listen together to what it was that the crab needed. He waited a while before answering.

"It needs to know that it won't be crushed if it stays out in the open," he said.

There was a new energy in the room as Harry's body, face, and energy came alive.

"It needs to know it won't be crushed," I remarked.

Referring to this dimension of experience as an "it" allows this kind of dialogue with oneself. Gendlin talks about this dialogue with the surprising notion that if you can talk to it, it talks back (Gendlin 1981).

"Yes!" he said. "It needs something to help protect it." "Doesn't it have a shell?" I asked. "The shell isn't enough," he replied. "So it needs some kind of shield." He nodded his head. "Yeah, something to keep predators away, so it could feel safe. You know, like a force field in science fiction. Something invisible that makes any attacker just bounce off it."

Harry seemed quite animated as he devised something specific that could shield him and allow him to be more assertive in setting appropriate boundaries at home and at work.

"I need to have rules, you know, like my own little union. Decent working conditions. No overtime." He went on. "You know, what I really need is to have a way to know when I'm going over my limit." He smiled grimly to himself. "Right now, I'm always working overtime," he said. "Everyone expects it of me. At work, at home, I can't say no. I just keep taking on more and more. And then I feel like going under that rock."

I smiled. I asked him, "Harry, when you go inside, is there a sense of too much? Can you tell when you've crossed the line?" He thought about it for a while. "Yeah, I think so. I get this feeling in the pit of my stomach, you know, like, a little voice saying, 'Oh no, Harry, not again.'"

We agreed that, as a first step, he would spend the next week just noticing when he crossed that threshold. "You don't need to do anything about it," I told him. "Just notice when you're going over that line."

Harry was able to take some steps in this session from feeling vaguely oppressed to connecting specifically with his conflicted feelings, which he expressed in metaphor. He found a part of himself which wanted to protest, and a part that was scared of asserting itself. Through coming up with his authentic gesture (no!) and his creative images of the crab and the protective force field, he was able to get in touch with the whole complex issue of his feeling overwhelmed. He also came up with a plan to notice when he started to work overtime. By gently acknowledging and getting to know these parts, Harry became more integrated, more aware, and less afraid of expressing himself.

In these sessions with Sally and Harry, Focusing was woven into the therapy in a way that enabled them to find and stay with their bodily felt sense; to speak directly from it, often using images and metaphors which are the language of the implicit; and to hear the meanings that were at the core of their feelings and behavior.

CLEARING A SPACE

There are times when clients make use of the first step of Focusing called clearing a space, a step where they spend time taking an inventory of what is in the way of feeling fine. This is a stress reduction method that can be the prelude to Focusing but can also, in its own right, be a powerful method of bringing presence to oneself.

Victoria was in dire need of such an inner compass when she first consulted me. She was a 42-year-old mother of four young children, and her lung cancer had left her feeling adrift and overwhelmed. Her illness had resulted in major chest surgery, and when she first came to see me, she was in a considerable pain.

"Well," she began before she had even settled in her chair, "I'm stressed out so much of the time. I'm not sleeping well, and anxiety about a recurrence makes me unable to plan even a month in advance. What I really need is some way to deal with all this fear. I try to think positively, but I'm afraid I'm not going to stay in remission. I've tried meditation, and it helps me to reduce the pain level, but it doesn't seem to lessen my fearful state—which is particularly bad the month before my check-up. And I don't want to take any more meds. I hope you have some new ideas."

I spoke with Victoria about clearing a space. I explained to her that it is a way to take an inventory of what you are carrying in your body that is between you and feeling fine. In this process, you discover each item that is interfering with your sense of wellbeing, and then place it at the right distance. As you place each item aside, you ask yourself—except for that, am I feeling fine? Going through the clearing a space protocol helped Victoria to attain a sense of calm that lasted for a couple of days. After that, often as she settled in her chair, she would say: "OK, I am really stressed out. Please help me to clear my space."

Although Victoria had a large circle of friends and family members who cared about her, she felt she could not be fully honest with them. The fears that she was able to find and verbalize with me as she cleared a space each week were ones she could not easily reveal to others. She believed these unspoken fears would be too upsetting for others to bear.

One day when Victoria seemed particularly agitated, I asked her to notice what was between her and feeling fine. The first thing she noticed was that, in her imagined space, there was a heavy menacing black cloud behind her, one that she could feel and, when she turned around, could even see. She described a clutched tightness gripping her belly whenever she saw the black cloud. I asked if she might begin by acknowledging the gripping feeling from a little distance away.

"Yes," she said. She was able to imagine placing the cloud a few feet away, behind the couch, tucked in a corner of the room. She then told me that the gripping feeling had lessened. This movement alone induced her to take a big exhalation, and I could see that the muscles in her face had begun to relax.

"OK, Victoria, except for the black cloud which you have placed a distance away, please see if you are fine." She frowned and slowly shook her head.

"So, let's see what else might be in the way today," I continued.

"Well," she said hesitantly after a long silence, "in my abdomen I can feel a kind of dark, sinking, sad feeling, like what if this could be my last Christmas with the kids? I am afraid that maybe I won't be around next year, and it is an unbearable thought."

I asked if she might want to acknowledge the dark, sinking, sad feeling and see if it might be possible to make a package out of it and put it at the right distance away. As she wrapped it in velvet and placed it on a shelf in the room, she and I both shed a tear. I reflected her heavy sadness and then asked, "Is there more?" She nodded her head.

The next aspect of fear that she experienced appeared as a tightness in her throat, as if, as she said, "I have something stuck there, and I can't swallow. It is about speaking to my kids when they ask if I can get cancer again. I want to be honest up to a point, but I can't get myself to say, 'Yes, it is possible.'"

"All right," I said. "Let's notice that tightness in your throat that doesn't want to be dishonest, but can't bear to frighten your kids. See if the tightness in your throat would like to be placed outside of your body for now; not to get rid of it, but to give yourself a free space to be in for a while. It is like getting respite from your problems." She nodded and made a gesture indicating that she had placed the tightness next to her chair. She then mentioned that her throat actually felt more opened, after she had imagined the tightness next to her rather than in her.

Finally, I asked if there was a background sense, kind of like the wallpaper we don't even notice anymore, but when we stop to look for it, we can see it plainly. She waited with her eyes closed and said, "Yes, there is a background sense of being preoccupied. Even when I am at the table at a meal with all the children, or making love with my husband or talking to a friend on the phone, I can feel the fear hovering overhead, preoccupying me."

I wondered how we might capture the preoccupation so she could place it aside—safely distanced from her. "Oh, that is easy," she said. "I think I can catch it and put it in a jar my kids use to catch fireflies." She imagined putting the jar in a suitcase and locking it away for the moment.

I reassured her that we would come back to work on those issues, but in the meantime, she could allow herself to enjoy what it felt like to be in the cleared space, a place where she didn't have to do anything and could allow herself to just be. I could see her breathing deepen, and her shoulders drop. Some of the lines of worry went out of her face, and her expression softened. I asked if there was a word, phrase or image that captured this clearer space. She smiled. "I'm back in the summer camp I went to for several summers as a child. There was a place in a pine grove that we called Chapel in the Woods. I am there and can feel the breeze, smell the pines, and I feel solid, safe and calm."

Focusing makes a space for all emotions, feelings, and responses, because by welcoming them, they can become guides and catalysts for change, and for forward movement. And forward movement is what is most needed in the process of psychotherapy.

HOW CLEARING A SPACE ENABLES US
TO DEAL WITH OUR FEARS

The process of clearing a space allowed Victoria to enter a protected space for a while and to recover the part of her that lived without worry and was truly calm. She found the capacity to reconnect with a deep-seated sense of wellbeing despite her physical pain and anxieties. She had been able to name and enumerate her fears and place them at a safe distance. By doing so, she had tapped into the aspect of self that is witnessing the fear, but not enveloped by it. As Albert Einstein is widely quoted as saying, you cannot solve a problem with the state of mind that created the problem. Clearing a space allowed her to find a new state of mind.

This process of naming and clarifying issues also helps us to identify and validate them as legitimate concerns. By allowing these issues to surface and come into the light of our compassion and caring, we give a home to a part of ourselves that needs acknowledgement. Engaging in this process of taking inventory of what the body is carrying allows us to release much of the bodily tension and free-floating anxiety that accompanies those issues.

Instead of dealing with fear as a clump of concerns, we separate them and will thus find them more manageable to work on when we return to the Focusing process. But for the moment, we remain at peace. And from the sense of peace that comes in a cleared space, people often discover a spiritual perspective on their concerns. Often people report feeling more equanimity, more gratitude, more hopefulness, more aliveness, and a greater ability to get a larger view of their situation. By spending time in the cleared space, they are dwelling in the present moment, which many spiritual traditions agree is the path to the sacred. Having seen the effectiveness of clearing a space in my practice, I undertook two pilot research studies with women with breast cancer (Klagsbrun *et al.* 2005;

Klagsbrun, Lennox and Summers 2010) that demonstrated positive changes in life-quality in women who practiced this step of clearing a space.

FOCUSING AND THE REALM OF THE POSITIVE

I have shown how Focusing can be a method of working with personal problems, but it can also be a catalyst for increasing joy, appreciation, gratitude, happiness, love, and wellbeing. Recently, I have been including the principles of positive psychology as an intrinsic aspect of a healthy psychotherapeutic model. Research on positive emotions shows that a positive feeling leads to desirable changes. According to Barbara Fredrickson's broaden and build theory, described in her book *Positivity*, positive emotions affect both personal and interpersonal domains (Fredrickson 2009). They broaden our attention and our thinking so we enlarge the scope of our thoughts and our perspective; they lead to more creativity in our thinking and actions; and they build cognitive and social resources in ways that help us to become more resilient.

I have found that Focusing is a wonderful way to find insights and to savor the positive aspects of our lives. When I have a wonderful experience hiking on a gorgeous trail, or see a great concert, it is even more powerful to pause afterward and ask: what about this hike or concert was so special for me; what spoke to me; what touched me? I then wait for my body to talk back to me. The experience takes on a new dimension and often the happiness these experiences induced lasts longer by spending time articulating the essence of what was so pleasurable or meaningful.

Focusing is, in essence, a way to hear from and appreciate the non-linear, non-rational aspects of you that are vital, alive and full of knowing. I have discovered that Focusing on positive aspects of one's life is as rewarding and compelling as Focusing on any other aspect of the self, and that paying attention to the positive provides a way to inspire and motivate movement toward health and wellbeing. Focusing is intrinsically an optimistic method; it has as its foundation the tenet that the body knows what is needed and that the body has a built-in tropism toward health. Focusing on the intricacy of the positive realm helps it to grow. The implicit dimension is one we sense not analyze and what we get from that is distinctly different from what we get from the intellect. By slowing down and listening for the "more," you get insights about what made something so positive, and you help yourself to savor the experience. Whenever a client comes alive or seems excited about something, I encourage them to stay right at that edge and to sense into those excited or alive feelings and to see what comes.

A father was finding himself moved that his grown son had decided to move back to the city where his parents lived, but he was ready to move on and talk about some difficult issues. I wondered if he could stay and see what was so moving there. As I saw a tear form in his eyes, I asked him, "Can you say what is so special about this for you?"

"I feel so much joy that we will get to be friends now," he said, and as he sat with that joy, he added, "and I feel redeemed too— like I must have been a good enough dad that he is choosing to live close and have his kids near me too. I wasn't sure I had been a good enough dad and this is a huge relief. I sort of feel, well, kind of whole again—like he gave me back a part of my heart that I didn't even know was missing." Now tears of relief and joy were flowing. So often when people dip into the implicit zone below their full awareness, they are surprised by what they find there. And they often speak in metaphors and images because imaginative language helps to symbolize what is freshly forming from one's felt sense.

These explorations of the positive in our lives are quintessentially spiritual. The experience of attending to those things, people, and activities we love makes us feel resilient, happy, and absorbed. Asking ourselves in a Focusing way what is it that we love reminds us of the best of ourselves and best of what life can offer us.

> Some say an army on horseback,
> Some say on foot, and some say ships,
> Are the most beautiful things
> On this black earth but I say
> It is whatever you love.

(Sappho 2007)

I now believe in serendipity. It seems that events sometimes conspire so that we find the right people or practices at the right time in our lives. I found Focusing 35 years ago when urgently searching for a new personal direction, and needing a more meaningful way to practice psychotherapy. I have come to rely on the philosophy and practice of Focusing for self-care; for the growth made possible through my Focusing partnerships; for a richer understanding of the intricate, implicit dimension of experience; for the special friendships made across the worldwide Focusing community; and, for the depth and texture Focusing offers to psychotherapy. For me, and for many of my clients, Focusing is a compass that allows us to navigate the inner islands of the self and discover in that realm a new sense of clarity and embodied aliveness—a place where we can "dip into the larger realm at the edge of thinking" (Preston 2008, p.351).

REFERENCES

Frederickson, B., 2009. *Positivity: Top Notch Research Reveals the 3 to 1 Ratio That Will Change Your Life.* New York: Random House.

Gendlin, E.T., 1962. *Experiencing and the Creation of Meaning.* New York: Free Press.

Gendlin, E.T., 1969. "Focusing." *Psychotherapy: Theory, Research and Practice, 6,* 4–15.

Gendlin, E.T., 1981. *Focusing.* New York: Bantam Books.

Gendlin, E.T., 1996. *Focusing-Oriented Psychotherapy: A Manual of the Experiential Method.* New York: Guilford Press.

Gendlin, E.T. and Tavris, C., 1970. "A small, still voice." *Psychology Today,* 57–59.

Klagsbrun J., Rappaport, L., Marcow Speiser, V., Post, P., Byers, J., Stepakoff, S., and Karman, S., 2005. "Focusing and expressive arts in therapy as a complementary treatment for women with breast cancer." *Creativity and Mental Health, 1*(1), 107–37.

Klagsbrun, J., Lennox, S., and Summers L., 2010. "Effect of clearing a space on quality of life in women with breast cancer." *United States Association for Body Psychotherapy Journal, 49*(2) 48–53.

Preston, L., 2008. "The edge of awareness: Gendlin's contribution to explorations of the implicit." *International Journal of Psychoanalytic Self Psychology, 3*(4) 347–69.

Rumi, J., 1995. "This we have now is not imagination." In C. Barks (trans.) *The Essential Rumi.* New York: HarperCollins.

Sappho, 2007. "Sappho's Fragment." In J. Powell (ed.) *The Poetry of Sappho.* New York: Oxford University Press.

CHAPTER THREE

INNER WORK AT THE EDGE OF THE *UNUS MUNDUS*

A Process-Oriented Approach to Conflict Facilitation

Joe Goodbread, Ph.D.

THE GUEST HOUSE

This being human is a guest house.
Every morning a new arrival.
A joy, a depression, meanness,
some momentary awareness comes
as an unexpected visitor.
Welcome and entertain them all!
Even if they are a crowd of sorrows,
who violently sweep your house

empty of its furniture,
still, treat each guest honorably.
He may be clearing you out
for some new delight.
The dark thought, the shame, the malice.
Meet them at the door laughing and invite them in.
Be grateful for whatever comes.
Because each has been sent
as a guide from beyond.

(Rumi 1995)

As I began working on this chapter, I was struck by a familiar, small inner voice that kept nagging me with a philosophical question: does it make any sense to distinguish between the inside and the outside of the human being?

Don't get me wrong—I *love* that voice. My philosophical nature has been a constant, if somewhat split-off companion throughout my life. It sometimes infuriates my friends, and has been the bane of my opponents while discussing the nature of psychology, psychotherapy, and the discipline called worldwork about which I will have more to say in this chapter.

But I feel that this philosophical voice is sometimes far too abstract for my workaday world, whether I am working with therapeutic clients, helping people and groups deal with thorny conflicts, or any of the myriad other practical tasks that seem to require clear-cut, understandable formulations rather than philosophical meanderings.

My intent in this chapter is to show how a kind of inner work, developed by Arnold Mindell, the founder of Process-Oriented Psychology (or process work as it is more commonly known) can be used as a tool by facilitators—those of us who work in emotionally charged fields, helping couples and groups sort out difficult conflicts and other serious tensions. I will illustrate this with thoughts and stories from my own personal experience.

Facilitators often struggle with a host of inner conflicts in their attempt to remain impartial toward the diversity of viewpoints and interests that contend in the situations in which they have been hired to facilitate. Mindell and his associates have, over the years, developed a robust set of skills and methods that facilitators can use both outside—interventions that are useful for the groups with which they work—and inside—for working with their own reactions to these outer situations. But behind these methodologies stands a much broader question that is more philosophical than procedural.

What is the relationship between the outer and the inner? And does this distinction even make sense when we examine it closely?

These are points that have permeated Mindell's writing over the past 30 or more years, and which I have been privileged to be able to discuss with him in detail as his ideas developed. Questions such as these have also informed my own writing on topics such as counter-transference, social marginality, and conflict facilitation (Goodbread 1997a, 1997b, 2010, 2013). In particular, my recent book, *Living on the Edge* (2013), dealt with a process-oriented approach to the process of social marginalization. The book was based on some 20 years of research with socially marginal groups ranging from inmates in psychiatric institutions and residents of homeless shelters, to ex-Soviet military personnel who helped clean up the reactor site after the Chernobyl nuclear disaster in 1986, and who were later severely marginalized by mainstream post-Soviet society. One of my main conclusions was that people and groups are marginalized by the mainstream when they are seen as carriers of experience that severely challenges mainstream identity.

When I see homeless people I may be shocked, appalled, or judgmental, but most likely I will fall into a very special sort of altered state in which I drive them to the margins of my awareness. I usually avoid contact with them, often making up stories about how they will hit me up for money that they will then squander on drugs and drink. In any case, I relegate them to the outer limits of the category of other, distancing myself from their world, while further reinforcing their marginal status.

Perhaps most relevant to this chapter, however, was my discovery that my philosophical commitment to the *unus mundus*— my conviction that we are all joined and entangled in a single unified system—breaks down when I am confronted by someone whom I categorize as other—be they, in my perception, homeless, mad, bad, or somehow contaminated by experiences that, if I let them in, would threaten to destroy my sense of equilibrium and security.

This immediately gives focus to a particular kind of inner work that I am ethically obliged to consider if I am truly committed to my membership in a unified world. And it is to this kind of inner work that this chapter is devoted. Although I had hoped to skip the more abstract bit, I kept being distracted by that inner philosophical voice that, just this morning, reminded me of a dream that I'd had a few nights ago, while struggling to find a unifying focus for this chapter. And here is that dream fragment.

Someone has served me a plate of spaghetti. And as I am about to tuck into it, I see a single hair lying on top of the mound of pasta. And on this hair is a single white louse egg.

Needless to say, this dream was one I'd sooner forget. Besides being unappetizing when taken literally—from the standpoint of consensus reality—it doesn't get any better when looked at from the attitude that each element of a dream is an aspect of the dreamer's psyche. I don't particularly want to identify with a plate of spaghetti, much less one with a hair in it—and let's not even begin to think about the louse egg.

Time for some inner work: since the dream is composed of non-human entities, and there doesn't seem to be much action, it might be useful to associate to the objects in the dream. And of course, some of my associations are a bit embarrassing to share openly in a published book, but in the spirit of the thing, here we go.

Spaghetti: I once was babysitting a neighbor's son many years ago. I didn't relate well to kids, but as the parents were leaving after his bedtime, they assured me I was there just to hold the fort till they got home. When they did get home, it turned out the kid had vomited his dinner in bed—it was spaghetti—but he had been too embarrassed to tell me. I nearly grew faint when I saw the mess. I had no idea what I would have done if I'd had to clean up it— and him—before the parents got home. So we are evidently in the realm of hopeless-looking, repulsive messes. That is an attitude that I sometimes have toward seemingly intractable conflict and other entrenched, unpleasant aspects of group life. If they get really bad, I would sooner forget them and lead a solitary life, but I don't always succeed, or have that option.

A hair: one of the minor intimacies of living with other human beings is the presence of hairs in places where we least expect them; in the soap dish, in a bite of food, in the shower drain. Housemates over the years have always reminded me of this whether as the recipients of my unintentional gifts, or as the donor of theirs. I remember one client of mine who said that he had divorced his wife because she left hairs in the soap dish. That strikes a chord. It has to do with conflict that develops because of unconscious or unintentional acts, like losing the odd hair. And then we are pushed to either marginalize our reaction until it explodes into something much larger like divorce, or to take a closer look at our minor entanglements as indicators of deeper underlying processes.

Louse egg: my first association to a louse egg is the story of Pan Ku, an old Chinese creation myth (Goodbread 2013, p.viii).

THE CREATION OF THE EARTH FROM PAN KU'S BODY

In the beginning, all was one, and all was chaos. The universe was like a big egg, containing the Yin and the Yang, and the sleeping giant Pan Ku. Pan Ku, feeling suffocated, awoke and cracked open the egg. The Yang, being light, went up and formed the heavens, while the Yin, being heavy, formed the earth. As the world began to grow, Pan Ku grew along with it, standing like a pillar separating heaven from earth.

When Pan Ku died, his breath became the wind and clouds, his voice the rolling thunder. One eye became the sun and one the moon. His body and limbs turned to five big mountains and his blood formed the roaring water. His veins became far-stretching roads and his muscles fertile land. The innumerable stars in the sky came from his hair and beard, and flowers and trees from his skin and the fine hairs on his body. His marrow turned to jade and pearls. His sweat flowed like the good rain and sweet dew that nurtured all things on earth. The lice on his body became the ancestors of mankind.

But this story has a highly personal meaning for me, since it has been at the core of my interest in the *unus mundus* and its breakdown at the edge of our personal identities. In my book *Living on the Edge* (Goodbread 2013), I use the evolution of humans from Pan Ku's lice as evidence that human beings themselves, like lice, are fundamentally marginal to the world. That human consciousness has the ability to both construct and destroy the unity of the world, depending on how seriously that unity challenges the integrity of the individual. That is my association to the louse—and so the louse egg is the potential for the coexistence of unity and individuality in this messy, sometimes disgusting but ultimately magnificent entanglement that is human coexistence.

My inner work therefore leads me to the need to embrace the philosophical voice that favors neither unity nor individuality, but the process—the flickering interplay of consensus reality, unity, and individuality—that constantly transforms my relationship to all of them, and in the process, contributes to their co-creation.

From the viewpoint of that voice, we human beings occupy a position at the edge of the *unus mundus*, forever vacillating between feeling part of nature and, when nature gets too challenging to our sense of self, retreating to a position of individuality. What inner work adds to this is the possibility of facilitating this otherwise spontaneous and often unconscious process. Instead of marginalizing the challenging other at the edge of our unity with the world, we can ride the wave of awareness to explore the other as an aspect of ourselves, to expand our sense of who we are and to make us more a part of the *unus mundus*, rather than less. And this process faces in two directions.

When turned inward, we call it personal growth, or in Jungian terms, the integration of the shadow; there, we are in the realm of Rumi's guest house. When turned outward, we call it worldwork, acknowledging the diversity of the world, its people and its experiences as a greater unity-in-becoming: the evolution of Pan Ku.

In the next parts of this chapter, I will describe some of the challenges that face the facilitator—who is to the world's individuation process what the therapist is to the individual's. And I will show, with some theoretical introduction, but mostly through personal experience, the many ways that inner work enables facilitation in conflictual situations that would otherwise be too hot to handle using procedural methods alone.

But first, I must say a few words about process work, which forms the core around which worldwork, and the special forms of inner work, which facilitate it, are built.

INNER WORK AS THE CRADLE OF PROCESS-ORIENTED PSYCHOLOGY

The foundations of process work were initially laid by Arnold Mindell in the early 1970s in the course of his attempts to use Jungian active imagination to explore physical symptoms. He was, at the time, a training analyst at the C.G. Jung Institute in Zurich, Switzerland.

I recall one of Arnold's early lectures on how he developed his concept of the dreambody—the network of relationships between dreams and the dreamer's subjective experience of their own body. He had noticed several key similarities between the way he and his clients described their physical symptoms, and the way they told their dreams. Beside the fact that both dreams and body symptoms arose spontaneously and were notoriously difficult to control, they also possessed similar structures. They typically depict dramas played out between an ego figure that shares a world of experience with the dreamer, and non-ego figures that act on the dreamer in various ways. Although this is obvious in dreams, it requires some explanation in the context of physical symptoms.

We typically describe physical symptoms as though something or someone other than ourselves is acting upon us to produce that symptom. For instance, I may describe a headache as a pounding one—as though something were pounding away at my skull. I typically identify with the victim or recipient of this pounding, although there is an agent or symptom maker implied in my description—the one doing the pounding. Mindell found that these two figures—the recipient and the agent of the pounding—are frequently represented in the person's dreams as separate figures. In the Jungian framework, the non-ego figure—the one doing the pounding—would represent a more unconscious side of the dreamer's psyche than would the dreamer, which would more closely symbolize the dreamer's conscious attitude.

Desiring to use his inner work skills to explore that similarity, Mindell tried doing active imagination with his body—talking to the part that was causing him discomfort in much the same way he would talk to a mysterious or troublesome dream figure. And he was less than satisfied with the results.

If the agent of the headache—the implicit character doing the pounding—could be made more conscious, then presumably it would be less troublesome. So Arnold tried doing active imagination with these figures that he and his clients experienced as being the agents of their symptoms. He tried holding conversations with them, in much the same way as one would do active imagination with night-time dream figures. And the results were disappointing. His painful or otherwise symptomatic body parts responded in voices that were only too well-known to him, telling him things that he already knew, recommending behavioral changes that were no mystery to him.

Active imagination becomes authentic when it is lively—when the messages we get from figures from the unconscious are new, unexpected, and numinous. Jung discovered the anima through just such a spontaneous active imagination. While drawing one of his mandalas, a feminine voice said to him, "It's art." And he disagreed. He held a spirited discussion with this new and unexpected voice, which led to a major new direction in his research. The voices Mindell encountered while doing active imagination with his body lacked this numinosity. Something else was clearly necessary to penetrate more deeply into the apparently parallel worlds of dreaming and body experience.

At about this time, Mindell made a discovery, which he describes in his book *Working with the Dreaming Body* (Mindell 2001). He noticed his young son picking at the scab of a minor injury. This was counterintuitive. Why was he reopening a wound that was already healing? Mindell realized that this is a common occurrence. Many of us bother and poke at painful spots in our bodies; we stretch painful joints and muscles, intensifying the usually unpleasant feelings in these places where common sense would dictate protecting them to lessen the pain. Mindell guessed that he was observing the somatic equivalent of what Jung called amplification, the reinforcement and expansion of dreamlike experiences to help them reveal their inner meaning. Could it be that our tendency to pick at healing wounds and stretch painful muscles was an attempt at spontaneous amplification, the beginning of an unexplored form of inner work that could be used to supplement the inner dialogue that was a mainstay (along with drawing) of active imagination?

Mindell pursued this idea, looking at traditional sources of patterns for amplifying dreams—fairy tales and myths, for example—from the viewpoint that they also referred to somatic experience. And that just as Jung amplified the visual and verbal action of dreams with dialogue and drawing, Mindell looked to a wide range of body-oriented therapies and meditation methods to find patterns with which to amplify somatic experience. The results of this work are summarized in his early foundational books *River's Way*, *Dreambody* and *Working with the Dreaming Body* (Mindell 1989, 1998, 2001).

The result of this early research was a body-oriented view of the psyche that recognized not only dreams, fantasies, and other products of the visual and auditory unconscious as aspects of a larger dreaming process, but saw somatic experience as offering a number of additional channels, expressing unconscious processes through deep body sensation and movement. And this brought with it a whole host of new amplification methods, all based on an awareness of how things felt and moved, in addition to how they looked and sounded.

Along with this expansion of sources of unconscious patterns came an expanded form of inner work. In addition to focusing on the content of inner dialogue—imagery and the like—this new approach emphasized awareness of the channel through which the information presented itself. And Mindell found that by simply focusing on the channel through which one was experiencing— was I hearing, seeing, feeling, being moved by something?—that new and coherent meanings emerged that were congruent with and supported the meaning inherent in the content of dreams and other dreamlike experiences.

Process work owes its existence as much to the search for a robust inner work practice as it does to its more obvious therapeutic application. And it is this inner work focus that contributes essential structures, insights, and skills to the safe and productive resolution of conflict, and to the facilitation of group individuation processes in emotionally charged, culturally diverse, and otherwise complex venues.

PROCESS-ORIENTED INNER WORK ON THE PATH OF THE FACILITATOR

Some 15 years ago, I attended a peacemaking and conflict resolution conference in Portland, Oregon, my adoptive hometown after 20 years living and working in Zurich, Switzerland. One of the talks was by a leader in the mediation community, who spoke of his initial excitement about mediation as a counterbalance to litigation as a way of resolving disputes. He saw the legal system as fundamentally unfair to the underdogs—the poor or otherwise socially underprivileged—in disputes with businesses, bankers, and other powerful stakeholders in society. But then he spoke of his disappointment in finding that as a mediator, he needed to be even-handed, supporting the rich landlord as fully as the poor tenant. He could not exercise the social advocacy for which he so yearned, needing instead to represent all parties fairly and even-handedly.

At the time, I was in the midst of my career as a practitioner of and trainer in process work. I had been Arnold's student in Zurich while he was initially developing his ideas, and was now, as his student and colleague, following him in his development of a later phase of his work that he called worldwork.

Worldwork is the application of process-oriented concepts and methods to working with groups of all sizes, with all degrees of ethnic, cultural, and other dimensions of diversity, on conflicts and other difficulties that challenge and ultimately transform the identities of such groups.

Worldwork grew out of Mindell's longing, developed early on in his study of Jungian psychology in the 1960s in Zurich, to make Jung's ideas useful not only for individuals, but also for groups in the midst of difficult, painful, and sometimes dangerous tensions and conflicts. Mindell was moved to study the power dynamics of groups and individuals by a tragic incident he observed during his psychotherapeutic training. His teacher, Franz Riklin, presented his point of view on an important issue before a meeting of the Swiss Jung Institute. Several senior members of the institute verbally attacked Riklin. Unable to defend himself, he collapsed and later died of a heart attack. Mindell was stricken by the loss of his mentor, and vowed to extend his understanding of psychology to include the dynamics of groups, a field which had been, to that time, under-represented in Jungian psychology.

Mindell developed the foundations of process work during the 1970s, primarily as a form of psychotherapy, but always against a background of interest in the relationship between the individual and the social and natural fields of which the individual forms a part. Worldwork was born in 1986 with a series of classes he presented in Zurich at around the time of the Chernobyl nuclear disaster, followed by the publication of his book, *The Year 1: Global Process Work*, in 1990.

Worldwork is based on the observation that conflicts in or between groups resemble in many ways intra-psychic conflicts. Typically, the sort of personal conflicts that we bring to therapists are between two viewpoints, both equally compelling, that create an existential crisis. Should I believe my internalized father's voice that tells me I am worthless and should be happy with my miserable job, or should I follow my dreams and risk everything on a new speculative venture? Should I remain shy and introverted, or risk getting entangled in new and possibly exciting relationships? Should I keep smoking cigarettes, or follow my doctor's advice and fight the painful battle against my addiction?

Similarly, groups in conflict divide into factions, each of which strongly represents its own viewpoint against the others. Should we open to outsiders, or keep the membership as it is? Should we trust our neighbors and open our borders, or should we build stronger fences to keep them out? Are we in favor of legalizing drug X, or should we impose even stronger criminal penalties for its use?

A huge difference between groups and individuals is that whereas individuals may seek out the help of a therapist to resolve their conflicts, groups usually wait until they are absolutely deadlocked, often on the brink of violence, before seeking help. And whereas individuals are often interested in using awareness to gain insight into their conflicts, each party to a group conflict is generally interested in winning over the others.

What is missing from the group in conflict is a sense of we—that we are unified and searching for a solution that makes us more of a group. Groups in conflict are usually more interested in resolving their conflicts—finding a solution that is just, or equitable, or even retributive—than in gaining insight into how and why they are having these difficulties, an insight that might help them find new and hopefully non-violent and sustainable solutions that enhance the relationships of the individuals and subgroups of which they are composed.

Furthermore, people suffering internal conflicts can often talk about their conflicts, taking a stance that is a bit detached from and able to reflect on the nature of their difficulties. It is to this detached, observing consciousness that therapy is often directed. People who are missing this detached viewpoint are sometimes considered to be poor candidates for therapy, and should their engagement in their parts be so complete that it crowds out the observing ego, they may be considered psychotic or otherwise mentally ill.

However, groups in conflict are lacking this neutral, detached, observing viewpoint more often than not. Members of the group are aligned with one or the other pole of the conflict, with little ability to or interest in reflecting on the meaning and possible validity of the other side's viewpoint. For this reason, groups in conflict often feel extremely inhospitable to their members, no matter what side they are on. They tend to polarize us into being less than the nuanced totality of who we are.

THE GLOBAL DREAMBODY

Just as sensory information—the subjective experience we have of our bodies through a host of sensory channels—leads to a coherent picture of a person's individuation process, so too does the individual serve as a channel for the global dreambody, the dreamlike aspect of the collective experience of groups. Groups tend to dream through projection: they attribute unwanted or disturbing aspects of their experience to other groups, or, when strong differences of opinion prevail within a single group, the fault lines form along which a formerly coherent group splits into two conflicting bodies.

But what is usually lacking in groups is an observing awareness—a person or subgroup that possesses a neutral viewpoint that hears, senses, and embraces the group's wholeness, knowing that the group, like an individual experiencing internal conflict, has everything it needs to unfold and recognize its wholeness. And where many inner work practices seek to enhance this overview and create coherence in the experience of the individual, it is the facilitator's job, in the practice of worldwork, to first fill the role of observing ego for the field in which she is facilitating, and then to help other members of that field to take over that function—to become participant facilitators who can help the group discover and manifest its own wholeness.

Facilitation comes in two "flavors." The first is the situation in which I am an identified facilitator, selected by the group to moderate a group discussion so as to help them resolve conflict, and, hopefully, empower them to make the resolution sustainable. A second typical situation is when I am a member of the group, have a definite viewpoint, and have, up to that point, contributed to sustaining and even escalating the group's conflict. But then, in the midst of the fray, I may remember the group's potential wholeness, and the part that I could contribute to either furthering that wholeness or sustaining the conflict. At that moment, I am on the brink of becoming a participant facilitator.

ENTER THE FACILITATOR

Mindell's goal in studying worldwork was to understand and develop the often-missing role of the facilitator, a member of the group who could assume what Mindell called a deeply democratic attitude that values all roles and viewpoints in the group, believing that they are parts of the group's wholeness, and ultimately part of a sustainable solution to the momentary difficulty. He emphasized that the facilitator is a role, and therefore open to be occupied at any time by any member of the group. A participant might at one moment ferociously defend a certain highly controversial viewpoint, and the next moment, might step into the facilitator role by expressing an interest and making space for her opponent's viewpoint.

What allows us to become facilitators in a conflicted group? Mindell believed that inner work was a key ingredient. To the degree that we are able to see the totality of the group's viewpoints, beliefs, prejudices, and experiences as aspects of our own personal worlds of experience, we are able to at least entertain the reality and meaningfulness of our worst opponents' viewpoint, no matter how much we disagree with it.

A CALL TO FACILITATE

Many years ago, a friend, who was also a colleague, was conducting a project at a prison. He and a social worker, who was on the staff of the prison, interviewed various inmates, trying to understand the complex social network in which the role of prisoner was embedded. My friend invited me to take part in some of these sessions, which I found fascinating because they gave me an insight into the complexity of the prisoners' lives, the background of the prison culture, as well as the role of the prison in the community, adding a third dimension to my tendency to stereotype the inmates merely as lawbreakers who got caught.

Prior to one of these visits, we were given a special assignment: to mediate a conflict between a prisoner who had, while released on furlough, brutally assaulted a social worker who, it turned out, had been his caseworker while he was still in juvenile jurisdiction many years before. This social worker was to appear with her lawyer, who was to read a statement requesting that the prisoner never have further contact with the social worker. We were to be present as witnesses to this ritual, although it was implied that we would intervene if things did not go smoothly.

As is the case with prisons, we were required to go through a screening process at the gate before being admitted to see the prisoner. And here the first difficulty developed. Just as I had been checked through, the guard consulted a list, and said that he was only to admit two visitors, and there were three of us. My friend, who had initiated the project, and who I assumed would take major responsibility for the day's proceedings, was not to be admitted. I tried to back out and give my place to him, but we could not convince the guard to admit my friend instead of me. I was on my own, and I was terrified.

At that time, I did not have much experience in facilitation, nor had I prepared to be a facilitator in this situation—I had assumed my friend would take on the job, and I would merely observe and assist him if necessary. And now the whole thing was landing in my lap. My first thought was, "Well, they're just people, treat it like any other conflict, and look for points of agreement behind the disagreement."

The prisoner—let's call him Hank—looked cool and relaxed, sitting at the steel conference table. The social worker, Margaret, looked nervous, on the verge of tears. Her lawyer, sitting beside her, looked stiff and furious: a man to be reckoned with. The tension in the room was palpable.

The proceedings began with the lawyer reading a prepared statement, in which he demanded that Hank never again contact Margaret, either personally, by mail or telephone, or risk dire legal consequences. Everyone looked rather uptight—except Hank, who sat slouched in his chair with a little smirk on his face.

Despite the superficially calm atmosphere, I felt my heart beating rapidly, and I was sweating. I was quick to explain this to myself as simple nervousness—I was unfamiliar with the surroundings: a bit afraid of Hank's history of violence, and of the stiff formality of the lawyer. However, I had worked in prisons before and had experienced the tension between inmates and prison authorities without being much affected. It occurred to me that I might be picking up a background feeling, a tension that was implied in the participants' non-verbal signals and mannerisms, but that was not made explicit. What could this be?

Hank spoke next. He assured the lawyer that he would not contact Margaret ever again. Although, if he wanted to, but of course he wouldn't...but *if* he wanted to, he would not have any trouble finding out where she was and getting in contact with her. He had his ways. It sounded to me like Hank was threatening her under the guise of agreeing to her lawyer's demands. I looked at Margaret, who did not appear to have any reaction to Hank's thinly veiled threat. But I was getting more upset by the minute. I did a brief bit of inner work, trying to pin down my own sense of unease. I was feeling things. My pulse was fluttering, my mouth felt dry, my muscles tense. I tensed my muscles a bit more, and realized that I felt afraid, as though I were bracing myself against a blow. So I decided to help the background feelings emerge a bit more.

I said something to the effect of "That was a strong statement. I notice that I felt a bit afraid when you said that. Maybe you'd come after me for some reason." And then Hank said, "I wouldn't come after you. And if I did, you wouldn't know it." The threat was real, and was becoming more explicit, even though he was still denying it. So I said, "Well, that *really* scares me." And then, I noticed that the atmosphere in the room had turned frosty. So I said, "Things are getting really tense here. Perhaps we all need to take a moment and notice what we're feeling." To my surprise, everyone took me up on my offer. Evidently I wasn't the only one suffering from the tension. After a few moments, Margaret began to cry. I asked her if she cared to speak. She first said how terrified she was of Hank, how deeply hurt she had been by his assault. But then she went further, and said how she felt betrayed by him, since they had had such a close relationship when she had been his caseworker before he turned 18. And then an amazing thing happened. Hank began to speak to her of how he had felt betrayed by her. When he turned 18, Margaret, who had been such an essential support in his life, suddenly vanished without a trace. She barely said goodbye, and then she was gone. No letters, no communication. He felt abandoned and angry. And vengeful. And it was this feeling of vengeance that had led to his later assault on Margaret.

Margaret was stunned by the story. She said that it had been hard on her too, but she hadn't realized how important she was to him. They had a very touching discussion about their feelings for one another, and their memories of what had happened around the time of their separation. The session concluded with Hank asking if he could write to Margaret occasionally to tell her how things were going. She said of course, she would be delighted to hear from him, and hoped that he would soon be released, and that things would go better for him.

This experience taught me a fundamental lesson about the value of inner work in facilitating outer conflict. To the degree to which I can believe in, trust, and then unfold my own inner experience, I become a channel or proxy for the unspoken, barely conscious viewpoints and reactions that make up the background emotional atmosphere of a group. How to make these experiences useful belongs to the skill set of worldwork. But the belief system, that I am the group, and that the group's and my experiences are part of a larger whole, is what gives rise to and enables the concrete skills and techniques that allow me to work with the group as one organic whole, instead of a simple collection of individuals with conflicting viewpoints and interests.

Microscopic inner work

A feature of the inner work that enabled me to facilitate the conflict between Hank and Margaret was its smallness. I had neither the time nor the venue for sitting quietly and meditating upon a solution. There was a great deal of pressure to find a rapid resolution of the situation; in fact, the pressure itself was part of the problem. At one point, I did indeed call for a moment of quiet reflection. But I was able to do this because the group had already become quiet, as if reflecting on Hank's shocking, if veiled, threat to Margaret. Part of my inner work consisted of noticing that sense of shock, the power of his threat, and the incongruently cool silence that followed.

When facilitating in tense interpersonal atmospheres, or in rapidly escalating group conflicts, it is essential that the facilitator be able to perform rapidly tiny bits of inner work that will help her apprehend and unfold her own experience as a piece of the larger outer process. I view these simple, quick acts of inner work as nearly microscopic fragments of much larger, systemic patterns that govern dyadic and group conflict. Let's take a look at what it takes for a facilitator to hone this skill of microscopic inner work, after which we will be in a better position to explore some of its variations that are useful in concrete facilitation situations.

A facilitator's attitude

Perhaps the greatest challenge to the facilitator is to maintain an attitude that Mindell has described as the guest house, a term he borrowed from Rumi's poem, which appears at the beginning of this chapter. The guest house is open to all who come, no matter who they are, what condition they are in, and what their attitudes and behavior are. One's guest house may be open or closed; when closed—when I, as a facilitator, am strongly biased toward one viewpoint or the other in a tense or conflicted field—I must be clear about this, and relinquish my role as facilitator, if only momentarily. When my guest house is open on the other hand, I have a special attitude that embraces the great diversity of viewpoints and behavior with which I am confronted, while growing attached to none.

Should I choose the path of the facilitator, I need to have access to the guest house attitude under conditions that challenge my openness. The following part of this chapter therefore deals first with an awareness project—inner work to determine whether my guest house is open or closed. Before we confront the challenge of keeping our guest house open, I'd like to return once more to the Pan Ku myth.

PAN KU AND THE UNITY OF THE WORLD

One reason that Pan Ku and similar myths are appealing is that they underscore the dream of a once and future unity. Many mythological, spiritual, and even scientific narratives emphasize the unity of all beings in a common origin. The Big Bang theory of the origin of the universe, Darwin's theory of evolution, Pan Ku, Taoism, the Judaeo-Christian Genesis narrative: all show the immense diversity of the world, its beings, and its people as originating from one tiny original place at one particular time. Whether implicitly or explicitly, each being carries a trace of all others in its present form.

This makes for a pretty good story, but in practice it has not been too successful for staving off lethal conflict. We are no less prone to killing our fellow human beings for knowing that we all come from a common ancestor. After all, envy-motivated fratricide appears in the Bible not too long after the creation of the world.

Although the trace of past unity has not been too effective in bringing us together, the dream of future unity remains a goal for many of our more effective and inspiring spiritual leaders. And it is the hope of unity that brings us together time and time again despite painful conflict, to try to reconcile our differences and achieve at least a temporarily enhanced coherence of our mutual worlds.

Conflict is often messy, like the plate of spaghetti and its associations in the dream I recounted at the beginning of this chapter. Aggression, violence, sarcasm, fury, and vengeance— these are but a handful of the emotional and behavioral states that emerge during heated conflict. How is the facilitator to maintain an open guest house attitude in the midst of all this turmoil? To add to her difficulties, people in conflict are apt to turn on the facilitator, unleashing on her the torrent of abuse that they have been directing toward their opponents. To keep her guest house open, the facilitator needs a strong belief in the possible future unity of the opponents, as well as a vision of their original unity—a common substrate of needs, wishes, and dreams that join them in their deepest humanity, despite the storms that rage on the surface of their relationship.

Here is where inner work is absolutely essential. Just at the moment when I cease to believe that the opponents whose conflict

I am facilitating will ever find common ground, I need to find that common ground in myself. I need to see—to know—to prove to myself that the entire conflict is taking place within me, and that the resolution of the conflict on the outside depends on my ability to embrace it in myself. I cannot expect to help the outer opponents resolve their conflict if I despair of somehow dealing with it in myself. And that is the goal of the inner work procedures that I will be describing in the following section.

I AM THE WORLD

In the quest for unity, it is often the facilitator who must reach for and explore that potential unity in order to make it accessible to the actual opponents. In a sense, this is what any empathetic therapist is skilled at—being able to understand and join in the client's world of experience, to become a partner in that world rather than a mere outsider trying to change the person's experience.

Identifying with the totality of the conflict differs from the approach I used with Hank and Margaret. There, I used my inner awareness to notice my reaction to the outer situation, and to make that reaction useful to the opponents in bringing forth their deeper experience—of yearning for a deeper connection with one another. I will now give an example of how an open guest house attitude proved essential for facilitating a very unpleasant conflict in which I was a participant.

My wife, Kate Jobe, and I were holding an introductory training seminar on the use of process-oriented conflict facilitation methods for managers in Mumbai, India, some 15 years ago. We were using a problem-solving approach. Participants were invited to present difficult situations, and we would work with them in front of the group to help them find novel solutions to entrenched conflicts.

A manager of a family-owned company asked to work. He was probably in his early sixties. He described a general tendency in Indian firms in which younger folks would leave the country to study at management schools in Europe or the United States, and would return full of themselves, demanding triple the salary of Indian-trained employees. He referred to these disparagingly as "high flyers."

He then described a specific conflict in his own company that involved one of these high flyers. Full of confidence, I proceeded to ask him questions that would help us find a solution to his problem. As I began proposing approaches we could take to the problem, he kept shaking his head while closing his eyes. Nothing I could propose seemed to fit the bill. I grew increasingly frustrated, and began to dislike him. I felt we were engaged in a power struggle, and he needed to prove me wrong. And I wanted to win.

But I was there to teach a more open attitude toward conflict. If I couldn't remain open to him, then my teaching was meaningless. I was under pressure to "walk my talk," to use my own methods to work on the conflict that was developing between the two of us in the moment.

I tried to put myself in his shoes. He was a successful businessman who managed his company in the old way—a way that had served the family for generations. And now he was confronted (in his view) with arrogant young people with no firsthand experience of running a business, and who claimed to know better than him. To add insult to injury, they demanded exorbitant salaries for trying untested methods that, in his view, would be the ruin of the company.

I realized that in his eyes, I was probably just the kind of person he was complaining about. This marked a subtle but radical shift in my own viewpoint. I no longer saw him as an opponent, but as a teacher. And from that new viewpoint, I saw myself as a pupil who was being examined by him. There was only one answer to the problem he had presented to me, since he had already successfully solved the problem using his own methods. He knew the answer, and was testing me to find out if I knew it. My guest house opened toward him.

To check my hypothesis, I said to him, "This is an examination, isn't it?" His face broke out in a broad smile, and he nodded. So I then said to him, "OK, let's see if I can find the answer." And I proceeded to go through various possibilities, ultimately failing, and asking him to tell me the solution that worked.

I thanked him for the solution, and then discussed with him how I was also a high flyer, who claimed to know better than he how to run his business. I apologized to him, and said that I wanted to learn from him. He then shifted his position, and asked me for my advice on the problem. This time he listened with interest, and we were able to discuss the merits of the various approaches.

This interaction marked a shift in the atmosphere of the seminar. What had started out as a relatively stiff and formal training workshop became animated and intimate, with participants asking our opinions, engaging in role play, and ultimately asking us to stay a couple of hours longer than we had intended. We had gained credibility by stepping into their world and understanding it through their eyes, ears, and hearts, rather than staying in our role as the foreign experts there to solve their problems and then leave.

Converting what started as a conflict into a mutual learning experience required that I find both the high flyer and the wise old businessman in myself—that I acknowledge and embrace both roles as aspects of my own world of experience. Before I did that, both the manager and the high flyers that disturbed him so much were troublesome others that I had to find a way to deal with. But when I was able to embrace both as unrecognized elements of my own inner world of experience, I was able to open to his world and join him in finding a constructive solution to his problems.

The facilitator's ability to maintain an open guest house attitude toward the entirety of the conflict and its participants can be crucial to finding effective resolutions. Just as I began to see the manager as an adversary who was frustrating my attempts to help him, facilitators often grow irritated with opponents and groups locked in long-term, escalating, and seemingly fruitless conflicts. The facilitator unconsciously slides into the role of adversary, whose presence irritates rather than helps an inflamed situation. To the degree that the facilitator can congruently step into the shoes of all the parties to the conflict, she becomes a trustworthy helper who, even if she momentarily steps to the side to support one viewpoint that is having trouble expressing itself, can be relied on to later come to the aid of the other side, no matter how unbalanced or unappealing one or both positions may appear to an outsider.

STABLE REFERENCE POINTS

When facilitation threatens to go off the rails, we frequently need a stable reference point to put us back in touch with our core values and our goals for the resolution of the immediate difficulty. The ability to do inner work rapidly and without drama can be, literally, life-saving in the midst of conflict that strikes at these core values.

In the following two sections, I will present two basic innerwork methods that are useful for quickly and reliably putting us back in touch with a sense of self, of being at home in our own skins, so that we are less vulnerable to being polarized by the conflict that may rage around us.

First, I will show how using inner work to remain in contact with our own somatic experiences can provide such a stable reference point. Then, I will discuss some of Mindell's newer research on awareness of the earth—of our path through life, and of our common roots—as a way of finding such a stable and impartial reference point.

BODY AWARENESS AS AN AID TO FACILITATION

Conflict facilitation can be a very lonely enterprise, especially when you are one of the parties in the conflict. I often have the feeling that I am on my own. My opponent is trying to defeat me. Not only my viewpoint on the topic at hand, but often my very hold on reality is being challenged. Where should I turn for support? One simple and reliable way of getting grounded—a kind of internal reality check—is to pay attention to what's happening in your body. In the fog of conflict, the mind is often at sea.

Conflict has a way of putting us into altered states of consciousness that make it difficult to think our way through the immediate difficulty. Internal critical voices rise up to question everything we are doing. The ghosts of old conflicts overwhelm us with dire predictions of what will happen if things go on as they are. We turn inward in largely unproductive ways just when we need to focus our attention on the outer situation. And although inner dialogue may offer a way out of this vicious circle, it can just as often exacerbate the difficulty. At such times, we need new information that is uncontaminated by the habitual internal dialogues in which we get trapped. It is then that looking to other channels—other sensory modalities—than the merely verbal or visual can be so helpful.

I once got a call from a former therapeutic client who had broken off therapy several years earlier.[1] She felt at the time that I focused too much on her strengths without empathizing sufficiently with her suffering—she felt perennially too weak to deal with life's daily demands. I had admitted to her that this was a fault of mine, and I'd tried hard to show more empathy. But I could not completely share her view of herself as weak and incapable of getting along in the world. She was physically strong, intelligent, and accomplished. And I had trouble ignoring the resolute strength with which she defended her weakness.

I was happy to hear from her. I looked forward to re-establishing our working relationship and the chance of making good on where I had failed her in the past. I was touched that she trusted me sufficiently to work on our earlier disagreement.

The following week, she showed up for the session. I expected at least an initial friendly greeting, but she arrived looking like a walking storm cloud. She brushed aside my attempts at cordiality and immediately got down to the business at hand. She sat hunched in her chair and began to lambaste me for having been insensitive, uncaring, and downright dangerous to her personal development.

At first I was shocked. I hadn't realized the degree to which she blamed me for her difficulties. But then I remembered my role as therapist and my obligation to listen carefully to my client's experience, putting aside for later my personal reactions.

But I had trouble listening. I felt wounded, misunderstood. She was unrelenting. She strung one accusation on another till they grew to a full-scale attack. I began to wonder, if she only came to attack me, why she had asked for a private session. She could have

---

1   This example appears in a somewhat different form in my book, *Befriending Conflict* (Goodbread 2010), which is a manual of inner work for conflict facilitators.

phoned me and voiced her grievances. Why pay me for a session if she only meant to read me the Riot Act?

Pay? Why, she actually saw this as a chance to redress old injuries. Surely, she said, I had once again misunderstood her. She hadn't asked for a therapeutic session, just a chance to say what was on her mind.

On top of my hurt, I was also furious. I knew that I had done my best to listen patiently to her and that I could not possibly be responsible for all the blame she was heaping on me. I felt she had misused my goodwill to avenge an ancient grievance. But I felt that exploding at her would not solve anything.

I was not only stung by her accusations, but also realized that I was partially agreeing with her. I often weather internal attacks for being insufficiently caring, or insensitive, or any of a dozen real or imaginary personal failings. Inner dialogue is simply no help to me in these situations. My inner narratives are so entrenched, so familiar, and so dismal that an attempt to deal with these inner voices is more likely to take me into a deep depression than shed new light on the problem. So while I was in the midst of my own inner dialogue, I decided to check around for new inputs, unexpected information that might help me find a way out of this dilemma.

Once I made this decision, the next thing I noticed was my body experience. I spent a moment focusing on what I was feeling. The first thing that came to mind was that I was hurt, angry, and afraid. But wait a moment—these were not the actual body experiences—they were rather my interpretation of what I was sensing. When I went back and focused on the sensation, rather than my interpretation of these sensations as emotions, I noticed that my heart was racing, my mouth was dry, and my pulse was pounding in my temples. I had a brief fantasy that if things continued in this vein, I might die of a heart attack. And I didn't want to die, at least not there, not then, and certainly not for her.

So I said to her, "I notice that my heart is racing and my pulse is pounding. I'm a little worried. I like you, I think you're a great woman, but I'm not willing to die for you today." She became very still and sat there with her mouth open slightly, looking bemused.

After a few moments she said, "I didn't realize I was that important to you, that I could affect you so strongly." And then I felt myself relax. I realized we had gotten to the core of the problem. She saw me as an all-powerful but uncaring authority figure who hardly acknowledged her existence. The only way, in her mind, that she could get through to me was by seeing me react clearly and powerfully.

I remembered this feeling myself when, as a child, I sometimes had to play nasty tricks on my father before he would take me seriously. It was not an ideal way to relate to him, but at least I felt that he saw me fully in those moments. But his angry reactions were not satisfying. I wanted love and acknowledgment, not anger. And because I got some reaction, but not a satisfying reaction, provoking him became mildly addictive.

It seemed that my accuser was motivated by a similar pattern. She needed to provoke me in order to feel seen and heard by someone with as much power and authority as she projected on me. If I had simply reacted out of the anger I felt, I would have only fed her addiction. She would have seen me as one more authority figure that put her down instead of taking her seriously.

By focusing on my body experience, I was able to show her clearly, but without anger, that she had a profound effect on me, and that the effect was not pleasant. This evidently helped her reflect on what she was doing, rather than simply provoking another round of accusations. If I had merely gotten angry, it would have encouraged her to try even harder. We both would have gotten caught in a cycle of escalation that would leave us hurt and resentful. I cannot say that we parted friends after this encounter. But nor were we enemies.

A week later, she called to thank me and to ask if I would be willing to resume our therapeutic work together. And work we did, cautiously at first, but later with a growing sense of trust and mutual respect.

My direct, uninterpreted experience of my body gave me new information, a way out of a vicious circle that might otherwise have resulted in both of us spiraling down into weakness, instead of upward toward newfound power.

LEVELS OF EXPERIENCE

In the past 15 years or so, Arnold Mindell's research into states of consciousness has led him to reformulate once again the classical dichotomy between the conscious and the unconscious mind.

During the early development of process work, Mindell found that the terms consciousness and the unconscious did not account for some of the experiences that he observed in his work with clients, and during his own inner work. He augmented these with two categories of dynamic process that described how we *relate* to our experience, in addition to identifying it as conscious or unconscious. Many of the phenomena that we call conscious refer to things with which we habitually identify—what Mindell came to call the primary process, because it is in the foreground of awareness. Those experiences that we experience as other, that disturb our sense of identity, he called secondary processes, to emphasize their position in the background of our awareness. Polarities could then be understood as secondary processes that challenged our sense of identity. By amplifying and exploring secondary processes, we come to experience them as our own. We withdraw projections, identify more with body experiences by which we formerly felt victimized, and generally expand the limits of an identity that may have grown too restrictive. This formulation points to two levels of reality.

The first, or consensus reality, deals with the world of appearances and generally agreed-upon meanings of experience. A body symptom is a sign of an illness, a conflict is something to be resolved by negotiation, and altered states of consciousness need to be terminated when they last beyond a certain reasonable period of time.

The second is the world of dreams and dreaming processes. It is governed by experiential polarities, projections, night-time dreams and daytime fantasies. It is the realm in which many forms of psychotherapy seek the solutions to consensus reality problems. It is the world that is generally identified with the unconscious.

To these two, Mindell added a third level, which he called sentient essence, based on his research into parallels between quantum physics and the nature of perception. Experience that occupies the world of sentient essence is close to the "unity" experiences I mentioned at the beginning of this chapter. Such experiences are essentially non-verbal, non-conceptual, and non-polarized. They are hard to verbalize and are closely connected with the deepest levels of body feeling and altered states of consciousness.

When we are able to descend to the level of sentient essence, polarities that have plagued us for years may dissolve, revealing a foundational experience that puts the formerly troublesome polarities in a new light, often resolving the tension between them and giving us new insights into our relationship to these polarities.

Although it is far beyond the scope of this chapter to explore the depth and breadth of this new and exciting direction in process work, I wish to give a brief example of inner work based on sentient essence, and how it can resolve with ease and grace pernicious, entrenched conflicts.

CUTTING A GORDIAN KNOT

I was once involved in a business venture with a group of close friends. We were very close to concluding a long-term, potentially lucrative contract with a client, but we had considerable disagreement among ourselves on one crucial point. I felt that the client had made numerous concessions to us on many contractual points, but that we had continued to press for ever more advantage on our side. I feared that if we pressed the client much harder, we would sour the atmosphere to such a degree that working with him would be pure torture.

My partners, on the other hand, argued that we had been badly burned in a similar situation on two previous occasions, that we were now in a strong position, and ought to press our advantage as far as we could. We had managed to negotiate most of the contentious points among ourselves, but remained divided on one crucial, final point. Our debate grew so heated, and so polarized, that I felt victimized and bullied by the partners with whom I had enjoyed such a cordial and creative relationship. But I could not let go of my position. Finally, one of my partners put his foot down, and requested that I remain silent during the impending negotiation, though before I had functioned as lead negotiator. I felt betrayed, hurt, and furious. Our internal conflict had spun out of control. We were divided, with only hours until we needed to present a united front to our client.

I decided to do inner work. I first played the role of my partners, whom I experienced as aggressive and demanding. I experimented with experiencing them as a part of nature—they came at me like a huge wind that tried to blow me off my feet. I played myself—a victim that was blown about by their force. When I explored my own role as a piece of nature, I felt like a sapling that was being violently blown about by the powerful wind of my partners.

So far, this resembled the actual polarity of the conflict, but it translated into a more emotionally neutral, earth-based framework. I then went further, and attempted to find the sentient essence that united me with my partners. I let my mind go fuzzy, and experimented with the movement of the tree, letting myself be blown hither and thither in a kind of hypnotic dance. As I danced the dance of tree and wind, I noticed that only my upper body was moving, that my legs felt as though they were planted deep in the earth. As much as the wind blew me about, I was securely rooted in the earth, and could give in to the wind, knowing that I would not be blown away.

The next day, during the final strategy session with my partners before meeting our client, I first experimented with being blown about by their arguments, and slowly focused on feeling rooted in the earth of my own core values. I then spoke clearly and unemotionally about how important sustainable relationships were to me, and that my core values prohibited me from endangering such relationships merely for financial gain. Something totally unexpected then happened.

As soon as I had spoken from my deepest values, my head suddenly cleared, as though I had emerged from a dense fog into clear sunlight. Before my partners could even respond, I asked them to repeat what the difficulty was, as they saw it. As soon as they explained the problem, I saw that I had misunderstood their demands. I proposed a very simple solution, which was immediately acceptable to them, and in complete accord with my interest in an amicable relationship with our client. The negotiation proceeded without a hitch, to everyone's satisfaction.

My inner work gave me access to a level that was more fundamental than our differences, where we were indeed one body with one another. And as often happens when we touch this level of unity, former polarities dissolve, making that unity experience available to everyone in the system. It is inner work done in the service of relationship and community.

WHAT'S INNER, AND WHAT'S OUTER?

So far I have been exploring inner work that prepares us for outer action. I would like to explore one more consequence of the unity principle that has underlain the methods I've presented to this point.

If my inner world of experience and the outer world of relationships, community, and conflict are really co-creative mirrors of each other, then inner work is really too narrow a description of the role of self-reflection in such a unified world. To work on myself is, simultaneously, to work on the world. This idea has given rise to a method of working with a field of conflict and relationship that I will call outer inner work. It consists of doing inner work out loud, in public, in such a way as to invite participation and comment from the assembled community.

This kind of outer inner work stems from Mindell's observation that when a group is deadlocked in a highly emotional conflict, the facilitator can substantially ease the atmosphere by finding both sides in himself, and acting out the conflict before the group. This resembles the method I described in the section I called I Am the World earlier on, but now the facilitator goes further by doing his inner work out loud. Although much can be said about the theory and practice of this method, I will have to content myself with an example from my own life, which I hope will bring across the essence of this method.

Some years ago, a group of friends and I were starting a training program in conflict work. We were quite excited about what we considered a novel approach to the program, and were getting together with someone who was interested in possibly hiring us to do the training. We had agreed in advance that we would give our potential customer only a small taste of our method, just enough to whet his appetite, and we would reveal the whole thing once we had an agreement to go forward with the program.

When we met with the interested party, things went better than we had hoped. The discussion became animated, resembling a brainstorming session among friends more than a cautious pre-negotiation. In my exuberance, I revealed a good portion of what my partners and I had discussed in private. The meeting ended, our potential customer departed, and just as I was basking in the afterglow of a successful meeting, I happened to notice one of my partners staring at me with a clenched jaw and a deathly pale face. This was someone with whom I had had some disagreements over the years of our association, but with whom I currently enjoyed a good relationship. So I suddenly grew afraid that I had done something to reignite our previously adversarial relationship.

"Well," he said, "you really did it this time!" I was stunned. What did I do? "You gave it all away! Now he doesn't need us, he can just do it on his own. I'm furious with you."

I found myself also getting furious with my partner. I felt he was raining on an otherwise glorious parade. But I was not in the mood to get into a fight, so I tried some rapid inner work. I found myself defending myself internally against a figure that sounded like my partner, but was familiar to me from long ago, like a parental voice that always scolded me when I got too excited about anything. Instead of dwelling on this, I brought it out immediately by getting out of my chair, standing close to my partner, and attacking myself. "Goodbread!" I said to myself, "You're always screwing things up by getting too enthusiastic and throwing caution to the wind. When are you going to learn that you've got to be cautious, honor commitments, and realize that you're working in a team?" And then I went back to my seat, faced my "attacker" and said, "I agree with you. I tend to get too rambunctious at times. But on the other hand, you know that my exuberance that you so mistrust comes from the same source as my creativity, which you value, which brought us here in the first place. If I squelch my exuberance, I'm afraid I'll lose my creative spark."

I went back and forth in this vein, while my partners looked on, spellbound. As I did this, I found myself becoming more neutral, as much on my adversary's side as on my own. Then he spoke. He said that he valued my creativity, that he valued me as a person, and that he was simply critical of my tactics. I felt that something had moved, although I was still discontent with the heavy mood that threatened to spoil our apparent victory. I used the shift in the atmosphere, the closer contact to him, to dig deeper, and to bring that exuberance into our immediate relationship. I told him that I needed to come to some resolution with him, that I needed him to love me despite my failings. He smiled and said of course he loved me, that we were friends from way back and nothing could change that. And then he admitted to me that he was a bit envious, that he wished he could be as trusting of others as I seemed to be. The atmosphere cleared, and we were able to conclude our meeting with cordial and cooperative teamwork on our further strategy.

PAN KU ONCE MORE

My intent in this chapter has been to show how inner work, approached from a minimalistic and process-oriented standpoint, can be a powerful tool for working with conflicts in a variety of venues, and with a diversity of facilitation styles.

Beyond contributing to creative resolutions of even long-standing conflicts, these methods revitalize the yearning that many of us have for a more coherent, unified world in which projections, marginalization, and conflict can be the starting point for both personal growth and healthier communities. In the best of situations, conflict reminds us not of our differences, but of our common origins—that unity is not only a once and future dream, but an ever-present background to all of our activities, no matter how mundane or troublesome they may initially appear.

REFERENCES

Goodbread, J., 1997a. *Radical Intercourse: How Dreams Unite Us in Love, Conflict, and Other Inevitable Relationships*. Portland, OR: Lao Tse Press.

Goodbread, J., 1997b. *The Dreambody Toolkit: A Practical Introduction to the Philosophy, Goals, and Practice of Process-Oriented Psychology* (Second Edition). Portland, OR: Lao Tse Press.

Goodbread, J., 2010. *Befriending Conflict: How to Make Conflict Safer, More Productive, and More Fun*. Portland, OR: Create Space.

Goodbread, J., 2013. *Living on the Edge: The Mythical, Spiritual, and Philosophical Roots of Social Marginality*. New York: Nova Science Publishers.

Mindell, A., 1989. *River's Way*. London: Penguin.

Mindell, A., 1990. *The Year 1: Global Process Work*. London: Penguin.

Mindell, A., 1998. *Dreambody*. Portland, OR: Lao Tse Press

Mindell, A., 2001. *Working with the Dreaming Body*. Portland, OR: Lao Tse Press.

Rumi, J., 1995. "The guest house." In C. Barks (trans.) *The Essential Rumi*. New York: HarperCollins.

CHAPTER FOUR

THE INNER VOICE OF OBSESSION

Listening and Responding

Richard Schaub, Ph.D.

Let's do an experiment together. Try to deny yourself a habit that is part of your life. For example, deny yourself the habit of eating late at night by staying in your chair instead of acting on the urge to get up and go to the refrigerator. A few seconds after staying seated in that chair of denial, a voice in your mind will start up. It will be the voice of your habit.

All mental patterns have a verbal component, and the inner voice you hear is really two brain sites in action: the site that has built up neuronally through repetitions of behavior, and the site that amplifies thought so that it becomes noticeable in your field of awareness. The inner voice of your habit of eating late has been established by countless repetitions of that action. Whether you're hungry or not, that voice is going to start up late in the evening.

You're still trying to stay in your chair, but now the voice is quietly convincing you to drop this experiment for tonight and try it again tomorrow night. This way, you'll still be staying true to your promise to stop your habit of eating late. You'll just begin tomorrow night.

Or the voice might take a different position. It will question the very idea of changing this habit at all. It will wonder why you are doing this to yourself, this denial of a totally normal, biological need to eat. Life is short, after all, and having a late night snack is hardly an act of self-destruction. Yes, your clothes don't fit anymore and, yes, it's generally agreed that soda and a box of cookies are not two of the nutritious food groups but so what? What's the harm?

We generally think of an obsession as a demanding, driven inner state of urgency. But it can also be the quiet voice I am describing above, the gentle nudge, the seemingly reasonable argument, the friendly advice. The proof of its power is that it is persuasive, that you listen to it, and that you do what it tells you to do.

You did tell your doctor and your partner that you are determined to lose weight and avoid future health problems. There is diabetes in your genetic family, and you certainly don't want to introduce obesity, high blood pressure, and a diabetes-prone diet into your life. Everything you promise to do to avoid future problems makes common sense, and you get lots of encouragement from people who care about you to follow through on your plan of breaking the habit of eating late.

There's a big flaw in the plan, however. It is that this habit began because it was an effective way to reduce your night-time anxiety and vulnerability. You didn't know exactly what your anxious feelings at night were all about, but you do know that eating seemed to be pretty effective in distracting you from the anxiety and making you feel, if not better, at least neutral. Neutral is close to numb, and that late night feeling of numbness helped you to fall asleep. True, you went to bed feeling bloated and, sometimes, even a little sick to your stomach, but the soda and the box of cookies or the half-gallon of ice cream or whatever else you found did put you out for the night. This origin of the habit is all but forgotten. The well-established inner voice is what you experience now. Before you know it, you're up out of your chair of denial and grazing in the refrigerator.

ALCOHOL ABUSE

Let's increase the level of difficulty by dealing with another obsessive inner voice: alcoholism. Overeating may cause you health problems, which is a poor choice to make, but it surely can't compare to the poor choices and problems in living that happen every single day when you are obsessed by alcohol and have the voice of alcoholism in your head.

The inner voice that reinforces alcoholic drinking has a lot of persuasiveness going for it. It suggests a far greater pay-off than the numbing effect of overeating. Getting drunk conjures up wild experiences, letting go of inhibitions, enjoying life, partying down, and not giving a damn about what others think. The promise of alcohol is so much more expansive and interesting than the late night sluggishness of soda and cookies.

Cocaine, heroin, anti-anxiety agents (e.g. Valium, Xanax), painkillers (e.g. Oxycontin, Vicodin), and other drugs can also become objects of obsession. In addition, there are obsessions without alcohol or drugs, including gambling, love and sex addiction, and pornography, which follow the same dynamic as the alcoholic obsession and compulsion. For convenience, I'll refer to alcohol and alcoholics as a way to discuss the inner voice of all obsessions.

The experts, Alcoholics Anonymous (1976), define alcoholism as a mental obsession and a physical compulsion. The mental obsession is the voice that tells you that you need a drink right now, and the physical compulsion is the behavior, the acting on the urging of the inner voice to get that drink.

So far, with that one drink, you are still in the realm of normal social drinking or the typical use of alcohol to calm down and relax after a hard day at the office. The voice, however, is obsessive, meaning that it makes the same suggestion over and over again. If you have raised children, you know how kids can get their mind fixed on a toy and nag you insistently to get it. In that insistent childish nagging, you have a parallel to what it sounds like inside the head of someone with an obsession for alcohol. If you walk into the store the next time and automatically buy the child a gift to pre-empt their nagging, you have a parallel to how the alcohol obsession turns into an automatic, compulsive action. You know the obsessive voice is going to be bothering you, and so you act on it to shut it up for a while.

At some middle point of alcoholism, you drink simply because that is what you do. The voice is quieted because you are acting on its command without any struggle. The compulsive behavior eventually becomes extreme: if it were physically possible, the person in the grip of this obsession and compulsion would drink constantly.

THE ORIGINS OF THE OBSESSIVE ALCOHOLIC VOICE

The person's obsessive thoughts about alcohol activate the physical compulsion to consume alcohol, but why does this voice develop in the first place? Why does a person become obsessed with alcohol? Most people can enjoy alcohol without becoming obsessed. What makes the alcoholic different?

This question becomes important when you are trying to figure out how to work with the obsessive voice in an effective way. To answer the question, we need first to review the theoretical models of alcoholism/addiction.

MODELS OF ADDICTION

There are at least 11 theories about the origins of an addiction (Gulino-Schaub and Schaub 1997, pp.20–27).

> The Medical Model: you have been consuming significant amounts of alcohol over a long period of time. Deprived of it, your central nervous system goes into a state of physiological craving (withdrawal). The craving is very uncomfortable and feels intolerable. To get rid of the craving that comes with withdrawal, you drink more. You are caught in a cycle of drinking, withdrawal cravings, and drinking to stop withdrawal.

> The Genetic Disease Model: you have a genetic, bio-chemical predisposition to alcoholism. There is alcoholism in your

family: if not in your immediate family, then perhaps in your grandparents. The genetic predisposition is activated by the use of alcohol.

The Self-Medication Model: perhaps due to past trauma, you have intolerable levels of anxiety and vulnerability that interfere with your daily functioning. Alcohol, marijuana, and so forth, smooth the edges of the difficult feelings and make you better able to cope. You use alcohol as your anti-trauma medicine.

The Dysfunctional Family Model: you learned from people in your family that one copes with anxiety and/or depression by consuming alcohol.

The Psychosexual Development Model: as an infant, you did not experience adequate nurturing at the oral phase of development and became psychologically fixated at that stage. The adult form of your oral fixation is the holding of the bottle or glass of alcohol to your lips and drawing in its relaxing effects.

The Ego Psychology Model: deprived of adequate nurturing and mirroring as an infant, you have a weak sense of yourself in a challenging world and cannot tolerate the pressures of life. Alcohol relieves the pressure.

The Character Defect Model: an early model offered by the 12-step program of Alcoholics Anonymous, it proposed that you are morally and characteriologically "defective" and require alcohol to pacify your "self-centered fears."

The Instant Gratification Model: as an alcoholic, you have a low threshold for frustration and need instant gratification of your impulses. This personal impulsiveness is reinforced by the collective culture of being conditioned to believe we can buy things to make us happy, and that we can have them at the click of a mouse.

The Trance Model: this is based on the pleasure principle of your brain. Once your brain has experienced the pleasure of intoxication, it stores the experience like a hypnotic suggestion and desires to repeat it.

The Transpersonal-Intoxication Model: based on the connection observed between artists and alcoholism, this model's thesis is that your alcoholic "thirst" is really a thirst for novelty, creativity and expanded consciousness.

The Existential Model: this model accepts that the human condition is innately vulnerable and anxious, and that alcoholics are people who experience this existential anxiety more acutely.

These models are of course greatly simplified. Their theme, though, is clear. Essential feelings of vulnerability, whether caused by biology, biography, or society, are at the heart of the origin of addiction. This emphasis on vulnerability is verified by my 35 years of clinical experience with hundreds of people in recovery. Patients repeatedly describe that the onset of their addiction was their initial discovery that alcohol took away their fears and made them feel relatively normal in life. Therefore, attention must be given to the person's vulnerability in order help them recover successfully. In other words, the challenge becomes how to listen to the obsessive voice, realize that it is being driven by feelings of anxiety and vulnerability, and provide a new, healthier answer to its demand for relief.

EARLY RECOVERY FROM OBSESSION

No family member, no doctor, no therapist has the power to stop an alcoholic from drinking. If you are being commanded in the intimate privacy of your mind by an alternately quiet or demanding inner voice which tells you to get a drink, smoke a joint, take a pill, and so forth, what outside person can break through into that inner world and dislodge the voice?

Though there are exceptions, most people's stories of recovery from obsession and compulsion start with hitting rock-bottom: they have become just too sick and tired to act on their inner voice. The voice is still there, but they have reached a point of exhaustion, usually including a build-up of relationship, employment, family, financial, and health problems, and they can't go on. Their obsession and compulsion has brought them to their knees. Their inner voice has lost the power to get them to act on it. But this does not mean that the voice goes away.

Once detoxified from alcohol, the alcoholic is technically a person in the recovery process. But now you are an alcoholic without alcohol being exposed to the pain of life without your "medicine." The very origin of the development of your obsessive inner voice— your feelings of vulnerability and not feeling good enough in this world—now come back to you in your non-medicated state.

This return of the vulnerable feelings accounts for the many early failures in recovery from alcoholism. Relapse—the return to drinking—is an unfortunate but typical part of the early recovery process. You may have stopped drinking temporarily, which was a great start to a new life, but the old feelings and the well-established obsessive voice in your head haven't gone away. Relapse is disheartening but understandable in view of the enormous life change you are making.

WORKING WITH THE OBSESSIVE VOICE

Help in early recovery needs to be psychoeducational. You need to replace the old mental obsession and the old physical compulsion with new ways of thinking and behaving. Above all else, you need to have new answers for the obsessive voice that knows only one answer to everything—drink.

The impressive effects of the 12-step program of Alcoholics Anonymous result from just this formula—providing training in new ways of thinking and behaving. The effectiveness of the 12-step programs is that they offer an accepting community in which the new thoughts and behaviors of sobriety are repetitiously taught. For example, when you notice that the inner voice is yet again counseling you to drink, you have been trained by the 12-step program to call another person in the program—a sponsor—and to tell him or her about the thoughts inside you that are guiding you toward discarding your recovery and drinking again.

If you accept the 12-step guidance, you will begin to build a new inner voice, that of a sober person. You won't yet feel like a sober person, but you will accept for the time being that you must imitate the thinking and behaviors of a sober person in order to salvage your life. You learn how to talk to yourself in your mind— self-talk—as if you are a sober person. Just as the old obsessive voice became established over the course of many repetitions of your old behaviors, the same repetitious reinforcement of your new behaviors, and the new thinking that goes with them, are required.

This sober inner voice needs to become strong enough to compete with the old, established inner voice of obsession. In terms of Psychosynthesis, the school of meditative psychology in which I learned about inner voice work, you need to practice identifying with (i.e. direct energy toward) your new, sober inner voice and practice disidentifying from (i.e. withdrawing energy from) your obsessive voice.

How do you do this? Let's first be clear about the mistake many people make. You can't argue with the obsessive voice. By its very obsessive nature it doesn't give up, and it will never completely give up. Bill Wilson, one of the founders of Alcoholics Anonymous, despite a long life in recovery, found that in the vulnerability and sickness leading toward his death, his obsessive inner voice returned to him to the degree that he was speaking from it, demanding that others bring him alcohol (Cheever 2005). The second reason you can't argue with the inner voice is that it has, in the words of Alcoholics Anonymous, an insidious logic that is hard to argue with. No matter what you come up with as a reason not to drink, it will find a way for you to reconsider why you are depriving yourself of something you love so much. Having taught awareness training and mindfulness meditation to many people in recovery— meditation methods in which you cultivate a witness attitude toward your mind's activities—I have heard the gamut of ideas that the insidious logic of obsession and compulsion comes up with to drink even while the person is sitting in deep peace on a meditation cushion.

Since arguing with the obsessive voice won't work, what will? A new voice informed by a new consciousness. If you are successful in building and reinforcing the new, sober inner voice, you will get to the stage where you will hear the two sides—the new sober voice and the old alcoholic one—competing for your attention. While this may sound difficult and crazy-making, it is a great sign that the new, sober inner voice is gaining strength.

A NEW VOICE, A NEW CONSCIOUSNESS

One of the reasons I began to apply my Psychosynthesis Psychotherapy training to the field of addiction recovery was because of its emphasis on the importance of spiritual development. The 12 steps of Alcoholics Anonymous have built into its teachings and system the concepts of internal relationships with a "higher power" (1976, p.5) and with "God as you understand God," and Dr. Roberto Assagioli, the originator of Psychosynthesis, worked from the premise that higher consciousness objectively exists inside you and can be discovered and experienced (Assagioli 1965).

I found that many people in recovery paid lip service to the higher power and God concepts of the 12 steps but did not actually have experiences that verified what they were asked to believe. For me, Psychosynthesis helped to fill that gap for the people in recovery whom I was working with in private practice. Among the many tools toward developing a new consciousness and a new voice, I began to utilize Assagioli's concept of guiding inner wisdom, which any person is capable of experiencing through very simple methods. My wife and I later on went on to write a book, *Dante's Path: A Practical Approach to Achieving Inner Wisdom* (2003), to describe the rationale and practices of guiding inner wisdom. I did this only after I had verified for myself, through many direct, personal experiences, that an inner voice of wisdom was actually available to me and that its guidance was intriguing and helpful.

The inner voice of wisdom is hardly a new idea. People of every time and culture have noticed a special relationship occurring inside them: the relationship between their everyday personality and a deep source of internal wisdom. Sometimes, at night, you might experience this wisdom as knowledge or guidance you receive in your dreams. Sometimes, during the day, a word or phrase or passing mental image might indicate that your internal wisdom is trying to get through to your conscious self. On some occasions, in a moment of true grace, a big piece of internal wisdom might break through to your awareness and illuminate reality more fully than you had ever seen it before.

Around the world and throughout the ages, people have been searching for ways to access this internal wisdom in order to experience the benefits it has to give. Tapping into that wisdom can reveal your purpose for living, your destiny; and with that new understanding your fears will relax, the right choices about the directions of your life will become obvious, you will live with greater peace, and more love will flow to and from your mind and heart.

There are many names for this deep source of wisdom. It is the mystic's vision, the artist's muse, and the scientist's intuition. The Old Testament prophets received it by seeing visions and hearing voices: Elijah referred to it as "the still small voice within," and when Moses ascended the mountain to receive wisdom about how to lead his people and asked for a name by which to call the source of his guidance, he was told only: "Tell them that 'I Am' sent you."

Tibetan Buddhists call this internal wisdom prajna. The Zen tradition refers to the "inner reason of the universe which exists in each mind" (Shaku 2002, p.46). Gandhi meditated in order to receive guidance from what he called "the inner light" of universal truth (Johnson 2002, p.171). The Kabbalah of the Jewish mystics calls this higher center of wisdom the Tiferet. Greek mythology spoke of it as the oracle. Dante, in his spiritual masterpiece *The Divine Comedy*, personified inner wisdom as his female guide, Beatrice (Dante 1981). As mentioned before, the 12 steps of Alcoholics Anonymous refer to the wisdom as your higher power. Carl Jung referred to it as the Self (de Laszlo 1959).

Assagioli's term for inner wisdom was the higher self and he founded Psychosynthesis partly to create a human science of the higher self because it was his belief that access to this higher self could be studied and taught as a practical, normal fact (Assagioli 1965). I eventually came to be more comfortable with the term "wisdom mind" in order to distinguish it from the rational mind in my discussions with patients and students.

To know that this inner wisdom exists and is available to you is certainly good news. The problem, however, is that this may be the first time anyone has told you about it. In order to form a relationship, you must first become acquainted with the other party—in this case your own inner wisdom—and then begin to nourish the bond between you.

The path to forming a relationship with your wisdom mind is not magical or mysterious. Rather, it is a creative process in which, through a series of discoveries, your experience of who you are is gradually expanded. You begin exactly as you are, stay exactly who you are, and, simultaneously, you become more. Your core personality doesn't change; you still function as "you" in the world and in your relationships with others on a daily basis, but you also begin to notice yourself gaining more perspective and purpose and feeling more at peace. Reality is no longer just the version presented to you by social convention—a life of surviving, functioning, and then relaxing from surviving and functioning. Rather, you will also begin to experience that there is a deeper purpose to your life, and that your inner wisdom is trying to guide you toward that purpose.

When I am asked about the origin of this inner voice of wisdom, I usually give two answers. If you think in terms of traditional religion, I say it might be the voice of God's will in your life. More scientifically, I say it is probably the voice of evolution that we can personally experience inside us. After all, if we accept that God and/or evolution exist, why wouldn't we have a way to experience it? As concluded by Assagioli and his more famous colleague, Carl Jung, it is through inner voices and inner visions that this impulse toward expressing the purpose of our life is displayed to us (Schaub and Schaub 2012).

STARTING TO STUDY THE VOICE OF INNER WISDOM

I trace my curiosity about the nature of this inner wisdom to a particular, early experience. When I was 19, I took part as a subject in a study of sensory deprivation at Princeton (Vernon 1963). It was conducted for the United States Army Astronaut Research. I had a spectrum of terrifying hallucinations and extraordinarily blissful experiences inside that tiny lightproof, soundproof room, and one of them was the emergence of a guiding inner voice that helped me through the frightening part of the experiment. The experience made a lifelong impression on me and stayed with me as I went on to train in Zen and mindfulness meditation and eventually came upon the recognition of inner wisdom in the work of Assagioli and Jung.

I was struck by the fact that Assagioli's commitment to inner wisdom work was because of the help it gave him during a very low and dark period in his life. He was born in the Jewish ghetto in Venice in 1888. Having lived through the loss of his father and then his mother by the time he was a teenager, he was guided by his stepfather, a physician, to become a psychiatrist. In 1909, he was named the Italian representative to the Vienna Psychoanalytic Society, founded by Freud, the father of psychoanalysis. Assagioli studied for a time in Switzerland, at the same hospital as Jung, but quickly became dissatisfied with psychoanalysis because, for him, it ignored the healthier possibilities inherent in human nature, including higher consciousness and spirituality. At the precocious age of 23, he broke with the psychoanalytic movement and began to formulate his own method of practicing psychotherapy, later founding the first institute for teaching Psychosynthesis in Rome in 1928.

In 1940 he was labeled a pacifist and imprisoned by the Fascists. Instead of breaking him, however, his imprisonment provided Assagioli with what he termed a blessing:

> the realization of independence from circumstances, the realization of inner freedom. We should realize the freedoms from fear, want, etc., but the right emphasis should be given that inner freedom without which all others are not sufficient.

My dedication is going to be to the task of helping men and women free themselves from inner prisons… (Gulino-Schaub and Schaub 2003, p.xvi)

Friends finally secured Assagioli's release, but his troubles were far from over. He remained under strict police scrutiny and, on the Nazi occupation, he was forced into hiding in the Tuscan hills. Shortly after the war, his only child died from an illness developed while the family was in hiding. It was not until 1950 that Assagioli was able to reopen the Psychosynthesis Institute, this time in Florence.

Assagioli was the first modern Western doctor to incorporate worldwide spiritual and meditative practices directly into his work with patients. By the late 1950s word of his approach had spread, professionals from around the world began to seek him out as a teacher, and, since that time, many others have begun to emphasize the importance of integrating spirituality into the paradigm for seeking mental and emotional health.

In all of his work and personal life, his inner voice of wisdom was key to him. His personal notes and diaries, which I had the privilege of reading while doing research in Florence, are filled with dialogues between his ego-personality self and his inner wisdom.

To anyone who has not yet experienced such a natural phenomenon, it might sound strange to think that someone is listening so intently to a voice inside his head. Such matters sound like psychosis, schizophrenia, not the experiences of a sane person. In fact, we all have multiple mental patterns urging us to do this and do that, whether it's to find your car keys or change your entire life. The inner life of our mental activity is routinely filled with all manner of chatter, thoughts, opinions, rehearsed speeches, and urges that come to us both as words and as mental pictures. As Dante has described it, his inner wisdom said to him one day: "For so long I have tried to reach you in vain in dreams and other means" (Dante 1981, p.325).

TEACHING THE INNER VOICE OF WISDOM

I have found there is only one effective way to help someone in recovery to engage with the new consciousness of their inner wisdom: to guide the person into a direct experience and work from there. I use the metaphor of higher power if the person has sounded comfortable with that phrase. If they've been fighting it and don't get what it means, I just use the more neutral idea of a deeper knowing about how to live.

I remember a man who had come to me at his wife's urging. She'd made the first call to me and told me that her husband had a serious cocaine problem. When he came in for our initial consultation, he spent the whole time talking about doubts about his marriage. At our second meeting, I asked about drugs and alcohol, and he blew my question off as if there was no problem in that area. I wasn't going to be a stand-in for his wife and confront him on his denial, but I also hadn't forgotten about it.

By our third meeting, our dialogue was drifting. We were having a pleasant enough conversation but it had no therapeutic direction. Not focusing specifically on the cocaine issue, I suggested that we try something different involving the imagination, and the patient was agreeable, but unsure of what he was getting himself into.

I asked him to close his eyes and to follow his breath. I then asked him to imagine a road or path, one that he knew or one that he created, and to imagine himself walking on that road or path. I then suggested that, in the distance, there was the appearance of a wise being, a wisdom figure, of any kind. I asked him to imagine that the being was coming toward him and to ask that being, "What's my next step?"

After I'd made my suggestion, I was quiet. I watched my patient's breathing and changes in his skin color as he proceeded into the imagined scene. At one point, his very pale skin became flushed with redness and his breathing increased, and then he calmed down again. When he felt finished and opened his eyes, he looked ready to cry. He stared straight at me and said, "I'm addicted to cocaine and I can't stop."

What had happened to him in that imagined scene, in that mental imagery exercise with inner wisdom? His path led into a forest and into a wood cabin. Inside, a very old man was throwing ashes on the flames in the fireplace. My patient asked the old man why he was doing that, and the wise old man was quick to respond: "You do that."

My patient didn't understand, and asked his question again. The old man threw so much ash on the fire that there was only one little flame left. Then the old man, putting his finger in his nostril, said again: "You do that."

My patient intuitively understood the finger up the nose as the snorting of cocaine, and his denial about his problem broke down.

Do dramatic things like this happen with the inner voice of wisdom? Actually, they do, fairly often, which is why I have used this method so much through the years with every conceivable clinical issue.

For the person in recovery, the experience of actually gaining help from their higher power through inner voice work is a source of great encouragement. It confirms for them that the 12 steps have properly taught them how to proceed on the road toward a new consciousness with its attendant new voice.

SUMMARY

The inner voice of obsession originates in feelings of vulnerability. In reaction to the vulnerability, you naturally seek relief. If you repeat certain behaviors, such as drinking to relieve your vulnerability, you certainly create a psychological habit and, as new evidence in brain research is suggesting, you also create a neuronal site in your brain that stores memory of the habit (Doidge 2007). The obsessive voice is the outcome of these repetitive behaviors and, in turn, reinforces them.

The answer then lies in slowly but surely depriving this inner voice of energy, which means not paying attention to it, and instead directing your energy attention toward the cultivation of a new voice of sanity and wisdom. In such cultivation, inner voice work cuts across psychological, neurological, and spiritual dimensions of our nature.

REFERENCES

Alcoholics Anonymous, 1976. *Alcoholics Anonymous.* New York: AA World Services.

Cheever, S., 2005. *My Name is Bill: Bill Wilson—His Life and the Creation of Alcoholics Anonymous.* New York: Washington Square Press.

Dante, 1981. *The Divine Comedy: Purgatory.* M. Musa (trans. and ed.). New York: Penguin.

de Laszlo, V. (ed.), 1959. *The Basic Writings of Carl Jung.* New York: Modern Library.

Doidge, N., 2007. *The Brain that Changes Itself: Stories of Personal Triumph from the Frontiers of Brain Science.* New York: Penguin.

Gulino-Schaub, B., and Schaub, R., 1997. *Healing Addictions: The Vulnerability Model of Recovery.* Albany, NY: Delmar.

Gulino-Schaub, B., and Schaub, R., 2003. *Dante's Path: A Practical Approach to Achieving Inner Wisdom.* New York: Penguin.

Johnson, R., 2002. *Gandhi's Experiments with the Truth.* Lanham, MD: Lexington Books.

Schaub, R. and Schaub, B., 2012. *Transpersonal Development.* Huntington, NY: Florence Press.

Shaku, S., 2002. *Zen for Americans.* New York: Dorset Press.

Vernon, J., 1963. *Inside the Black Room.* New York: Potter.

CHAPTER FIVE

AN INTRODUCTION TO GESTALT THERAPY THEORY AND PRACTICE

Susan Gregory

Maria looks small sitting on the couch, hands tightly folded in her lap, legs twisted around one another, feet with her heels lifted and toes digging into the carpet. Her hair partially covers her slim face; and her eyes are cast down, only occasionally darting up to look around the room. Maria is 30 years old yet appears, on this day, to be 16.

She has come from Europe, accompanying her husband for his work here in New York. She was a psychotherapist in her country, having been given an introduction to gestalt therapy and related humanistic modalities during her training. She has one year left in New York and has come to me for further study and practice of gestalt therapy.

At this moment, she is describing her previous therapy training to me and, as I lean forward to hear her quiet voice, her eyes suddenly dart up and a broad smile spreads across her face. "Do you play the piano?" she asks excitedly, her hand waving toward the instrument that stands in another part of the room. "Sometimes," I say, "when I'm singing or teaching singing." "Oh," her own vocal tone shoots to a high pitch, "I'm glad to hear it. I was afraid to tell you that I am a poet, and used to teach poetry in the university before I became a therapist.

"In my therapy training my supervisor told me that I was too expressive and needed to become more restrained when working with clients. My supervisor said I was behaving too much like an artist. I am relieved that you practice an art form also."

"And so did both Fritz and Laura Perls," I tell her. "Fritz was an actor before he went to medical school. And Laura was a classical pianist who played on a professional level and made a choice between a musical career and becoming a psychotherapist; she never stopped playing the piano, though."

"Really?" asks my student, her eyes opening wide. We look at each other for a moment. "I thought that perhaps I had chosen the wrong profession; I still write, you know," she says, looking down at the floor.

"Gestalt therapy values the whole human being," I respond, "in all our creativity and varied interests." And with that exchange, Maria and I begin to co-create our work together.

CO-CREATING GESTALT THERAPY

Gestalt therapy was co-created by Drs. Fredrick (Fritz) Perls and Laura Perls, husband and wife who left Germany in 1933. They went to live in Johannesburg, South Africa, where throughout World War II they practiced therapy, collaborated in writing their first book *Ego, Hunger and Aggression* (1945/1992), and developed a new therapeutic theory and practice, which they later named gestalt therapy. In Germany, Fritz and Laura had been practicing psychoanalysis in traditional ways, with the client lying on the couch and the therapist sitting behind him or her, listening and saying little. While in South Africa, Laura began to have her patients sit up while she sat opposite them. Grounded in her Berlin studies with eurythmics and bodywork with Elsa Gindler (Gregory 2001), Laura included in her work attention to her patients' posture and movement qualities while inviting them to become aware of these aspects of their own functioning. Laura later said, "You must be a body to be somebody" (Perls 1992, p.x).

Laura Perls developed movement and voicing experiments for use in therapy sessions, in which clients might be helped to bring awareness to, and at times even exaggerate, what they had been doing unawares. Laura would sometimes invite clients to try new postures, movements or gestures and to speak with her about what they were experiencing while trying them. The purpose of this was not to improve movement but to help the client become aware of the details of her or his own functioning, along with the feelings and thoughts that arose at the same time. These ways of working, which Laura and Fritz were using, are described as *heightening awareness of what is*, and *encountering the novel* (experimenting with something new).

Laura reports that during their years of exile in South Africa, Fritz and she would spend each weekend conversing about their work, developing and writing about a system which grew into a new approach to practicing therapy, an approach in which the client was seen to be the expert on her or his own life, and in which activities were as important in session as were the client-therapist conversations through which they were explored and processed (Perls 1992).

Because of their need to escape from Nazi Germany, Fritz and Laura worked in South Africa for over ten years, in relatively professional isolation, far from the influence of Freudian psychoanalysts in Europe with whom they had originally trained. By the end of the war they were practicing a new mode of psychotherapy, which, while growing from psychoanalysis, also departed from it. It became, as Laura put it, a therapy that was experiential, experimental, and existential (Perls 1992).

After World War II, Fritz and Laura settled in New York City. In regular gatherings at their apartment they began to host conversations about therapy, its practice, theory, and underlying philosophy. People participating in these discussions included physicians, psychologists, educators, graduate students, artists, writers, actors, and musicians. This eclectic group of intellectuals and artists discussed theory and practiced together, processing what they were doing, and seeking to develop a new vocabulary to describe the new work they were undertaking in individual and group therapy.

When the weekly meeting had grown to 40 people, Fritz and Laura divided the group in half and each half began to do therapy with and then train 20 people. The first gestalt therapists developed from this effort; and together with Fritz and Laura they formed the New York Institute for Gestalt Therapy.

In 1951, guided by an outline of ideas, which Fritz had brought with him from South Africa, the writer and social activist Paul Goodman, who was a member of the Perls's weekly discussion group, wrote the theoretical half of what was to become our founding text, *Gestalt Therapy: Excitement and Growth in the Human Personality* (Perls, Hefferline and Goodman 1951/1994).

The other half of the book was a set of sensory awareness experiments that the reader could undertake on his or her own. These were written by Fritz, and tried out ahead of publication by Ralph Hefferline's students at Columbia University. Years later, I recognized many of these experiments as having originated with bodywork pioneer Elsa Gindler, who taught Laura in Berlin in 1930 (Perls 1993). In New York, Fritz studied for a while with Charlotte Selver, who had briefly been Gindler's student in Berlin.

Within a few years, Fritz began to travel, teaching groups of psychoanalysts, educators and graduate students around the United States and Canada. Fritz was frequently in residence at the Esalen Institute in California, occasionally coming back to New York, where he stayed with Laura. They lived separate lives from the late 1950s on; and so gestalt therapy developed into two separate styles of practice, reflecting Fritz's and Laura's differing personalities and ways of working. Yet both the East Coast and the West Coast styles of practicing gestalt therapy remained true to a set of core gestalt therapy principles, which were laid out in *Gestalt Therapy* (Perls *et al.* 1951/1994).

Because the "parents" of gestalt therapy effectively split, there was for many years a split in the gestalt therapy community worldwide, the "children" being loyal to one or the other of the founding practitioners' styles. This schism in the field has begun to heal only within the past ten years. Now, because gestalt therapy is more than 60 years old, we are able to look at how it has developed differently in different locales, and how we gestalt therapists worldwide may respect and understand one another with the support of the underlying principles of our theory.

SOME CORE PRINCIPLES OF GESTALT THERAPY'S

Gestalt therapy is meant to treat the whole human being, not just the mind. Ahead of its time, gestalt therapy developed from radical psychoanalysis, as described by Philip Lichtenberg (1969) in *Psychoanalysis: Radical and Conservative*. Gestalt therapy was a response to the times in which it was founded. Paul Goodman, using Fritz's outline, wrote the founding text (Perls *et al.* 1951/1994). Paul was a social thinker and therapist whose many books looked toward encouraging a freer and more personally authentic life style for the socially restricted men and women of the 1950s.

In gestalt therapy theory, we say that figures form and are perceptible in relation to the ground from which they emerge. We understand that figures (*Gestalten* in German) can only be perceived against a ground, the two are thus interdependent. The words figure/ground are taken from art, as well as from the studies of perception by gestalt research psychologists in Germany between the wars (Ellis 1938).

From its beginning, therefore, gestalt therapy was a therapy of implied relationship, since one part of the whole could not be perceived without the presence of the other. In gestalt therapy, we speak about needs and interests being foreground or background, of something being figural for the client or therapist. We speak of emergent gestalts, of sequences of contacting, which include sensing, being aware, choosing, taking action, and assimilating or dissolving the figure. This language is intended to be descriptive and never evaluative.

In gestalt therapy we speak of figures of interest being the leading form through which we do our work with clients and awarely live our lives. The dissolving of figures into the ground, called destructuring in gestalt therapy, changes the ground and is thus part of a dynamic relational process, today described in dynamic systems theory (Oyama 2000).

In the 1950s, the idea of an individual following her or his figures of interest, rather than being merely obedient to societal norms, was revolutionary and quite in contrast to ideas of adjusting, fitting in, or being mentally well, which was the medical model through which mental distress was evaluated then. Psychoanalysis at that time spoke of adjustment to society's norms, and to some extent still does.

By contrast, gestalt therapy spoke of creative adjustment, meaning an individual or group adopting the best possible decision or action in the moment, given the constraints and/or opportunities in the field. These constraints and opportunities may be aspects of the environment or of an individual's capabilities, the two together composing the field.

The concept of field in the 21st century has changed from that which existed when Fritz and Laura first developed gestalt therapy. Individuals in Western society today recognize few personal constraints and often struggle with problems in life related to speed and perceived rulelessness, and from the consequences of our now living in a liquid society (Bouman 2000). The consequences of these struggles can be seen in our most recent economic and environmental emergencies. Assistance through gestalt therapy for individuals and groups contending with emergencies is as available today as it was more than a half-century ago when it first came on the scene. This is because gestalt therapy eschews fixities, but rather encourages clients to grow with awareness of the changing field.

Although he was trained as a medical doctor, Fritz and Laura departed from a medical model of describing mental health or illness. Gestalt therapists look at: how well a patient understands her or himself; how able he or she is to make choices based on the opportunities and limitations of the moment (constraints in the field); how aware of his/her own bodily sensations as well as mental processes he/she is; how aware of the field the patient is part of and in what ways he/she interacts with it; how fluidly he/

she is able to adjust to changes while developing a clear sense of self, within what we call the organism/environment field.

In gestalt therapy, the set of experiences where a person is interacting with the environment is called the contact boundary. This expression, while appearing to be a noun, is actually a set of verbs and interactions that describes experiences. Thus our emphasis in gestalt therapy is on activity, described in verbs, whether in the therapy session or outside it. Our emphasis, too, is on the development of choice-making, which we call alienating and assimilating, as well as on awareness and ability to describe relationships of the elements of figure/ground.

Gestalt therapy has an ever-developing theory, which helps us describe experience; it is thus phenomenological. The therapy helps therapist and client understand where our work together may be moving ahead or be stuck, and to evaluate the kind of stuckness, which we call interruptions in contacting, and help us experiment with whether or not we wish to undo those interruptions and how. The emphasis in gestalt therapy is thus on "how" and not on "why."

Contemporary gestalt therapy values sensing, feeling, thought, and action in equal measure. We evaluate human functions through a process which we call the aesthetic criterion—that is how flowing, harmonious, energetic, and bright we experience a person's functioning to be at the present moment. "Aesthetic" here does not refer to beauty, but rather to balance and authenticity (Bloom 2003). We are less interested in how correct, healthy and "well adjusted" our client's behavior may appear to be to others. The aesthetic criterion looks at a patient based on what she or he says and does—or through the experience of therapy comes to say and do—about what is wanted or needed in living right now.

When the patient is able to articulate and then actively try to fulfill that which she or he wants, given the existing constraints and opportunities in the field, then we say that the patient is creatively adjusting, and may be understood according to the aesthetic criterion. Thus, he or she establishes their own parameters through which therapy may be judged to be or not to be successful for him or her.

Gestalt therapy is frequently mistaken to be only a set of procedures, which we gestalt therapists call experiments. Gestalt therapists may utilize experiments in therapy sessions to activate clients and get them to experience that which they were previously only talking about. These experiments may include chair work (drawn from Moreno's *Psychodrama* (2008) as utilized by Fritz), awareness exercises (drawn from the work of Elsa Gindler who taught Laura Perls in Berlin, as well as from Fritz's time in a Zen monastery in Kyoto), movement experiments (some of which come from dance therapy, body-mind centering (Cohen 1993), and other expressive and bodywork modalities), and numerous other active approaches including imagining, drawing, sculpting, singing, writing, drumming, taking a walk with the therapist, going to a store with the therapist, and so forth.

In Gestalt therapy, these active experiments are not seen to be ends in themselves, as they are in some forms of arts therapy, but rather to be ways for the client to experience self in the now and to explore what the experiences mean to him or her. This exploring is a discussion, which we call processing, and it is an essential component of gestalt therapy. What the client makes of the experiment, in a slow exploration of experiences, is what makes the work relevant and useful to her or him, and gives him or her self-agency.

The therapeutic relationship is the medium through which growth and change may occur. What client and therapist may each be imagining about the other, which qualities inspire, intrigue, puzzle, disgust, or frighten the client or therapist may provide a route to explore the client's inner life, style of communicating, and what outcomes the client hopes for from the therapy.

The ways that he or she walks in, sits, shakes hands, smiles, frowns, listens, speaks are filled with personal history which can be attended to in the therapeutic relationship. The here-and-now in the consulting room is regarded as the prism, through which all the important themes of the therapy may be found and explored by client and therapist.

The consulting room is ideally a safe place where all that is important to the client (as well as to the therapist, although that part will be professionally bracketed, except where judged by the therapist to be usefully revealed for the client's growth) can be explored and experimented with—both in terms of knowing more brightly what is (leading to paradoxical change; see Beiser 1970) and inventing and experimenting with new behaviors and ways of thinking. In a gestalt therapy session, we may converse, move, imagine, or engage in any number of creative activities (Zinker 1977), all in the service of the client encountering the novel with the support of the therapist in the here-and-now. We understand that here-and-now is the only place/time in which change can actually occur. The therapy session provides exploration; and assimilating change takes place later, outside the consulting room.

HOW I BECAME A THERAPIST

I was growing up in Brooklyn while Laura and Fritz Perls, along with Paul Goodman and a group of intellectuals and artists, were developing gestalt therapy in Manhattan. My exposure to intellectual life was through my parents' single shelf of books and their well-worn collection of classical records. These we listened to every Saturday while we all cleaned the apartment. Also, when I was young, my mother kept a scrapbook of poems she cut out of newspapers and magazines. And for a couple of years I remember her painting watercolors. During those years, my father was an amateur actor and appeared in modest productions. These were my introductions to "culture," as folks in my working-class neighborhood thought of it in the 1950s.

From an early age, I sang; I sang while I washed the dishes each night beside a window, which opened on to an alleyway. The neighbors in the alleyway heard me and eventually formed a committee to urge my parents to give me singing lessons. This community action set the path for my life.

While Laura Perls was playing classical piano in her apartment on West 96th Street, I was studying voice with my teacher on West 93rd Street and my language coach on West 74th Street. Both teachers were immigrants from Berlin, as were Fritz and Laura. I also studied breath and bodywork with Elsa Gindler's longtime teaching assistant Carola Speads, another Berliner. She lived on West 85th Street. I don't doubt that these "muses who fled Hitler" (Zinker 1977, p.26) traveled in social circles whose paths intersected with those of the Perls', though it would be decades before I would learn who Fritz and Laura were.

In New York City, I attended the High School of Music and Art, City College and, after many years, stepped upon the stages of both the Metropolitan Opera as a competition finalist and the New York City Opera as a principal artist with the company. (I was hired by another émigré from Berlin, Maestro Julius Rudel.) My musical career was founded upon the training available in New York City through classical musicians who had settled here just prior to and after World War II, along with many other professionals, including Fritz and Laura, who all were part of that intellectual migration to New York. I took advantage of this musical and language training throughout the 1970s.

When, in the 1980s, I left the New York City Opera to care for my infant daughter, I began to teach singing. It was then that I experienced a phenomenon that surprised me. Some students would stop mid-lesson and ask for my advice or help on life matters. Others would begin to weep while singing and would then share with me the pain that was welling up from within them. For several years I tried to be commonplace, helpful, soothing, encouraging, dispensing advice, picking songs for them that mirrored their moods. This was not enough, though, and rarely helped in the long run. I was the only professional in many singers' lives: and they were turning to me for help. Finally, I decided to train during the evenings to become a gestalt psychotherapist. I chose gestalt therapy because of its history of accepting artists to its training programs. It took four years for me to become a therapist.

In 1991, I entered private practice while continuing to teach singing a few hours a week. Twenty years later, having just finished a term as president of the New York Institute—the institute which Fritz and Laura had founded—and having been visiting guest faculty at gestalt institutes in Europe, South America, Australia and New Zealand, I continue to teach a few singing students every week when I am in New York. I still concertize occasionally as well. Singing is part of my life no matter what other work I am doing; I have published articles on the health-giving properties of singing (Gregory 2004, 2009, 2011). I feel inspired by the example of Laura Perls, who, although she had a distinguished career as a psychotherapist and teacher, never stopped playing the piano privately on a professional level.

GESTALT THERAPY IN MY EVERYDAY LIFE

Gestalt therapy theory and practice are part of both my work life and my everyday life, though that distinction is a false split in gestalt therapy theory. My whole self is as present with a client as with a friend, although the choices I make for colloquy are different. With the client, our conversation focuses upon his or her concerns and needs. It is my professional responsibility to hold mine in the background, or bracket them. Although I do not speak of my needs and concerns, except in the rare instance in which I determine that such sharing may be supportive to my client, all the aspects of my life are always present in the consulting room: inchoate yet there, they are part of the field. Likewise my work style, my ways of seeing and describing, are present, though rarely directly spoken of, when I am conversing socially. It may be deep background, of which I am at that moment unaware, or near the surface, where I am aware yet am choosing not to make it figural. Gestalt therapy theory and practice is always present with me:

When I wake up in the morning, before arising I check in with myself physically and emotionally to know what I am feeling right then; that is an aspect of gestalt therapy practice.

When I am at work and walk with awareness to the door, noticing my breathing, my feelings and thoughts and then bring that awareness to greeting the client as I open the door; that is an aspect of gestalt therapy.

When I am in line at the grocery store, looking around at the people in front of me and noticing the moods they are in and what seem to be the intentions of their behaviors; that is an aspect of gestalt therapy.

When I take an extra few seconds to connect with the cashier, through looking at her, through body language, through asking how she is, through exchanging a smile if she wants to; that is an aspect of gestalt therapy.

When I lift up my grocery bags, awarely balancing the weight to carry them effectively through the crowd of people at the exit; that is an aspect of gestalt therapy.

When I reach home and notice that I am tired and need to rest, sitting down to feel my breathing and to sense my muscles as well as my mood; that is an aspect of gestalt therapy.

And it is gestalt therapy theory and philosophy when I return to these kinds of awarenesses after a period of absent-mindedness during the day; when I smile and realize that as a human being I am apt to lose awareness frequently. Accepting that with understanding is an aspect of gestalt therapy.

I enjoy my life being filled, most of the time, with awareness and choice-making. Physically, Elsa Gindler's work taught me to be aware and to experiment. Cognitively and emotionally, gestalt therapy theory and practice taught me to be aware and to be able to talk about it. It is how I live, most moments of my life, in an integrated way—awake, aware, choiceful, given the opportunities and limitations around me.

How I live, and how I practice Gestalt therapy, are one and the same. I live my life the same way I do my work, and that, also, is how I teach new therapists to work and live. Each of our lives is a whole gestalt, and the interconnectedness of those gestalts is the relational field of our work and of our world, as, for example, is the field co-created by Maria and I.

Maria is preparing to return to her home in Europe. We have been working together for a year and she has grown a lot as a person and as a practitioner. Last night in supervision class Maria had been both bold and kind; she had challenged her "patient," another therapist-in-training who was hesitant about trying an experiment she had proposed.

"Would you be willing to talk about how you feel when you hesitate this way?" (exploring process is as important as exploring content in Gestalt therapy) asks Maria with warmth and firmness. "No," he says, "because to talk about that would be to talk about the personal information I am wanting to withhold. I need to have a wall here." He draws a line in the air with his hand. "OK," she says in a steady, clear voice, "let's both know that together." She draws an imaginary line also. They sit gazing at one another for a moment.

The silence in the room is full. She has spoken clearly, giving support and respect to her client. She is sitting up straight in her seat, sounding kind and caring, her gaze straight at him, eyes bright, her hair swept away from her face, hands resting loosely in her lap, feet flat on the floor. She looks and sounds her age. She is calm, present and settled. The model client smiles at her in appreciation. I see that Maria's professional work as a gestalt therapist has begun well; and I feel satisfied that I am succeeding in creatively teaching gestalt therapy to the next generation.

REFERENCES

Beiser, A., 1970. "The paradoxical theory of change." In J. Fagan and I. Shepherd (eds) *Gestalt Therapy Now*, pp. 77–80. New York: Harper.

Bloom, D., 2003. "Aesthetic values as clinical values in Gestalt Therapy." In M. Spagnulo-Lobb (ed.) *Creative License*, pp. 63–78. Vienna: Springer Verlag.

Bouman, Z., 2000. *Liquid Modernity*. Oxford: Blackwell.

Cohen, B.B., 1993. *Sensing, Feeling and Action*. Northampton, MA: Contact Editions.

Ellis, W.D. ed., 1938. *A Source Book of Gestalt Psychology*. Highland, NY: Gestalt Legacy Press.

Gregory, S., 2001. "Elsa Gindler: Lost Gestalt ancestor." *British Gestalt Journal, 10*(2), 114–117.

Gregory, S., 2004. "The song is you." *British Gestalt Journal, 3*(4), 24–29.

Gregory, S., 2009. "You must sing to be found." In K. Luethje (ed.) *Healing With Art and Soul*, pp. 141−151. Newcastle upon Tyne: Cambridge Scholars Press.

Gregory, S., 2011. "A Gestalt therapist teaches singing." In D. Bloom and B. O'Neill (eds) *Continuity and Change*, pp. 197−202. Newcastle upon Tyne: Cambridge Scholars Press.

Lichtenberg, P., 1969/2010. *Psychoanalysis: Radical and Conservative*. Wollongong, Australia: Ravenwood Press.

Moreno, J.L., 2008. *Psychodrama*. Wikipedia, wikipedia.org/wiki/Jacob_L._Moreno.

Oyama, S., 2000. *Evolution's Eye: A Systems View of the Biology-Cultural Divide.* Durham, NC: Duke University.

Perls, F., 1945/1992. *Ego, Hunger and Aggression.* Highland, NY: Gestalt Journal Press.

Perls, L., 1992. *Living at the Boundary.* Highland, NY: Gestalt Journal Press

Perls, F., 1993. "A life chronology." *The Gestalt Journal, 6*(2), 5–9.

Perls, F., Hefferline, R, Goodman, P., 1951/1994. *Gestalt Therapy: Excitement and Growth in the Human Personality.* Highland, NY: Gestalt Journal Press.

Zinker, J., 1977. *Creative Process in Gestalt Therapy.* New York: Vintage Books.

CHAPTER SIX

JOURNAL OF TRANSFORMATION

My Living Relationship with Ira Progoff's *Intensive Journal®* Method

Carolyn Kelley Williams

INTRODUCTION

The *Intensive Journal* method is the creation of Dr. Ira Progoff (1921–1998), a depth psychologist and social historian who, in the early 1960s, was looking for a practical tool for evoking personal growth and help people develop their lives. The instrument Progoff found most useful for this work was a looseleaf psychological workbook with colored page dividers that, over time, came to have some 21 sections, as well as specific procedures for working in each section. Progoff created a program to introduce the method and teach its use in workshops, after which people would be able to work on their own. The method and its structured workbook have since been used by many thousands worldwide.

I first encountered the *Intensive Journal* method in 1985 by way of Progoff's book, *At a Journal Workshop*, the basic text for the use of the method (Progoff 1975, 1992). I was leading a discussion at a conference for my professional association, and my topic was the personal journal as a writer's tool. In the list of related readings, I included Progoff's book, which I had not seen before. I have kept unstructured personal journals almost since I first learned to write, and as I leafed through *At a Journal Workshop* for the first time, I was intrigued by the section headings, which suggested a variety of new ways of looking at my life: Intersections: Roads Taken and Not Taken; various dialogues—with Persons, Works, Body, Society, Events, Wisdom Figures; a Life History Log; Meditation Log; Twilight Imagery; Spiritual Steppingstones. Synchronistically, a few weeks after the conference, a friend mentioned that she had attended an *Intensive Journal* workshop at a retreat center only blocks from my home. Another workshop was offered there soon, and my life was about to be transformed.

At the age of 47, I was in what Dr. Carl Jung would have called the second half of my life, the appropriate time to focus on my inner life. Though I was in favor of that, the pages of my schedule book were black with commitments for the next five years. My professional life as a medical editor in Chicago was all-consuming; I was working 12 to 14 hours a day at my office and grinding my teeth during the three or four hours a night I slept. I was struggling with addictions and I was without a spiritual life. I was somehow holding everything together with brains, heroic effort, and rigid self-discipline.

People often seek out *Intensive Journal* workshops at times of transition; perhaps they are facing a career change, dealing with retirement, ending a marriage or beginning one, experiencing physical challenges, or suffering a dark night of the soul. Having social support during these life transitions and challenges is one of the most important benefits of the program. To live in a secular culture such as ours means that we are very much on our own when it comes to making life transitions and becoming fully realized human beings. In a sense, we are fortunate, for the very lack of a rigid social structure also means the opportunity for creativity in finding our own meaning, and realizing our unique existence within the context and circumstances of our individual lives and capacities.

The atmosphere that is created in an *Intensive Journal* workshop as people work together in meditative silence provides a supportive environment for doing inner work; the workshop becomes a place to gain a deeper sense of what our individual lives are seeking to become, without doctrines or interpretations being imposed by others. The recognition of meaning arises from our experience during the writing itself, and we come to understanding in our own way, according to our particular needs and beliefs (Progoff 2010).

Our relation to the *Intensive Journal* workbook itself becomes, with time, a "living relationship" very similar to a musician's relationship with his or her instrument; the more the instrument is used, the greater are the possibilities of what the two can achieve together. After the experience of a workshop, says Progoff, the workbook becomes "much more than a book in which you write. It will become a companion, a portable alter ego, and an intimate friend who will respond and discuss with you in dialogue the decisions of your life" (Progoff 1992, p.44).

So it has been for me. With my first *Intensive Journal* workshop in 1985, a conscious, creative, and healing relationship with my inner life was initiated. I left the workshop filled with hope, for the first time in many years, especially for my life as an artist. Since graduation from Northwestern University in 1961, my creative energy had been poured outward into the requirements of my career. During that first workshop, I discovered a devotion to the *Intensive Journal* process that has grown ever more compelling and rewarding over the decades. A new awareness of my inner life has evolved and a process of inner dialogue, inherent in the way of working with this method, has allowed me to evoke and experience resources of creativity, renewal, wisdom, and deep meaning as never before. With ever-growing skill in using the process of Twilight Imagery, I have become mindful of the continual flow of images coming up from the deeper-than-conscious range of experience and speaking to me of my life possibilities in symbolic language, and I have learned ways of understanding the rich messages and inner guidance these symbolic images afford me.

Using the processes of the *Intensive Journal* method, I have come to realize that, though in one sense, I live with conscious purpose and intention, in a deeper sense, my life can be thought of as living me, and the inner potentials of my deeper life are far more vibrant with energy and meaning than many of the goals I consciously set for myself.

Progoff's term for this life that speaks to us from our depths, "the life that is true to its own nature" (Progoff 1992, p.34), recalled to me my life as an artist—the one I had envisioned for myself in my youth, when to be an artist seemed the highest calling, the life for which I had prepared myself and studied early on, until graduation from college and the need to get a job sent me off in another direction.

As Progoff was developing the *Intensive Journal* method, he realized that gaining access to the dynamic energies moving in the depths of persons, so as to promote growth, requires a way of working, and an understanding of the nature of the psyche, that is broader and more encompassing than in many approaches to psychoanalysis. A psychoanalyst, seeking to help a person move beyond blocks or inhibitions toward a more creative and fulfilling life, might seek to uncover particular personal traumas that have been repressed and therefore comprise a hidden motivation behind the blocks and inhibitions and insecurities of neurotic behavior. Referring to this perspective, Progoff says: "The depths of the psyche, [therefore] have essentially a negative aspect, for they are conceived in terms of the pathology of personality" (Progoff 1973a, p.6).

A more encompassing view of persons was provided by Jung, whose work had relevance for Progoff in developing the theoretical basis for the *Intensive Journal* method. Jung recognized in the human psyche not only the personal unconscious, but also a collective unconscious, or objective psyche, a deep repository of the patterns, life-energies, and creative potentials that we all share as human beings but that we live out in the world in our own unique ways. Although we all have personal repressions and inhibitions that may surface as neuroses, of far greater significance is the awareness of the vast resources of replenishing life-potentials residing in our depths (Jung 1989).

It is those potentials that our work in the *Intensive Journal* process allows us to realize so that we can help them find outer expression in the world through our works and relationships. As we work in the various sections of the workbook, each with its unique vantage point, we are able to understand symbolic material in the context of our life as a whole. Further, the structure of the workbook itself provides a protective framework so the energies of the deep psyche, which when unregulated can have an unbalancing effect in a person's life, become instead rich resources for creativity and growth.

Therefore, when we experience fears or blocks or confusions, and seek to move beyond them by means of the workbook and its processes, we do not analyze them from an intellectual, exterior, objective perspective in order to remove the painful emotions. The techniques we use in our work are *nonanalytical*.

To explain this term, Progoff compares the analytical (but not referring to Jung's analytical psychology) with the nonanalytical approach using the metaphor of restoring the flow of water in a stream (the dynamic movement of our life-energies) that has become blocked by a boulder (a repressed experience from our past). In analysis, we would chip away at the boulder so as to break it into pieces small enough to allow the stream once again to flow. In the nonanalytial approach using the *Intensive Journal* method, we would increase the flow of water from the source (that is, we would access energies and images from the depths of our personality), until the stream became deep enough and had sufficient momentum to flow around and over the boulder (Progoff 1985).

What this image illustrates is that in the *Intensive Journal* process, by gaining access to the deep source of symbolic imagery as we record our sleep dreams and the waking dreams unfolded by Twilight Imagery, we are able to reach deeper levels of awareness that may then bring forth new insights, not only into our personal psychology, but new kinds of insight into the nature of life. As Progoff writes:

A larger perspective opens [and] a new quality of relationship can be established to the events of the past. The continuity of life renews itself, and we have a fresh opportunity. In the light of our new recognition of the inner movement and meaning of our lives, it actually seems that we can now begin our life anew. That is what the ageless symbolism of rebirth has been trying to say to people since the beginning of religion. (Progoff 1992, pp.14–15)

Our growth as persons and the transformation of consciousness necessary for significant change depend upon our having access on an ongoing basis to these strong inner resources of life-energy. A closed container, such as the deep atmosphere of an *Intensive Journal* workshop, the protected environment of the therapy consulting room, or the skillfully evoked sacred space of traditional ritual process, is essential to build the inner momentum and draw on factors strong enough to evoke true psychological transformation. Progoff (1992) further realized that the energies and potentials arising from our depths are not always experienced and expressed in the outer world in the same way, and he therefore organized the *Intensive Journal* according to four distinct dimensions:

1. In the *Time/Life Dimension*, our life-energy is manifested through outer and inner events, circumstances, and decisions that together comprise the facts of our personal life history.

2. In the *Dialogue Dimension*, our life-energy is expressed through what the theologian Martin Buber would call I/ Thou relationships, our way of connecting in a depth way to the inner, essential selves of the significant persons and other important relationships of our life.

3. In the *Depth Dimension*, our life-energy is manifested through imagery, defined broadly by Progoff to include far more than visual images, that is, to include the symbolism expressed in sleep dreams, as well as the imagery we encounter in waking dreams that we experience during the Twilight Imagery processes in our *Intensive Journal* work.

4. In the *Meaning Dimension*, our life-energy is expressed as our yearning toward connection to the larger-than-personal, expressed in our beliefs and values, in our spiritual journey, and in our reaching toward the transpersonal aspect of personal existence.

Each dimension has specific workbook sections and special techniques appropriate to the kind of work to be done there. The structure and containment of the workbook give the work the capacity to generate new energy, an inner dynamic experienced according to the perspective associated with each of the four dimensions.

In the following sections, I will speak specifically of ways I have experienced the transformative energies associated with each of these four dimensions in my work with the *Intensive Journal* method, and I will mention some of the most significant insights, artworks, enlargements of consciousness, and depths of relationship that have accrued as a result of my devotion to this practice. The method is a practice to which I have given devotion regularly, approaching it with reverence, absolute trust, and, indeed, on occasion, awe and fascination. For me the process itself possesses a quality of the sacred.

1. THE TIME/LIFE DIMENSION: INITIATIONS, AWAKENINGS, AND TRANSFORMATIONS

Two profound initiatory ordeals stand like bookends at either end of my 51 years at Northwestern University, where I was first an undergraduate and then a professional person. What I now recognize as the first initiation was experienced when I was 18, and a freshman. During that ordeal, I suffered a sense of dismemberment and the stripping away of everything I once was that is essential to initiation, but without ritual elders, language or conceptual grasp to recognize and fully understand what was happening to me. At 18, I writhed about in the cauldron of transformation as courageously as I could, but half a century would pass until I had the *Intensive Journal* method to reveal to me the meaning of the experience.

The second initiation occurred at the age of 69, when I retired from the career that had been based at Northwestern University Medical School. It was no less of an ordeal, with no less a sense of psychological dismemberment and stripping away of everything I once was, but I was able to undergo this second initiation far more consciously, with the conceptual grasp of what an initiation necessarily entails. This time, I had the guidance of wise elders—most importantly Progoff—and understandings I had gathered along the path of my long spiritual journey. I had the technology of the sacred to hold me and allow me fully to experience the ordeal, enduring it with eyes open and mind awake. This time, I recognized that losses and sufferings were necessary to move me into the self-chosen life rising up from my depths, with its blessings of time and life-energy to devote to what I truly love.

Back in 1956, however, having undergone a crisis of faith during my freshman year at Northwestern University, I had my first encounter with psychotherapy and with life as an atheist, for I was now without God, and my valedictorian golden-girl persona had slipped off of me. I was in intense psychological and spiritual pain. The source of my existential upheaval was, by today's standards, quite commonplace. But in the 1950s, to seek Spirit in spirits of alcohol and the Sacred Feminine in a decidedly earthy relationship with a woman was shocking to some important people in my life, and was painful for us all.

Those college years were also intense with intellectual exploration and cultural riches. My companions were Thomas Mann, James Joyce, T.S. Eliot, Fyodor Dostoyevsky, William Shakespeare. And all these years later, working in the *Intensive Journal* process, I find that my college years are an archeological dig, in the layers of which I continually find the bones and postholes of early forms of my most meaningful creative and spiritual work.

Before Progoff developed his method, he gave workshops sometimes using fairy tales and myths as teaching tools and would ask participants to try to tell the story without the betrayal by the stepmother or the failure of the girl to return as promised to save the beast, and they found they could not (Progoff 1973b). In the context of his method, betrayals, failures, losses, and mistakes in judgment must happen to us for our lives to unfold their lessons. Sections of the *Intensive Journal* workbook, such as the Dialogue with Events, and Intersections: Roads Taken and Not Taken, and Spiritual Steppingstones, become the places to which we turn to uncover the deeper meaning of our losses and seemingly wrong turns. We enter into dialogue with the events and circumstances of our existence, inviting them to speak to us from their perspective and teach us what we need to know, perhaps softening their impact upon us.

Jung, in the chapter of his autobiography entitled "Confrontation with the Unconscious," describes the period of inner uncertainty and disorientation following his break with Freud, a period of which he says:

> The years when I was pursuing my inner images were the most important of my life—in them everything essential was decided. It all began then; the later details are only supplements and clarifications of the material that burst forth from the unconscious, and at first swamped me. It was the *prima materia* for a lifetime's work. (Jung 1989, p.199)

Without the *Intensive Journal* method, I might have closed the door on a painful, though intense and interesting, period of my life and left it unexcavated. But with this way of working, I am able to mine that earlier time for the resources and origins of my understandings of the shape and functioning of my own spirit; I am able to appreciate those years as an alchemical vessel where the raw material of inner experience could eventually be refined and turned into gold.

Many decades later, in 2007, this time armed with the *Intensive Journal* method as my instrument and practice, I began preparing myself consciously to submit to the initiatory ordeal that would draw to a close the cycle of self called my career. I set for myself an initiatory task, the creation of a stained glass mandala with imagery that came up from my depths during my journal work, to prove my worthiness to be a full-time artist. I sought out the erudition of scholars who had written specifically about the initiatory process:

Mircea Eliade, Edward Edinger, Jungian analyst Robert Moore, Joseph Campbell, Heinrich Zimmer. I understood the experience itself, however, on an immediate, personal level in the context of Progoff's teachings and method, which would support me through what became the most challenging ordeal of my life.

We can prepare ourselves intellectually and conceptually for initiatory experiences, but living through them is another matter. During the two years after my career ended, my husband, Fred, fell seriously ill, and it became necessary to sell the home we had loved for 40 years. My life-energy drained out of me and there was no remnant left, it seemed, of the person I once was, and no promise of the person I hoped to become. Work on my mandala and everything else in my life was put on hold as Fred's illness took me to his bedside. I wrote and wrote in my workbook as I sat in the ICU, with the hum of the ventilator and the dialysis machine and the eerie light and chirp of monitor screens. Miraculously, over the months, Fred's health returned, and we moved to a suburb of Chicago. Then, with the greatest part of the danger past, in the peace and gentleness of fragrant summer nights, I fell into a time of profound exhaustion, unspecified grief, fear, and existential shuddering at so close an encounter with death and the loss of everything that once was.

Yet Progoff had given me what I needed to endure a time like this. According to Progoff, the psyche functions by means of Cycles of Connective Experience that begin just where I found myself, in a place of disconnection, disorientation, emptiness, and depletion (Progoff 1985). It is our nature to experience this disconnection from meaning from time to time. Invariably, the experience of disconnection itself sets up, in our psyche, a yearning, and something in us scans the inner and outer landscape for an image of hope, a sign of the next step on the journey, a new direction. It is especially important to pay attention to our dreams at such times, for our inner life speaks to us in symbolic language. For me, the workbook became an invaluable container for this kind of experience.

In *The Dynamics of Hope*, Progoff (1985) speaks of three aspects of the theory that forms the basis of his method, and he describes the function of what he calls our organic psyche.

Dialectics is the tendency of opposites to form and build the energies of movement within a human existence. Our lives, says Progoff, move in a dialectical manner between hope and anxiety and back again; further, this dialectical movement is cyclical.

The downward part that moves from the affirmative to the negative is one half of the cycle but the nature of a cycle is that it contains two parts. After moving downward and reaching bottom, it remains in this "valley" phase for an indeterminate period—for as long as its contents require—and then, without being prodded from the outside but moving in its own timing, it reverses direction. It moves back upward again, going once again into its opposite. (Progoff 1985, p.16)

Depth is the dimension of human experience that expresses itself by means of symbols, as we see in sleep dreams and in the twilight range of waking dreams.

[Depth] is not a level in the psyche literally and spatially; but it is indeed a level in the human organism in *principle*. It is present and it is *deeper* down in the psyche in the sense that it is more fundamental than those mental contents that are in closer relation to surface consciousness and to sensory contact with the outer world. The depths contain what is implicit in the psyche, what is potential there, what is working in the background of individual development toward fulfillment by means of growth. (Progoff 1973a, p.8)

Holistic integration is "the tendency of the life process, both in the world of nature and in human society, to form new and ever more refined units, or integrations, of life" (Progoff 1985, pp.12–13). These new integrations, or *emergents*, as philosopher Henri Bergson has called them, were never in existence before and could not be planned; they are essentially creative. According to Progoff, the inner movement of our psyche is invariably toward wholeness (Progoff 1992). If we can open ourselves to an awareness of this movement, we will have an ever-enlarging and increasingly integrated sense of who we truly are.

One of the functions of the *Intensive Journal* workbook, with its exercises, is to [help us] maintain our perspective as we move through the valley of anxiety and hold us [in its protective containment] until we move into the upward phase of the cycle where the opposites are able to renew themselves. (Progoff 1985, p.18)

If we can allow the dialectical process to take place without stepping in to stop the movement artificially, we will experience an enlargement of consciousness; an emergent will come into being, and an expression of creativity will occur.

This is what I experienced. My workbook provided a place to make my lament and describe my journey down into the valley, with the accompanying experience of emptiness, the anguish of non-being, and my fears that the darkness would never end. But, indeed, the very act of lamenting brought a shift, a movement upward. And, as Progoff had said would happen, there came with it "an image of something that is to be given tangible form in the outer world. It is for the future, and it is envisioned whole" (Progoff 1985, p.14).

Hope returned, and with it, an image, an emergent. This image arose from my depths during an *Intensive Journal* workshop, taking form as a vision of eight stained glass windows for a Chapel to the Sacred Feminine. At the time, I was dazzled by the power and intensity of this image. Without having any idea how I would undertake such an enormous project, which seemed far beyond my experience and skill as a stained glass artist, this energy-charged image called me back into life. It was "for the future."

The Chapel to the Sacred Feminine became the initiating image for my next cycle of self. Later in this chapter, I'll speak more about its meaning, and how I discovered, by means of my journal work, evidence of its long history in my psyche.

2. THE DIALOGUE DIMENSION: PERSEPHONE AND THE I/THOU RELATIONSHIP

Inner dialogue is a central concept for Progoff; indeed, he named the organization that administers his public programs of personal and professional growth Dialogue House Associates. His concept of dialogue has a range of meanings, from an exercise used in certain sections of the *Intensive Journal* workbook to a profound way of being in the world and relating to every aspect of our life. Ultimately, it means entering into a dialogue with our life itself, and asking the life living us what it is seeking to become.

Dialogue involves a way in which we experience our inner and outer life, in which we encounter the world of human relationships, nature, society, and the cosmos. The idea is that anything in the field of time has a beginning, then grows and develops in certain ways and, at some point, undergoes a falling away and ending or transformation into something else. In that sense, it has a life history, and can therefore be treated as a person with whom we can enter into dialogue. We allow it to speak of its inner purposes and intentions and to share with us its perspectives. We relate to the other, whether it is a person, our body, a social group, a wisdom figure, even an event, as a Thou. The depth of discoveries that result from the dialogue script we write will depend upon the psychological and meditative deepening of our level of awareness in preparation for such an encounter. That preparation is a skill we develop with experience in working with the method (Progoff 1992).

For me, one of the most important of the dialogues in the workbook is the Dialogue with Works (Progoff 1992). The Work that has been my partner in dialogue for many years is a novel I entitled "The Realm of Persephone," the first draft of which I completed more than two decades ago. It came from a deeper-than-conscious, mysterious place in me, and I am still struggling to shape it into a conscious literary work. The story is what the Germans call a *Bildungsroman*, a coming-of-age tale, which is set not only in real time in the outer world but also in the inner world of my main character, Zoe Thomas, a 35-year-old administrative director of a small scientific research society. A parallel existence unfolds in her unconscious, to which she is pulled down by way of fainting spells during which she comes awake as her 12-year-old self in the Realm of Persephone, an often-terrifying treasure trove of extraordinary experiences and fabulous characters. She is drawn downward into her unconscious again and again as her psychological containment fragments after the death of her adored father.

For the Ancient Greeks, the realm of Persephone described in *The Homeric Hymn to Demeter* was a mythic underworld where Hades, the god of hidden riches and stores of wealth under the earth, makes the abducted Persephone his queen (Foley 1994). The task, in the classic tale, is to restore Persephone to the world of light. To the Greeks, she symbolized, among other things, spring, new life, and renewal out of the death and darkness of winter. The story of Persephone and her mother, Demeter, goddess of agriculture and fertility, was central to the Eleusinian Mysteries, which were celebrated in Eleusis, Greece, for more than 2000 years. From what little we know, for the actual rites were never written down, the initiatory rituals had to do with rendering a transformation of consciousness, reconciling initiates to the idea of death, and offering an experience of spiritual rebirth.

In my story, the task of Zoe is to make conscious what has happened to her in childhood, an abduction, and then come to terms with repressed events that only now, with her father's death, are breaking through into awareness and throwing her conscious life into chaos. Like the initiates at Eleusis, Zoe must undergo a transformation of consciousness; she must integrate new awarenesses gained through her ordeals in the underworld, undergo a spiritual renewal, and make peace with what happened in her past so as to live in the present with more authenticity, claiming at last her fully realized existence.

The Persephone manuscript is the second long literary work I have undertaken, and both the first manuscript and the second begin with the same opening lines:

As she stood on the front porch of the Ohio home of her childhood, on this February morning, and her father had just died, she noted that a storm was brewing, and the winter sky was purple. And her mind took her back to an Easter morning when she was a young girl and she had stood on this same porch, and a storm had been brewing then, too, and she was wearing a beautiful new dress of Easter colors. But this winter storm depressed her, stirred feelings of dread. This February porch did not comfort, or shelter. No. These February steps were icy and dangerous. They had not been shoveled and salted as her father would have done if he had not been dying.

In the first story, Zoe then turns and enters the house and goes upstairs to where her bereaved mother lies resting. The tale that unfolds, which I have entitled "The Good Daughter," is about the relationship between a widowed mother and her grown, only daughter. For the first time, they must relate without the ameliorating influence of the husband/father between them. When the mother shows signs of dementia, the two women gradually reverse roles; the mother becomes a dependent child and the daughter becomes the mother. With her mother's overwhelming need, Zoe struggles with resentment and compassion, anger and aching love; she finds herself doing battle with death on behalf of her mother. In her mother's face, so like her own, Zoe watches herself age and become infirm. After her mother dies, Zoe struggles to free herself from the restless ghost, which impels Zoe to wear the dresses she had bought for her mother, and tortures her by creating symptoms in Zoe mimicking Alzheimer's. The tale ends with exorcism and Zoe's uneasy peace.

"The Good Daughter" manuscript was written before I had the *Intensive Journal* method. A literary agent acknowledged my writing skills but, perhaps from her perspective as the agent for authors in the biological sciences, felt the book would be more salable if I were to bank on my cachet as a medical writer and revise the manuscript as a scientific text on Alzheimer's disease. I didn't want to do that. I told her I wanted to write about a spiritual journey. "Not a good idea," she said. "You aren't Shirley MacLaine."

I began again, but in an unanticipated way, and with an unexpected result. Sitting in a week-long *Intensive Journal* retreat led by Progoff himself in Chicago, working in the way we do with

Twilight Imagery and doing an Imagery Extension, I found myself on the same front porch described in that opening paragraph of "The Good Daughter," but, as I worked, I was led in a meditative way back into the house, and, to my surprise, I was drawn into the basement, where my real-life father had had his writing office for many years. The basement was the Realm of the Father, in my personal mythology.

During that workshop, I read aloud from my writings in the workbook and Progoff asked if I was familiar with the Demeter-Persephone myth. I was not. But after the workshop, I sought out *The Homeric Hymn to Demeter*, and the ancient tale of the abduction of the young Persephone into the underworld became the central image not only of my creative writing but also of my personal healing work for the many years of my life.

This is not the story of a first-time novelist creating a Pulitzer Prize-winning literary achievement. This is a story of a long dialogue between artist and artwork, an artwork that, like a person, has a life history and its own purposes and intentions. While the artist has been creating the artwork, the artwork has created the artist.

As I worked on the Persephone manuscript, I began each writing session by intentionally deepening my level of awareness, using techniques I had learned in *Intensive Journal* workshops. I was determined this time not to write to please my ego or to position my story, or to think in terms of a book tour and film rights for what had begun to feel to me like a sacred process, a kind of entering into a mystery, my own Eleusinian mystery. I experienced a going-down into depths where I encountered a source of creative life-energy in the far reaches of the psyche. Progoff's method had given me access to this transpersonal realm, and its energies allowed me to come to my writing day after day, even while I was meeting the enormous demands of my career. I surrendered the results of my day's efforts, placing the work, and my intentions for whatever would unfold, upon a metaphoric altar in an ego-sacrificing gesture. When I finished the first draft, I became convinced that, working in this way, I did not fully understand what I had accomplished;

something of value was there, yet I felt unprepared to take the manuscript to the next level as a literary work.

When I wrote dialogues with the manuscript itself, and posed the question, "What are you asking of me?" the voice of the Work said I needed more understanding of how psychological healing takes place, more ability to see what I was doing as an artist, more skill as an editor. It told me I needed a deeper and more psychological understanding of the Demeter-Persephone myth and its implications for a modern person. I needed greater understanding of the implications of this magical story for my personal healing.

Accordingly, I returned to therapy, this time with a Jungian analyst. I renewed my reading of myth, and discovered an enormous literature surrounding Demeter and Persephone and the Eleusinian Mysteries. I worked in the workbook to uncover aspects of my childhood that had not been accessible to me before. My psychological work with my therapist, which lasted for more than ten years, focused on healing the wounded feminine.

Twice, over a couple of years before my retirement, Fred and I read my Persephone manuscript aloud to one another. As I listened to the story unfolding, I experienced wonder, even delight, for though the manuscript is not yet a polished literary work, it has for me a luminous intensity.

Its strength is also its problem. Because of the Twilight Imagery techniques I used in the writing, it is a waking dream, a very long dream, and, like a Grimm's fairy tale, it is filled with strange symbolism and mysteries to be intimated rather than analyzed, and it seems to hold messages still difficult to decipher. How could it be edited? What is meaningful detail? Until I know how to make those kinds of decisions, my long dialogue with this work will continue.

3. THE DEPTH DIMENSION: SWAMPY, THE RAKISH CRONE

One night, many years ago, I had a brief but vivid dream in which I was standing with friends at a cocktail party, and a smelly, disreputable old woman with wild hair and flouncy skirts walked up to our group and went directly to the most proper and refined of us, a friend who in real time was a soldier and in civilian life is excessively neat and self-disciplined. In the dream, the old woman kissed this man and pushed her tongue lasciviously into his mouth. He and the others drew back, aghast. I, however, put my arm around the old woman and defended her, asking them what was so terrible about what she had done.

In returning to the dream, working in the way we do in the *Intensive Journal* process, I entered into dialogue with the old woman, asking her why she had appeared to me. Her answer was, essentially, that she felt everyone (I knew she meant me) needed shaking up a bit and needed not to be so proper and controlled and in their heads. What she said had a ring of truth for me, and she was so engaging and charismatic that I have continued my dialogues with her for many years.

With time, the old woman has become a Wisdom Figure for me. What prompts an inner dialogue visit with her is a feeling of physical and emotional depletion, a profound exhaustion that overcomes me from time to time. Our dialogues, which involve vivid Twilight Imagery, usually take place on a rocky beach, a cove at the bottom of a high cliff. She almost always is accompanied by a flock of ravens, which she calls "my girls," and she sometimes comes along wheeling a shopping cart filled with sea creatures and seaweed, right at the edge of the water. Often, she grabs my hands and "dances" me on the shore, and at her touch, I feel my body infused with radiant energy, a heat that I experience as light.

During our many encounters, I have discovered that this old woman from my depths can control weather and is a shapeshifter, a trickster. At first, I called her the Rakish Crone, but when it occurred to me to ask her what her name is, she said "Swampy." Later, reading Mary Oliver's (1992) poem, "Crossing the Swamp," I realized how right it is that the Rakish Crone calls herself Swampy. In the poem, the poet makes her way through the slick, glittery mud of a swamp, where she experiences a sense of renewal, and she feels she might have a chance at resurrection, a new opportunity to take root and bud again.

To what in my life is this drawing my attention? I had learned from Progoff to ask as I worked: *What does my life seem to be asking of me?*

The answer came to me: Swampy offers me a kind of rebirth and new blossoming, by means of her untamed, swampy earthiness. She urges me to laugh and be wild and sing and carry on, play my drum, make love. When I take myself too seriously, she pokes fun at me, teases me, and jars me out of my stuckness. When I become mired in the mundane, the secular, the constraints of consciousness, she is the powerful, transpersonal, elemental force of nature, of the winds and tides, storms and darkness encountered at the edge of the great ocean in which the minuscule human ego is swallowed back again into the vast, boundless deeps.

A few years ago, I thought I would write a one-woman show and put Swampy on stage, but she quickly let me know, in our dialogues, that to do such a thing would not be appropriate. She is not a character in a play, she said, and she must be treated with proper respect. She made me understand that the great powers of the deep unconscious must be related to with humility, reverence, and awe, for the Rakish Crone has been evoked from sources far deeper than, and beyond, those of waking consciousness. Those powers are potentially as dangerous as Yahweh was to Job, as Moby Dick was to Ahab, as Mephistopheles was to Faust, and as all of the gods have always been to mortals who have made the mistake of thinking they could encounter a god as an equal and survive unscathed.

Recently, I wrote a dialogue with the Rakish Crone, the first dialogue in more than a year. In the past, she didn't always come when, in Twilight Imagery, I went down the face of the cliff on the steep, muddy path to the cold, wet sand of the cove. I wasn't sure she would come this time, but she did, with her ravens. I was grateful to see her. She was jocular, as ever, and talked about me in the third person at first, teasing. But when I told her my fear of being old and helpless, and I wept and poured out my anxieties about disease and mortification of the flesh, she surprised me by promising that she would help me if ever I truly needed her; she promised to be my protector. And it came to me that perhaps the ravens are dark angels, and are also protectors. My fear was lifted for a while.

Over time, I have experienced resonances with Swampy in surprising places. For example, I have recognized her in Jung's Philemon, the fantasy figure of an old man with whom Jung had long conversations during what he called Active Imagination (akin to Progoff's Twilight Imagery) (Jung 1989). I have also recognized Swampy in Baubo, the old woman who appeared to Demeter and, with ribald jokes and outrageous behavior, made the grieving mother laugh. I have recognized her in Hecate, the crone aspect of the Triple Goddess, guardian of crossroads and caves and the dark wisdom of endings. I have recognized her in the Morrigan of Celtic mythology, who appears on battlefields with her ravens to harvest fallen heroes. I have recognized her in Baba Yaga, the witch of Russian fairy tales, who could be both fearsome and helpful (von Franz 1993).

These resonances with mythic figures suggest that in my encounters with the Rakish Crone, my psyche has reached into a deep place beyond the personal. Yet Swampy is mine, an Inner Wisdom Figure experienced uniquely by me, in my own imagery, speaking directly and individually to me of my own sorrows and losses, times of depletion, discouragement, and grief. She finds the words to comfort me, to lift me up, to revitalize me through her touch, and to infuse me with new life energy.

As Progoff writes in *The Dynamics of Hope*:

> …what is happening in such situations [as an encounter with a numinous dream figure is that] a transformation of consciousness is brought about. It is a transformation in the sense that it provides a new and larger perspective in which to see the situation of the life. The actuality of the events remains the same, but the circumstances are reset in a context of universality and timelessness. Then, the situation of the life, which has been experienced as encompassing and enclosing the person, is loosened, giving the person psychological breathing space and opening new possibilities. In the phrase of Benedict Spinoza the situation can then be seen *sub specie eternitatis*, in the light of eternity, perceived in symbolic forms that are readily translatable into the terms of one's own life. (Progoff 1985, p.31)

Indeed, my encounters with the Rakish Crone could be thought of as encounters "in the light of eternity," in the timeless place at the shore of the oceanic unconscious, not existing in the physical world, but real nonetheless. These encounters always feel as if I had been in the presence of the sacred. "Awareness of existence in the light of eternity," says Progoff:

> carries with it overtones of spirit. It may indeed be that this breaking open of the walls of time in the act of symbolic perception is a main aspect of what is being indicated when such experiences are referred to as spiritual experiences. (Progoff 1985, p.30)

The dialogues with Swampy have become a long teaching on how to live my life, influencing the kind of psychotherapy I chose (a woman Jungian analyst), books, workshops, and spiritual practices (a women's ritual group celebrating Celtic seasonal festivals, my dedication to meditation practices, my reading of mythology), even the musical instruments I have played (dumbek and frame drum). Those encounters have influenced my approach to writing poetry and fiction, and myriad other decisions I made, especially during the late 1980s and 1990s, as I struggled to turn my life in a new direction. My work in the *Intensive Journal* process gave me an inner knowing that these changes were right and necessary, and as I experienced the Rakish Crone, with her teasing and cajoling, speaking her crazy wisdom, dancing with me at the edge of the ocean, my inner life gradually began to express itself outwardly in more embodied, passionate, and creative ways.

4. THE MEANING DIMENSION: STAINED GLASS, THE SACRED FEMININE, AND THE ONE RADIANCE

I began working with stained glass relatively late in my life, yet I have come to believe the impulse to work with stained glass has a long history for me, traveling within me like a deep current for many years, perhaps even centuries, in my genetic material from forgotten ancestors. Or, could it be, other lifetimes spent creating rose windows dedicated to Our Lady, the Goddess, in the great cathedrals in twelfth-century France, and at last moving upward into the outer world to find expression in my life only in recent years? Even more than writing, my work in the stained glass studio wipes out the experience of time. I stand bent over the glass in a kind of rapture, discovering the texture, grain, and special radiance of each piece, perceiving the way it must take its necessary place in the pattern. Finally, after months, even years, of effort, I lift the finished artwork to the light, and in that moment, something of eternity breaks through the temporal. The physical object, glass, interacts with light, with all the symbolic meaning light has held for humankind through the ages, in such a way as to create a moment of holiness.

There is, in the *Intensive Journal* workbook, a section called Gatherings, where we gather together a record of those times in our lives when we have felt a sense of connection to something larger than personal, times when we have had an experience of what might be called the sacred. Depending on the person, that moment may be in nature, with a teacher, in a mathematical equation or a science laboratory, with a beloved partner or grandchild, in a religious observance or in public service, listening to music, walking through an art gallery, or gazing into the eyes of a cherished animal. Our work in Gatherings brings to our awareness such moments, and in the paragraphs where we recapitulate those experiences, we gain intimations of what is, for us, most high and holy (Progoff 1992).

Working in Gatherings, I realized that throughout my life I have experienced a sense of connection to the sacred many times as I have stepped into deserted cathedrals and chapels, my heart opening in the silent luminousness of stained glass. I also realized I have felt a sense of connection to the sacred as I have stood before the paintings of Vincent van Gogh, to whom even the worn boots of a laborer, the weary faces of the Potato Eaters, were expressive of holiness. He recorded experiences of the sacred, as if they were Gatherings, in his paintings, which seem to say that for him, one radiance shines through all things. This perception, coming to me in a workshop, prompted a poem.

VINCENT VAN GOGH

Long after the last letter,
long after the gunshot, the wheat field,
the sun pale in a menacing sky,
the three roads leading nowhere,
despair-dark crows,
that difficult life reveals itself
an act of deepest faith,
each brushstroke praise,
each painting a prayer:
Let my love be
absolute.

Long after the trials
of the pilgrim in his desert: Terror,
lust, the lure of convention (comfort,
every need met,
every painting sold)—

one radiance
shines through all things.

And the answer, seeming to be,
No. Never.
becomes, in the final balance,
Yes.

In Gatherings we also recapitulate times when we have felt a sense of disconnection. Here again, church windows held symbolic meaning. The windows of the Congregational church where my family and I worshiped as I was growing up were clear glass. To my Puritan ancestors, stained glass and incense and the ecstasy of mysticism invited idolatry, and the clear glass of our little church seemed to stand firm against such sensuous lures. My parents found sanctuary in that church. I did not. I felt disconnected and separate;

I felt there was no place for me, though at the time I could not have said why.

As a young person, I did not know I missed stained glass and incense, but I sensed that there was no Sacred Feminine in the atmosphere of my church. The theology was about Father and Son. The Virgin Mary, revered by Catholics, seemed unimportant to Congregationalists. Our minister was a man, though an eloquent one; Jesus was a man; the Disciples were men. The few women in the Bible stories I read were silent, or fallen, like nature itself, and requiring forgiveness and correction by men or by God the Father. Nowhere did I encounter representations of the Sacred Feminine.

When I was about eight years old, an inner prompting caused me to begin refusing to say, "Our Father, Which art in Heaven" when it was time in the service to do so. My mother would look down at me encouragingly, and I would clamp my jaw tightly closed and turn away. During my freshman year at Northwestern University, I shook my fist at heaven and cried: "There is no God!"

As we work in the Meaning Dimension of the *Intensive Journal* workbook, having written our Gatherings, we then consider our spiritual journey in a more formal way. We list our Spiritual Steppingstones, some eight or ten points of reference that reflect the range of faith and doubt that we have experienced since childhood, our inner quest for wisdom and truth in our life. Though I have drawn together many such lists over the years, which differ from one another because of the different perspectives from which I have written them, each has included my earliest experience of the sacred in the beauty and sanctuary of my mother's garden. My mother was, indeed, Demeter for me as a young child, the Goddess of Growing Things. She knew the Latin names for flowers, and she nurtured her garden as she nurtured me in those early years of my life, tenderly, and with intense caring.

Often, I list a curious event for a Spiritual Steppingstone— myself, at about four years old, frantically pedaling my tricycle away from my mother along the sidewalk, weeping loudly and inconsolably. At the time, my mother had suggested that I accompany an older friend for a day of kindergarten, since I would soon begin school. My mother told me that story years later, still puzzled by the intensity of my grief at what seemed an innocent enough suggestion.

Looking back, now, in the light of my *Intensive Journal* work, I recognize how prophetic that moment was. The weeping child, who had no direct outer experience upon which to base her grief, seemed to have an inner knowing that she was about to leave the sacred world of the Goddess. Going to school would take me into the world of the Father, the world of ideas and achievement. There, the feminine was not valued, and in that world, I would often feel like a motherless child.

Reflecting upon my Spiritual Steppingstones, I realize that at college, experiencing the death of God the Father, I had simultaneously felt an intense and powerful yearning toward the feminine, which for me was the Sacred Feminine. But without the awareness at that time in my life of the symbolic meaning of my actions, I expressed my yearning on the physical, literal level. Understanding its deeper, symbolic meaning would come only later, after years of alienation from the feminine in a spiritual desert, when I began the long work of recovery and healing. In 1985, with the *Intensive Journal* method, I began to reclaim the lost Sacred Feminine and consciously to reintegrate it in symbolic form into my creative and spiritual life. Gradually, my *Intensive Journal* work has moved me toward an awareness of continuity and deep inner intention in my life, and a growing sense of wholeness.

At the conclusion of an *Intensive Journal* workshop, we turn to the final section of the workbook, Now: The Open Moment, and call upon the capacity of the psyche for holistic integration, inviting it to draw together all the life-energies and Molecules of Thought and Imagery (Progoff 1992) that have been stirred as we have worked, to offer us an emergent, an image for the next stage of our unfolding life.

Working in that same way now, as I write this, I think again of the child in the sanctity of Demeter's garden, the weeping child on the tricycle, the death of God the Father and my yearnings toward the Sacred Feminine in college, the bookend initiations at Northwestern University, "The Good Daughter" manuscript, which sought to be about a spiritual journey but failed, "The Realm of Persephone" manuscript, which is a spiritual journey but is not yet a literary work, my encounters with Swampy, the Rakish Crone, at the edge of the deep, the confrontation with non-being and the near death of my husband, and my bliss in the stained glass studio. All of these become, in this Open Moment, a single, creative whole, held in the image of a Chapel to the Sacred Feminine, drawing me into my next cycle of self.

I have, in fact, created six of the eight chapel windows I saw so many years ago in my mind's eye during that *Intensive Journal* workshop, though to call them windows is too grand. They are stained glass panels, each 16 by 24 inches, and an actual chapel to house them will never be built. Instead, the panels are suspended from a wrought-iron frame, divided into four hinged sections so as to be self-standing. Thus, a small chapel can be set up in any space large enough to accommodate it. Perhaps that is exactly right, in a world where the sacred is imminent everywhere, and one radiance shines through all things.

In such a world, all the discrete and seemingly unrelated events of my life, the life that is true to its own nature, which I record and reflect upon in my workbook, can be experienced as one great inner movement, an ever-evolving process of becoming whole. Of all I have learned through my years of devotion to the *Intensive Journal* method, this awareness is Ira Progoff's greatest gift to me.

REFERENCES

Foley, H.P. (ed.), 1994. *The Homeric Hymn to Demeter: Translation, Commentary, and Interpretive Essays.* Princeton, NJ: Princeton University Press.

Jung, C.G., 1989. *Memories, Dreams, Reflections.* New York: Vintage Books.

Oliver, M., 1992. *New and Selected Poems.* Boston, MA: Beacon Press.

Progoff, I., 1973a. *Depth Psychology and Modern Man.* New York: McGraw-Hill Book Company.

Progoff, I., 1973b. *The Symbolic and the Real.* New York: McGraw-Hill Book Company.

Progoff, I., 1975. *At a Journal Workshop: The Basic Text and Guide for Using the Intensive Journal Process.* New York: Dialogue House Library.

Progoff, I., 1985. *The Dynamics of Hope: Perspectives of Process in Anxiety and Creativity, Imagery and Dreams.* New York: Dialogue House Library.

Progoff, I., 1992. *At a Journal Workshop: Writing to Access the Power of the Unconscious and Evoke Creative Ability.* Los Angeles, CA: Jeremy P. Tarcher, Inc.

Progoff, I., 2010. "Creativity and Spirit in History and Today" [audio CD of recorded lecture]. Brentwood, OH: Dialogue House Associates.

von Franz, M.-L., 1993. *The Feminine in Fairy Tales* (Revised Edition). Boston, MA: Shambhala Publications.

CHAPTER SEVEN

THE FAMILY WITHIN
An IFS Journey
Susan McConnell

There are many remarkable stories of how the Internal Family Systems (IFS) Model has changed the course of people's lives. I have heard numerous dramatic stories from students in IFS training all over the United States and Europe. The students tell of having come across a few sentences in their graduate school family therapy textbook about the IFS model. At that, they closed their books and went online in search of IFS training.

Rather than sweeping me away in an instantaneous conversion, the model has quietly reverberated in my inner life, my relationships, and my work. Over time, I would experience this safe and effective entry into the rich complexity of the inner system. I would come to understand that my relationships, personal and professional, could become a vehicle for my own psychological and spiritual growth. I would feel the joy that there was room for me to shape the emergence of the model, as well as be shaped by it.

I first learned of IFS from a colleague. I was intrigued to learn that the founder of this innovative model lived just outside of my home city of Chicago. Although I did not feel an overpowering urge to add this particular model, one thing did grab my attention.

I heard that the founder, Richard Schwartz, had developed his model from listening to his clients. When the strategic and structural family therapy approaches he was trained in didn't always lead to the promised results with his bulimic clients, Dick set his training aside. Instead of imposing his methods on his clients, he listened to them describe their inner and outer worlds. Many of them referred to their inner experiences in terms of parts. Synthesizing many clients' experiences within his framework, he developed a powerful new model (Schwartz 1997, 2008; McConnell 2013). I am drawn to pioneers, heretics, and collaborators. I admire risk takers. I imagined the courage it took for Dick to risk his status in the field of marriage and family therapy. I wanted to meet this man willing to have his clients be his teachers. I wanted to know more about his model whose source is a deep, respectful listening to clients' inner experience, and that honors the clients inherent wisdom.

I jumped at the opportunity to join a consultation group he was leading. The group offered consultation for our clinical cases as well as an introduction to IFS. On entering this ongoing group, I felt safe with the members and with Dick as the facilitator. I trusted his unassuming, understated persona and his accepting, compassionate nature. I was inspired by his patience and passion in teaching us his emergent model. I had hopes this would be a supportive place for my more challenging cases.

In preparation, I read one of Dick's books, *Internal Family Systems Therapy* (Schwartz 1997). The model made intuitive and intellectual sense to me. By following the fascinating journeys into the inner worlds of his traumatized clients, the deceptively simple process was revealed. It included accessing the sub-personalities engaged in extreme roles, compassionately witnessing their stories, helping them release their outmoded emotions, behaviors and beliefs, and finally restoring them to their preferred healthy roles. The steps of this process resulted in increased balance and harmony in the system.

This non-pathologizing, empowering approach struck a chord. I appreciated the assumptions that even the most extreme parts had positive intentions, and that each of us has a core self, which, however buried, is the source of our wisdom, creativity, and healing. I was not, however, convinced that I had a bunch of little people inside me, wringing their hands in despair or vying for control.

With 20 years of sitting on my meditation cushion, and almost as long in the client's chair in therapy, I was on familiar and mostly friendly terms with my inner voices, emotions, and beliefs. But I hadn't conceived of my inner experiences as discrete sub-personalities that I could see, hear, dialogue with, and have a relationship with. I was quite familiar with my inner struggles and conflicts, but I hadn't thought of them as parts warring with each other and engaged in relationships as complex and intriguing as any family's.

I was willing to suspend my skepticism (or, in IFS language, I asked my skeptical part to step back). As I focused on a feeling, a thought or physical sensation, images and memories eventually rounded out my inner experience to reveal what could be called a part. I spent some time with this part. I discovered that it had a history, a set of behaviors and beliefs, and its own way of organizing itself in my inner world, as well as in relation to the outer world. I eventually got acquainted with other parts, each with their own individual personalities, needs, and ways of relating.

As we brought our cases to the group, Dick worked with our own parts that were being triggered by our clients. One day, I presented a case of a woman that was particularly challenging for me. I described her re-enactments of destructive behaviors that persisted despite my many various therapeutic interventions. I hoped the group or Dick would give me some new ideas. One of the group members labeled my client, with a particular tone of voice, as borderline, as if that meant I couldn't expect her to get better.

Dick firmly directed my attention to my inner experience. As I listened inside, I felt a compulsion to continue to recount her exasperating behavior to these empathic listeners. Reluctantly shifting the focus back to myself, I had to admit I was judging her. Dick coached me to ask my part: "What are you afraid would happen if you were not convincing us of how difficult this client is?" I went inside, focused on the muscular holding in my body, felt the hard, defensive energy, and asked the part what it was afraid of. I was surprised to hear the part answer: it feared I would be revealed as an inadequate therapist. My part judged my client so I would not be judged. My part didn't want me to feel ever again that awful feeling of not being good enough.

As I continued to dialogue with the judging part, it told me that it had been trying to help me for quite some time. Dick guided me to appreciate it for its intention. The part liked that. It had expected to be criticized by me, by Dick, or by the group for being judgmental. The part felt it was finally getting the acknowledgment it deserved. I felt more spaciousness in my body and my mind.

Dick then suggested I invite the part that held the belief of not being good enough. I felt that one near my heart—a sensation of tightness and pulling inward. I stayed with the sensation and the feeling of "not good enough." An image arose of myself at the age of six being coached by my father to say my Ss. The six-year old tried and tried and never seemed to say them the way he wanted to hear them. She eventually ran to her bedroom and sobbed secretly into her pillow. She had carried that shame for decades. Tears ran down my face. Dick asked me how I felt toward that six-year old.

At first, the question surprised me. I learned later that this question, in addition to "What is the part afraid would happen if…", are central to the process, and both questions may be asked many times in a session.

How do I feel toward her? In that moment, I felt I was she. The question helped me to differentiate just enough to recognize that I was indeed not six years old. How do I feel toward her? Not what do I think about her. The question evoked the possibility of a relationship between this little girl and me. No one had been there for her then, understanding her pain. But I knew what she needed. I felt a warm, open sensation in my heart that flowed toward this little one trying to get it right. The little girl felt my compassion and came to my arms. I held her and let her know I liked the way she talked. I told her she didn't need to keep trying. I had a sense that she left behind that scene and joined me in the present. When I brought my focus back to my relationship with my client, I considered I could stop trying to get her to change and see what could happen if I could simply open my heart more to her.

This experience opened up a new world for me in my therapy office. Dick had told us that if we were in Self,[1] we were doing IFS. The methods he was teaching us were the form of the work, but being in Self was the essence. Not fully understanding the form, I decided to focus on this state of being in Self, which I understood as the state when all our parts step back. I began to pay more attention to my inner state instead of focusing overly on my clients. When I wasn't enjoying my clients—when I felt tension, boredom, or frustration—I saw that it was my parts that were having these feelings. I became fascinated with getting to know my parts that emerged with various clients. Clients would evoke in me an "uggh" or an "ah, an easy one!" and both responses were trailheads that led me on a journey of discovery.

My clients have been my parts' greatest detectors, teachers, and healers. Some clients have had the courage to confront my parts directly, others have led me to my parts more indirectly. A "resistant" client sniffed out a part of me I didn't know that at first was a part. I so much wanted him to be free from his reportedly miserable life that I was subtly pushing him to change. Our work had come to a standstill. As long as my part was in the therapist chair, my client's part could not experience the unconditional acceptance that is a hallmark of this model. Instead of condemning, controlling, or suppressing my part who had the agenda, I appreciated it for its concern for my client and for me. I asked it to trust me in this relationship. In our next session, I appreciated the positive intention

---

1   Self is capitalized in IFS when referring to the true nature or core of a person that exhibits leadership qualities of compassion, curiosity, and acceptance.

of his part despite how much it constrained his life. His part softened, and our work could then flow.

I discovered even more parts clustering around the issue of competency. In addition to the one that fears I'm not good enough, another is defended against that idea. Another wants me to refer out, and yet another tries the self-improvement approach. I found helper/pleaser/fixer parts. I became familiar with parts that want to distance me from certain clients—parts that need to feel one-up. These parts fear I may tumble into the abyss of my clients' neediness, terror, despair, and grief. Although these parts were pulling me in all different directions, what they had in common was they were all trying to help me. They didn't want to interfere with or constrain me. They were trying to protect me, or protect other parts of me.

I learned that we call the protective parts either managers or firefighters, depending on their strategies. Managers are pre-emptive, trying to make sure bad things don't happen, while firefighters are reactive, showing up when the bad thing has happened. We all have these protectors, and their job is to try to control or change the situation so we don't keep suffering, or to help us out when we are hurting. They work very hard at an impossible job. They usually get criticized or vilified. No one wants to be described as critical, controlling, prickly, withdrawn, or aggressive. The protective parts want to be appreciated for their intent. They don't believe it possible to change their roles, as tired as they might be. Secretly they long for play or rest, but they can't see how that could be possible. They dutifully and diligently strive to protect the more vulnerable parts of the system that have been wounded. As long as they and the ones they protect carry burdens (beliefs, behaviors, sensations, and emotions) they are trapped in their self-defeating roles.

I appreciated the beautiful logic to the concepts. It was a while, though, before my own protectors were not reflexively triggered by other peoples' protective parts. Their controlling or demanding parts evoked my resistant parts. Their critical parts evoked my defensive parts; other parts tried to suppress these parts in a futile effort to protect my image. That takes a lot of energy, and it didn't fool my clients. I had to go to another group of parts, the vulnerable ones within me, whom the protectors were trying to protect.

The vulnerable parts that absorbed hurt and pain we call "exiles." They are called exiles since the system tries to keep them hidden—out of harm's way, and out of the way of causing any harm. They carry the wounds of trauma and faulty attachment in emotions, behaviors and beliefs—commonly feelings of shame, worthlessness, and loneliness. My six-year-old exile absorbed the message that she would never be good enough. My six-year-old protectors learned to hide that feeling, to hide that she had been hurt, and to keep trying in spite of it all.

Until the exiles' wounds can be healed, the protectors believe that they need to keep them locked away, but being locked away, the exiles can't get healed, and the protectors don't get a break. It's like there is a lonely, hungry baby inside the house guarded by a Doberman who believes that it is his job to make sure no one enters, who assumes everyone who comes toward the door is a dangerous intruder. It doesn't work to ignore the dog, or tie him up, or trick him. His trust must be won. The one to befriend the protector is the Self of the person.

This Self that is at the core of everyone, beneath or behind all the parts, is one of the most significant aspects of this model. Dick, having learned about parts from his clients, also learned about the Self from his own clients' experiences. He would typically ask clients to ask their parts to step aside to allow other parts to be heard from. At one point, when all the parts stepped aside, there was a presence, which his clients described as simply "me, or my self." He and his clients discovered that when this Self-energy was freed up, the inner system had an amazing resource that could witness the parts' stories, soothe their hurts and worries, and provide reassurance and leadership in the system. In that state they could heal their own parts. Self could help the vulnerable parts find creative and ingenious ways to let go of the burdens they had carried from traumatic or developmental wounds. Once the vulnerable, exiled parts were unburdened, the system of protectors—often working against each other—could also let go of their rigid roles. They were then free to move into a collaborative, harmonious relationship with Self and all the other parts.

IFS uses the term Self differently than what is normally thought of as self. The self described in much of current psychoanalytic thought is called parts in IFS, and can be synonymous with ego. Freud used the term "the I" (*das Ich* in German), translated into the Latin *ego*. Similarly, Eastern philosophies may use self and ego interchangeably to describe the personal self, which is regarded as illusory and the source of all suffering. The Buddhist notion of self, with its attachments, aversions, and deluded perceptions, IFS also calls parts. On the other hand, IFS uses the word, Self to refer to that presence that has awareness of the parts, but which is not defined by them. In other words, Self is that "you" who is aware of the parts which you are experiencing.

Since I had experienced what Dick called Self-energy, I easily understood how his clients intuitively knew this was their true nature. For me, this state is an embodied, grounded sense of feeling connected and unified with myself and all of life—feeling loved and loving. I had felt this in its strongest, purest form in Buddhist retreats. I was excited to learn that working with the parts that stood in the way of Self could access this state. Through a wholehearted acceptance of the most vilified and shameful aspects of myself, I could attain a state it would take me all weekend on a cushion to find.

As a Buddhist, I wondered about the difference between Self in IFS and what we Buddhists called no-self or emptiness. Self-energy is very much the same as the enlightened state of boundless awareness that can be experienced in sitting meditation. But our parts want more than for us to observe them like passing clouds in the sky. They want us to be able to pick them up, retrieve them from places where they are stuck in the past, hear their stories, and see their pictures. So I understood that Self, essentially empty, manifests as form when our parts need form.

I recognized it was my Self that had held the six-year old in that session with Dick in the consultation group. An important shift in my emotional life was to bring acceptance and compassion rather than suppression to my fear, anger, and other socially objectionable attitudes. What a relief to let go of trying to hide or correct my inadequacies! That question, "How are you feeling toward that...?", increasingly helped me to identify the lack of acceptance as parts of me. These parts could step back and trust me to help the fear or anger. Over time, many of my parts experienced having "me" there with them to hear their stories and provide comfort, reassurance and wisdom. I experienced more coherence, and, paradoxically, more integration as I came to know more of my parts.

The concept and experience of Self expands the model from a strictly psychotherapeutic one to include the spiritual realms. The assumption of IFS is that everyone has a Self. Yes, *everyone*. I was surprised by this assertion that the Self is there even in extremely traumatized people. Although it may be buried so deeply it may never be experienced in their lifetime, Self is there. There is always the potential for its release. Until the client's parts are healed enough to separate out, the therapist's Self acts as proxy for the client's. Self is present at birth, but doesn't have the physical and mental resources to help us out in the difficult times we all encounter in early life. So the attachment wounds are not only between parent and child but also between the Self of the client and the client's parts.

With more Self-energy in my system, I was ready to begin using IFS with my clients. Introducing the language and concepts of the model to my clients felt fairly seamless. Most of my clients didn't miss a beat when I used phrases like, "So a part of you is feeling afraid of what he will think of you, and another part doesn't care." The language and concepts of IFS made intuitive sense to them. They provided a more structured sense of their inner world. They were relieved to conceive of their thoughts and feelings as belonging to a part rather than to all of them.

I realized my job was to help my clients be good therapists to their own inner families. I knew that my clients' healing was not dependent on my pithy insights and interpretations, but rather on their ability to bring compassionate witnessing to their inner worlds. When my clients' parts were able to step back enough to let the light of their Self shine in their inner system, the part's positive intention underlying its destructive behavior was revealed. The wound it carried in the form of a belief, emotion, or behavior could be released. The part, now free of its burden, could be restored to its original or preferred function within its system. The parts that were organized in the system to protect the part or protect the system could also be transformed. This unburdening and restoration of the original qualities resulted in more Self-energy being freed up.

Clients who had been tortured by critical demeaning parts, by self-destructive parts that were causing them to cut or starve themselves, could see that these feelings and these behaviors belonged to a part of them that was desperate for their help. They learned that we didn't want to get rid of any parts, and that is not possible in any case. All parts are welcome when there is enough Self-energy to greet them with compassionate curiosity.

I found that holding this belief that everyone has a Self is, in itself, a therapeutic intervention. There can be a kind of emotional contagion in relationships whereby parts evoke parts in the other in an endless, vicious volley. Self-energy, too, is contagious. When parts experience the presence of Self-energy in the dyadic system, more Self-energy is released, and more parts step back.

By identifying my reactions to my clients as parts, and witnessing the parts in the consultation group, or promising to spend time with them later, my parts were increasingly willing to step back and let me be more present with my clients. I could then easily draw from my stores of experience, wisdom, compassion, intuition, and creativity. In other words, my parts got out of the therapist chair and I was left.

With me in the therapist's chair, I could guide my clients to free up their own Self-energy. With a Self-to-Self connection between therapist and client, compassion resonates and reverberates throughout both persons' systems. The empathic attunement is like a duet of Self-energy. Therapy becomes a delightful, agenda-free process that is transformative for both parties.

I felt more at ease with my clients. It was easier for me to be calm, to be curious about the parts' perspectives on the world, to wonder what the parts needed to be able to step back and allow the Self of the client to lead. My role shifted. I felt less responsibility to make the change happen, and more ability to respond to what was happening. When the client's Self emerged, the process of therapy felt like floating down a river on a summer's day.

Attempts to be in Self often result in being in a part that is trying to manifest the qualities of Self. We call these parts pseudo selves. Truly accessing the Self, however, can often be a major excavation project. Not a reconstruction project, but a process of respectfully and skillfully sifting through layers of interrelated parts to uncover the Self, and restore the rightful roles and harmonious relationships of the parts.

MY SESSION WITH ANDREA

My client, whom I will call Andrea, is a white woman committed to working against racism. She wanted to explore any potential obstacles to her effectiveness in her anti-racism work. She found some fear of black people stemming from her growing up white in Chicago during racially volatile times, and sensing the rage from the black people around her. She was experiencing some fear activation in her body as she talked about this. I asked her to find the part that holds this fear and to focus on it in her body.

A 17-year-old girl emerged as the one who holds this fear. She showed us a park near Lake Michigan where she was nearly raped by a young African American man wielding a knife. The night before she had told her boyfriend, whom she later married, that she loved him. Her heart was full and open. That summer's day she was on the swings in the park near her home when the man approached her.

In the session, Andrea at first alternated between several parts with little access to Self-energy. There was the adolescent girl who felt alone and terrified. Here comes the magic question—"Andrea, how are you feeling toward her?" She had difficulty answering the question directly. A persistent distracter part tried to change the subject. A disassociating part numbed her out. I also sensed a part of her that was trying to get me to take care of the girl. When she did eventually answer the question of how she felt toward the 17-year-old, she said she was angry about how self-reliant she has had to be. She also doubted that she could help the girl. There were a lot of parts, and, at this point, no access to Andrea's Self.

I spent quite some time with these parts, appreciating them, developing a relationship with them, and asking them to share their fears. To get at the parts' fears, I asked the other magic question— "What are you afraid would happen if you were to step back and let Andrea talk with the 17-year-old?" Eventually the parts were willing to separate out enough to see what Andrea would do. Andrea was by then feeling some compassion toward the girl. My intention at this point was to continue to develop a relationship between Andrea and the girl. I asked the girl how she felt toward Andrea. At first the girl appeared not to acknowledge Andrea. I coached Andrea to let the girl know she understood how alone and scared she feels. The girl demanded to know where Andrea was back then. Andrea apologized for not being there in the way she can be there today, with all her resources. Andrea felt a softening in her body.

Then I asked how spatially close the young girl was to Andrea. She said she was right next to her on the swing. I recalled Andrea had been swinging before this man approached her. I encouraged Andrea to feel the swinging in her body, to feel the pleasure of the sensations and to spend several minutes enjoying that.

I suggested that we ask the girl to show us just one little piece of the story at a time, so we can really hear her, so we can take it in and digest it. I knew that exiles often tend to overwhelm the system with their energy. I had learned that we can ask the exile in advance not to do this. Although at first I doubted this was possible, I found that most often they are able to modulate their arousal as they show or tell their stories. The 17-year-old girl showed us how scary it was for her to feel so small and powerless next to this large man with a knife. She shook and cried. Andrea let her know she understood. Then the girl fast-forwarded to when it was all over. The girl joined Andrea on the swing. Andrea let her know they had survived it, comforting her with the rhythm of the swing that synchronized with her breathing. We asked the girl if she wanted to leave the park and come into the present with Andrea. She was eager to do that. We invited her to leave her fear behind at the park. Andrea's body was relaxed and open at the end of the session.

In future sessions, Andrea heard more pieces of the girl's story. She identified beliefs she had absorbed from that instance of her powerlessness. She associated the opening of her heart and her opening to pleasure with the fear of being seriously hurt. We unburdened the 17-year-old's belief there was no one to help her. She felt she had worked through her fear of African American men and was able to continue her anti-racism work in her community.

Andrea's Self, like the Self in each of us, has all the resources needed for the resolution of the trauma. Her parts doubted it, but once they stepped aside it was obvious that Andrea knew exactly what the girl needed from her to heal her trauma. Andrea's protective parts emerged during the time of the trauma, when the young person's limited resources were overwhelmed by the event. These protective parts hold the intensity of the life-and-death nature of the event and are determined to do everything in their power not to let this young part get hurt again.

But these protectors, being essentially the same age as the wounded, traumatized part, are limited in what they can do. They can help the client dissociate, like they did at the time. They can try other ways to distract from the pain of the trauma held in the body, using substances and other behaviors to numb, suppress, and soothe. They can be hyper-vigilant, avoidant, and controlling of the environment. My aim was to help the protective parts trust Andrea to help the part that holds the trauma.

Until the Self is available for the client, the parts that hold the trauma in their bodies and in their emotions are exiled, isolated, and frozen in time by these same parts that are intending to help them. Yet these wounded exiles are desperate to have their stories told. Our life force moves inexorably toward healing, even when a whole army of parts holds it down. When the exiled emotions find a crack, they often burst forth from this pressurized environment, in turn triggering the protective parts to push the energies down again. This explains the biphasic nature of the trauma survivor in the concepts of IFS. This phenomenon of braking and accelerating, or braking while accelerating that is so disruptive to our client's lives, can be mediated by the Self of the client, along with the Self of the therapist.

Self-energy is an embodied experience. It is what is left when the parts feel safe enough to separate—both protector parts and the ones they protect. But it is more than an absence of parts. Self-energy is experienced in the body as a calm, centered, openhearted feeling. There is warmth, flow, connection, and confidence. As Andrea's therapist, I paid attention to my body, my breath, my grounding, and my center. Throughout the session I scanned not only my client's body but also my own for evidence of my own parts that might hinder the process. I noticed tension in my neck and diverted my breath to help it relax. I eased the knot in my stomach as I resonated with the fear from her encounter with the man with the knife.

Our clients, especially our trauma survivors, have parts with excellent radars for others' parts. Their hyper-vigilant parts are watching for any sign that they may be hurt in a close, interpersonal relationship like a therapeutic one. All of our parts, like crystal goblets, tend to vibrate to the frequency of other parts in close proximity. So when the therapist is radiating embodied Self-energy, the client's protector parts experience this energy somatically, and they move in the direction of more openness and relaxation.

MY SESSION WITH ERIC

Eric had a serious childhood disease that temporarily disfigured him and left him with many burdens. Now, a healthy 50-year-old pastor, he identified many of his protective parts and had a respectful, trusting relationship with them. They had names: couch potato, philosopher, booster, and savior were among them. His parts held beliefs that his body was bad. They carried feelings of humiliation and fear. They were working to keep the exile, "the Boy on the Couch," right where he was. They believed the boy needed to stay on the couch or he would get sick again and die. The parts feared that if the boy left the couch, his system would be flooded with emotion, and that he wouldn't be able to function.

The parts also feared they would lose their jobs, and wouldn't be seen as valuable.

After listening to the concerns of these parts, the protectors eventually let the boy leave the couch. With my guidance, Eric helped the boy unload the burdens of believing that his body was bad and the fears of dying. The boy pranced around the room and now wanted to be called Jason. Eric felt a surge of energy run through his body. As a result of this unburdening, the next week Eric became more active in his life in many ways, including writing and painting from and for his parts.

Although we had carefully received permission from his protectors to unburden Jason, Eric experienced backlash from his protectors. Couch potato kept him on the couch nearly all day. Apparently they had fears and concerns we hadn't adequately listened to. He wrote couch potato's lament and sent it to me:

> The couch is empty. The one I've worked so hard to protect isn't here. He's gotten up. He's taken off his sick clothes. He's gone outside into the world. Doesn't he know how dangerous the world is? I remember all those blows we took, people whispering about us behind our back, kids laughing at us and calling us names because we were disfigured. I worked so very hard to limit our participation in that cruel world, to keep us safe on the couch, safe from competing with other kids and losing, safe from the pity of adults. How could he even think about leaving? The couch was safe. The couch was familiar. The couch was comforting. I feel frantic. I can't protect him if he's not on the couch. I can't do my job. What will happen to him? What will happen to me?

Couch potato wasn't the only protector upset by the unburdening. Savior caused him to cut the skin of his arm. Savior said he thought things were going too slowly in therapy and the cutting brings immediate relief. Later, savior admitted that he is not in favor of what we did with the boy on the couch. He thinks what we are doing is dangerous. Eric offered his view that the therapy is radically transformative and is the most hopeful thing we've ever done.

Eric feels love and appreciation for savior. Philosopher and booster are judgmental of the cutting, but they agree to trust us to deal with savior. Savior tells Eric that he is aware of a deep hurt that he can't soothe, and so creates the kind of wound he can soothe. Once the deep hurt is uncovered, savior won't know how to take care of it.

We tell savior that Eric, with my support, can take care of the deep hurt. Savior will consider that. We thank him for being willing to talk with us and to consider trusting us with the deep hurt. Savior agreed to let us know when he feels the urge to cut or harm his body in any way.

We check in with other parts to see if they have any reactions to what we did today. Philosopher is pleased with what happened. He feels what we are doing in therapy is prayer. He says we are accepting and loving all that is as created in the image of God. He valued us bringing savior into the light so he can be claimed as part of God's creation and be dealt with redemptively. Booster is happy that Jason is off the couch so Eric can be more active, and is hopeful that savior will stop the self-harming.

Therapy as prayer! Clients frequently come to realize the spiritual nature of this model of psychotherapy. They experience our work together as transcending symptom-focused, results-oriented clinical techniques. The concept and experience of Self-energy is a quantum leap into a realm described by sages and seekers over the millennia. All the esoteric, religious, and spiritual traditions speak of the divine within us. What we in IFS call Self may be called Buddha nature or no-Self, Atman, the Beloved, Christ Consciousness, Higher Self, Inner Light, or the Tao.

IFS as a systems approach sees Self in every level; parts have a Self, as does each individual. Self-energy flows in any relationship that is a Self-to-Self relationship. A group of individuals can process through the various stages of its development and can attain a state of cohesion that can be described as allowing the Self of the group to emerge. A Self-led group can become a force for transformation and healing in the larger community. At the cosmic or universal level, Self is experienced as divine presence or oneness.

SELF FIELD

Over the years of exploring inner worlds—others' and mine, I have experienced a more nuanced and expanded sense of this state of Self-energy. I experience Self as not limited to within me or within another person. I can connect with it in the earth, and in the sky. I can breathe it in to parts that need it, and breathe it out. I can rest in it as it surrounds me in a Self field. Self-energy transcends the individual body, the individual personality. It is vast, limitless, and omnipresent.

In the thirteenth century, the poet Mevlana Jelaluddin Rumi described this relational field as a deeply spiritual place:

> Out beyond ideas of wrong-doing and right-doing
> there is a field; I'll meet you there.
> When the soul lies down in that grass,
> the world is too full to talk about.
> Ideas, language, even the phrase *each other*
> doesn't make any sense.
>
> *(Rumi 1995)*

People throughout the ages have longed to live in this place and have found many paths to it. My journey of expanding my awareness of the client's inner world to include my inner world, and finally the field between us, has been one such path. I have embraced my parts that need to know, to diagnose, and that need to feel I am not as disturbed as my clients. I have befriended my parts that need healing to happen, that need my clients to prove to me that I am a good therapist. They have trusted me to heal the ones they have protected.

My parts, feeling appreciated, valued and welcomed in the therapy room, trust me to be present. As my trying/helping/doing/pleasing parts relax, I experience more openness and receptivity. I am beyond "doing" IFS. I am being with rather than doing to. Beyond diagnosis or healing, beyond transference and counter-transference, beyond therapist and client, beyond time and space, Self and other, Self and parts, is the luminous field, this non-separate, relational field.

My involvement with IFS has gone far beyond the therapy office. After a year or two of involvement in the consultation group, Dick informed me that there was going to be an IFS training session starting in the fall and that I might consider applying. I was not consciously considering committing to another training program, but politely said I would think about it.

That night I had a dream. I was speaking with colleagues at one end of a table who were mostly not paying attention to me. I looked down toward the other end of the table and noticed Dick was sitting there alone. I decided to get up and ask him about the training. He told me there was one training session of 30 people and another made up of only four people. The session of four people was the one he wanted me to be in. The music started and I asked him to dance. I was leading. He smiled and said to me that he liked not having to lead all the time. I awoke and pondered the dream.

I finally got up the courage to share the dream with Dick, and he listened intently. He told me that the Chicago training group was full, but that he was looking for four assistants to help with the session. He seemed to be suggesting I could be one of the assistants. I could hardly take in what he was telling me. I finally had the presence of mind to ask him what the assistants' responsibilities were. He replied that they would lead small groups that might include demonstrating the model with a group member, adding an experiential component to illustrate the didactic pieces from the morning session, and answering questions from the group about the model as they were beginning to apply it clinically. That all seemed doable to me, and Dick told me to show up for the first day.

IFS TRAINER

As I recalled Dick saying in the dream, "I like not having to lead all the time," I realized that neither Dick nor I could teach in all the sessions that were burgeoning all over the United States and Europe. With laptop in hand, I followed Dick all over the country, recording talks and developing experiential exercises for these embryonic sessions. As the structure and tone of the sessions developed, I produced a training manual for the trainers. I mentored staff who assisted me, and led staff development retreats for the Center for Self-Leadership. We now have a staff of almost 50 lead and assistant trainers and a couple of hundred program assistants.

For over 17 years I have taught the IFS model to psychotherapists, health professionals, pastoral counselors, dance and art therapists, bodyworkers, and other professionals seeking personal and spiritual growth. In addition to the basic and advanced courses, I have developed and taught workshops and retreats that focus more fully on the somatic aspects of the IFS model, which is my particular life-long passion. I call this somatic IFS, and offer it as an adjunct for those who want to experience the depth and dimension the somatic aspect brings to the IFS model.

SOMATIC IFS

When I initially began to teach the IFS model with Dick in 1997 as a body-centered therapist, it was important to me to know I could fully include the body at every step of the process. Dick assured me he welcomed my contribution. With his encouragement I developed somatic IFS. Somatic IFS is a synthesis of 40 years of study, teaching, and clinical practice defined by attempts to integrate what Descartes and other philosophers tried to keep in separate realms.

In a typical IFS therapy session, the body is included. The client may hear or see the part, or experience the emotions of a part, and is asked where the part resides in the body. Also, during the unburdening process, the client is directed to find where the burden is held in or around the body. Somatic IFS includes the body more comprehensively, in every step of the process.

My experience is that transcending the dualism of mind and body with my IFS clients has enhanced and deepened the effectiveness of this model. Years of exploring IFS and the body with my clients and students have revealed the body to be an invaluable resource for grounding in Self-energy, for accessing and witnessing parts, and observing and anchoring numerous somatic shifts with each transformation. My shifting relationship with my own body, mining the wisdom in the depths of my tissues and cells, has been a vital ongoing part of the development of somatic IFS. My personal experience with healing my own mind/body splits, embodying my internal family, has shown me that a deep exploration of the relationship of mind and body leads us to the spiritual realms.

As my somatic IFS training has evolved over the years, it has grown beyond including the body in the steps of the process. Attending to the inherent intelligence of the body has a powerful affect, and the body has taught us a great deal about ourselves, others, our relationships to each other and to the whole that informs the process of psychotherapy. It is clear that when engaging in the process of psychotherapy, we are delving into a somatic state of relatedness as physiological as breathing, birthing, and dying. A psychotherapy that doesn't fully include the somatic aspects of the person limits the fullest potential for transformation.

GIFTS OF BEING AN IFS TRAINER

These training sessions have taken me all over the United States, Costa Rica, and also to Great Britain, France and Germany. One of the greatest joys of my life has been to witness the transformations of the students as they experience the sessions. They sign up to learn a model, and a year or two later, their entire lives have changed. They find a more sustainable, energizing way of being therapists. Their personal relationships and spiritual lives deepen. They become part of a Self-led community. They experience the Self of the group, as it emerges over the course of the sessions through the stages of forming, norming, storming, performing, to transforming.

Another gift of being a trainer has been to have one of these trainers as my life partner. We have a common language to process our differences and more quickly return to a Self-to-Self connection. Could we take what we have learned about a Self-led therapeutic relationship outside of our therapy offices and into the bedroom, the kitchen, and even into the streets? Could we sustain Self-energy for longer than a 55-minute session?

When our parts take over, as they have been known to do over the course of a 30-year relationship, we feel the strong urge to control, criticize, withdraw, to accuse. We are familiar with the escalation of anger, fear, and distance. We know where it all leads, to fantasies of changing the locks and dividing the furniture. The IFS model is a resource in these times. Just to remember that these are parts, not our true Selves, is a start. Even so, our parts don't want to stop doing what they do. But we do stop. We look inside. Or at least one of us does. That is all it takes.

The narrative details of the latest conflict are irrelevant. It could be any misunderstanding, miscommunication, or lack of attunement between us. This time, I take a breath, and turn my attention to my inner experience. My parts are on a roll. I ask them to step back, reminding them of the inevitable outcome. They aren't listening to me. They don't care about effectiveness or even hurting my partner. I notice the tension in my body, the shallowness of my breath. I take several moments to find calm, and wait for my breath to slow and deepen. I feel a thread of appreciation toward my part for its diligence and persistence. I recognize it wants the best for me. Inwardly, my experience is like an appreciative smile toward the part. I ask it to trust me to be there to take care of me too. I try to remember my partner has also been taken over by a burdened part. I attempt to recall a loving, or at least a less contentious moment between us in the past. I feel a bit more spaciousness in my heart.

Sometimes I can accomplish all this in a minute and a half. Other times it might take me several hours or even days. The next step is to make an effort to speak for my part rather than from it. I say, "A part of me has been trying to make you wrong. It doesn't want me to be wrong. It fears if you are right, you will get to do what you want to do, and I won't get to do what I want to do. I guess underneath that is a part that must be feeling pretty afraid and powerless."

When one person is going inside with sincerity, it tends to disable the energy of the argument. To separate from a protector part and speak from Self for the part is a good start. We then have a chance to identify the vulnerable exile. We all find it much easier to have compassion for the softer, more vulnerable parts of each other. It is much more effective to ask our protector parts to step back and let us speak for the feelings and needs of the vulnerable ones.

There is more space to hear different needs and different points of view. There is more creativity to discover collaboratively solutions to what had felt like an impassable barrier.

In the heat of a conflict when parts have nearly taken over our bodies, our voices, and our thoughts, it is helpful to remember that these are parts. They are not our whole selves. Their perspectives are skewed. They are always well-intentioned, but often bring on what they were trying to avoid.

Our parts' natural tendency is to focus outside. Parts with burdens don't automatically look to the Self for what they need. They look to other people for redemption. They look to people they perceive as powerful enough to give them what they desperately need. They appoint people to make them feel worthy, beautiful, or smart. They appoint others to be nurturing or protective. The parts need the person to guarantee that they won't feel again what they felt so long ago when the hurt was so crushing. When the other person inevitably disappoints, the parts that appointed them are... dis-appointed. They react in outrage. They may try desperately to get the other person to change. The unsuspecting other will feel judged, unaccepted, insufficient, and tired of trying to please. Their parts may cause them to attack back or to withdraw. These parts further wound and disappoint the other.

Over time, my parts have grown in their trust in me. The vulnerable ones trust me to care for them, and have let me help them come out of their isolation and unburden their hurt. Their protectors no longer have so much to fear about these vulnerable ones getting crushed by rewounding. The parts are more trusting of each other and more tolerant of their different needs and viewpoints. They trust me to listen to them all and to come up usually with an acceptable solution. Often, they know the better option is to have me give the part what it needs rather than trying to get it first from some other person. This means that my partner is less burdened to meet the needs of my parts.

Supported by a strong community, with common resources for the inevitable challenges, our relationship has experienced expanding currents of Self-energy. We value relationship as a vehicle for our own psychological growth and for our spiritual awakening.

The ripples of Self-energy widen. As all of us in the IFS community, along with the model have grown and matured, there have been many exciting developments. The model has garnered the enthusiastic recognition of therapists, social scientists, and educators as a robust and innovative method of healing. IFS is the primary treatment modality at some residential youth homes and eating-disorder treatment centers. Many members of the community have published articles and books including introductions to IFS, using the model with couples, with children, and IFS and spirituality. Some trainers have developed and expanded aspects of the model and incorporated their own experiences, such as a training session for working with couples and my somatic IFS training. Universities have underwritten research on IFS therapies' effects on veterans suffering from post-traumatic stress disorder and individuals with rheumatoid arthritis. Independent studies have expanded IFS to other fields such as the healing of survivors of civil wars and genocide. The model has been applied in international conflicts, and has been a valuable tool for the peace-building efforts of a non-profit Israeli organization. I have felt deep satisfaction as graduates of my training sessions, with the increased confidence and creativity of their Self-led systems, have brought their unique applications to so many corners of the world.

In spite of my slow start, IFS has truly rocked my world, and increasingly, our world. I still have parts with burdens, and still act from them rather than from the Self that could be in the lead. However, as I am more accepting and open-hearted toward what shows up in my inner world, I can extend that toward what shows up in my office and beyond. My parts have renewed hope from the widening ripples of Self-energy.

REFERENCES

McConnell, S.L., 2013. "Embodying the Internal Family." In M. Sweezy and E.L. Ziskind (eds) *Internal Family Systems: New Dimensions.* New York: Routledge.
Rumi, J., 1995. "Out beyond ideas of wrong-doing and right-doing." In C. Barks (trans.) *The Essential Rumi.* New York: HarperCollins.

CHAPTER EIGHT

IN MY FATHER'S GARDEN

J. Tamar Stone

This dance of the Selves is an amazing process,
and we see the dynamics of the world around us shift
as our internal world changes.

(Drs. Hal and Sidra Stone)

"You have rheumatoid arthritis and will be on drugs for the rest of your life." Dr. Green smiled, then launched into a monologue about what pills and injections I would need to function with minimal pain.

"No," I said under my breath: to the doctor, to the medical status quo, to the diagnosis. This one moment would catalyze not only a relentless exploration of my health and physical wellbeing, but a revolutionary leap in my consciousness—and ultimately the discovery of my lifework.

My father, Hal Stone, would become my most influential mentor and colleague. My mom, my brother, and I were his early research subjects as he developed a psychodynamic technique for giving voice to the sub-personalities living inside us—the dominant ones born to protect us in their particular way, by helping us fit in. Voice Dialogue was born from his eclectic background in traditional and

Jungian psychology, and the various holistic and transformational therapies that emerged during the human potential movement of the sixties and seventies. Over the next 30 years, in partnership with his second wife, Sidra Stone, he would evolve the Voice Dialogue Process, based on the Psychology of Selves and the Aware Ego Process, into a new paradigm of consciousness—one that's been easily integrated into other systems of thought by spiritual and business pioneers.

The living room of my childhood home was my dad's laboratory. He would direct me to move from chair to chair to sofa, and allow to arise, in each seat, one of my dominant sub-personalities: the Critic, the Thinker, the Pleaser, the Creative.

Conversing with each Self, he would elicit their feelings, thoughts, interests, and observations. This was much more fun than slumber parties with my girlfriends, this doorway into my father's world and my emerging inner world.

Evenings and weekends I'd accompany my father to his transpersonal psychology talks and conferences throughout California. I was a bona fide groupie. Even my teenage girlfriends thought it was cool and would sometimes join us. It was the seventies, and somehow we knew we were on the cutting edge of consciousness.

Despite my fascination with my father's work, I had a strong aversion to becoming yet another psychotherapist in my family (my mom and brother, too, were psychotherapists). Even as a child, I knew I was a non-conformist, born to do something that hadn't existed yet. Still, I loved the human condition, so I entered a four-year undergraduate program in psychology, and immediately felt at home, alive, in my interactions with professors and classmates. I was a natural in the roles of counselor with my classmates and mediator in the model United Nations club.

This informal and formal training served me well when Blue Cross of California, having hired me as a customer-service agent, quickly identified my facility with others' pain and anger, and redirected all the irate callers to me. Within a year, upon completing my master's degree in psychology, I was promoted to the position of corporate trainer, the first step in a promising career in training and development—or so I thought. Many months of acute muscle and joint pain, chronic fatigue, and an incremental weight loss—my body screaming the professional unhappiness I wasn't admitting—sent me to Dr. Green.

Receiving the diagnosis of rheumatoid arthritis was an existential moment: first, because I'd thought it was a condition suffered by people three times my age; second, because I could have bought into the predominant field of medical thought. True to the philosophy of the Psychology of Selves, I was wrestling with two distinct opposites: the Self vulnerable to the seduction of turning my authority over to the "expert," and the Self rebelling against a lifetime sentence of prescription drugs. Standing between these two polarities and not identifying with either, I began to work a "muscle" I didn't know I had: the Aware Ego.

The day I realized that my body had been trying to tell me something—that taking nine aspirin to get myself to an unfulfilling job was insane—was, as they say, the first day of the rest of my life. That same day, my father invited me to participate in the three-weekly Voice Dialogue groups he conducted in his garden.

In the garden, I woke up to how asleep I'd been; or, in the language of the Psychology of Selves, I realized how identified I'd been with the Selves that had no clue about the essential role of the human body.

In the garden, I met my Pusher first, the Self most instrumental in running my body down.

"How long is this gonna take?" my Pusher asked the person assigned to a practice dyad with me.

"What's your rush?" the facilitator inquired.

My Pusher insisted: "Judith has phone calls to make and errands to run."

"It sounds like you're her engine."

"Yes, I fuel her legs. Judith can count on me to get the job done. Thank God for coffee."

Fidgeting in my chair, I realized that my Pusher is the one who, sharp and strategic, bought stock in Starbucks. My Pusher is also the one who, for my daily exercise, ran up and down eight flights of stairs, in heels, to the Blue Cross cafeteria for lunch and breaks. My

Pusher adopted my father's gospel "to burn on all seven burners" for a successful life.

After a half hour of animated conversation, the facilitator asked my Pusher if it would be okay if I moved to another chair to allow the emergence of the opposite Self—the one I'd subconsciously disowned because my Pusher had become so dominant. In a chair six feet away, I immediately felt the crackling electricity of my Pusher dissipate, replaced by the sensory awareness of a Self so completely different energetically—my Being Self, who didn't speak or even move for several minutes.

"I don't feel compelled to *do* anything in this moment," my Being said with quiet authority. "I love the cool grass under my feet. I love the hum of the Cessna overhead."

"Were you present during Judith's childhood?" the facilitator asked.

"Yes, when watching the sun rise with her brother and playing with Robbie the black lab and Binky the cat."

"Do you have a sense or a memory of when you got elbowed out?"

My Being sadly replied, "When doing well on tests and report cards became more important than anything else."

"It sounds like the Pusher has been running the show for a long time," the facilitator observed. "What do you need so that Judith can restore balance in her health and wellbeing?"

"More unscheduled time. Time to not have to do anything. Time for spontaneity, inspiration, and creativity."

The facilitator instructed me to return to my original seat, between my Pusher and my Being, where I felt, for the first time, how my Pusher was separate from me. From this position of a more Aware Ego, I could appreciate its role in my life without being identified with it, and integrate my rediscovered Being Self, allowing me access to a fuller range of expression from which to make more authentic choices.

Blame my Libra moon and rising sign, but I love mathematics, its balance and symmetry. Among the features I relish about Voice Dialogue is the premise that, for every dominant, or primary Self, there's an equal and opposite Self that is repressed or disowned. The shadow holds as much value as the light; all Selves are created equal; there's no such thing as a good or bad Self. After two years of these sessions in my father's garden, I surrendered to my lineage: I came to see that I *was* a psychotherapist, that Voice Dialogue is an amazing language for navigating our unconscious via the Selves, and a universal language for relationships that enables us to be accountable for ourselves and to others.

In my father's garden, while meeting the Pusher, the Thinker, the Perfectionist, the Responsible, I found myself curious about their hijacking of my body, and which parts of my body were screaming the loudest for my attention.

"Will you humor me?" I asked my dyad partner one day. "I'd like you to treat my body as you would any Self, and be present to and curious about her, because she needs a voice."

My body chose to recline—on a chaise-longue with a blanket—as, I would later learn, most bodies in this culture want to do when given the choice. My body removed my earrings, watch, and shoes, and asked for a pillow to place under her knees.

"How are you?" the facilitator asked.

Tearing up, my body replied. "I'm really tired. She's so busy. She's constantly on-the-go, and doesn't give me a chance to catch up. She reads all these health books, but doesn't run the information through me."

"How is it to have a voice right now?"

"I have so much to say, but what's even more important is finally being recognized. Everything she does happens through me; every Self gets expressed through me, yet I feel the most ignored."

"Has this always been true?"

"Judith comes from a family of heads," my body asserted. "Big heads on little sticks. While other families camped, hiked, biked, and gardened, Judith's family read, processed their feelings, and analyzed their dreams. Can I tell you what *I* want?"

"Absolutely." The facilitator seemed relieved that my body intuitively knew how to engage in this dialogue.

"I want her to stop being a vegetarian. I need protein; I need her to put my wellbeing over her moral values. I want her to go to bed when I'm tired rather than avoid going to sleep because she dreads waking up to go to her job. I want her to do Pilates instead of yoga; it's the one exercise that doesn't cause me pain right now."

"What else?"

"I love Judith's high thread count sheets and cotton clothes. I love that she sleeps with the window open and takes hot baths with essential oils. I need more sun and less sugar." My body took a few deep breaths. "If there's enough time, my hands would love to speak."

The facilitator nodded her agreement. My hands moved the pillow from under my knees to my belly, and propped themselves on it like a king and queen on a throne.

"Mutiny!" they cried out, surprising both of us. "If she doesn't listen to us, we're going to give her more pain."

"What isn't she hearing?"

"Her boyfriend is oblivious to us. He doesn't deserve our sensual, healing touch. She spends way too much time shuffling paper and doesn't do enough to express us creatively. She doesn't appreciate that we scratch her itches, cook her meals, write in her journal every morning. We want more sun, too."

When I moved back to my original seat, I felt an energized, kinesthetic presence I'd never experienced before. I realized I'd stepped through a doorway into a new world. And that world was Body Dialogue.

Within a year, I incorporated the Body Dialogue Process into my Voice Dialogue practice and was teaching it at the annual Voice Dialogue summer camp. The bodies I dialogued with thrived not only on being recognized and honored, but on being befriended.

The body wants to be our partner, supporting us the way a best friend or significant other does. And like our best supporters, the body sometimes tells us things we won't face up to. Take my hands: they alerted me to my then boyfriend's insensitivity; and after I broke up with him, they experienced less aching and more mobility.

The body can and wants to be heard before it's hit with a condition as severe as rheumatoid arthritis. A cold whispers to me that I may have some unshed tears; my headaches typically begin in my back, behind my heart, alerting me to unacknowledged feelings of vulnerability. Body imbalances—ailments and illnesses—aren't punishments but cues to a life out of balance.

When our physical, mental, or emotional state feels out of whack, we can do an inventory of our family of Selves to determine who's running the show. Our sub-personalities express themselves not only in our daily life via our health, behaviors, routines, roles, and relationships, but also in our dreams. When I worked for Blue Cross, for example, I had a recurring dream that the brakes in my car wouldn't work; now I understand that my Pusher was out of control. The acronym HALT, taught in the 12-step model, helps me remember to take care of myself before the stress from being too hungry, angry, lonely, or tired sends me into the default mode of one of my primary Selves.

It's easier to recognize our dominant Selves than our disowned ones. We can be sure a repressed or disowned Self is operating in the background when we judge or overvalue another person. In fact, we actually attract into our world people who mirror our disowned Selves, so that we can accept those sub-personalities in ourselves, integrate them, and become whole. For example, my college roommate's sloppy habits used to drive me crazy: she'd let dirty dishes pile up in the sink and leave her cosmetics strewn on the bathroom counter. I know I've come closer to embracing my inner slob when I allow myself to spread out a project on the coffee table and leave it there overnight.

Throughout my career as a psychotherapist, consciousness teacher, and Voice Dialogue facilitator, I've wondered how anyone successfully navigates their relationships—with Self and with others—without this universal language. When we allow the conscious expression of all our Selves, we allow others' full range of expression, conscious or not, and accept responsibility for our part in the dance of relationship. When the language of the Selves is shared, the territory of the relationship becomes a no fault zone, in which people are accountable for themselves, to the other person, and for the third entity that is their relationship.

In my father's garden, I began to grow a conscious relationship with my Selves, my body, and my lifework. I continue to be awed and inspired by the profundity of Voice Dialogue—and, by extension, Body Dialogue—as a consciousness model that expands and integrates our inner and outer worlds.

CHAPTER NINE

HAKOMI IN MY LIFE

Donna Martin

OF BEING WOVEN

The way is full of genuine sacrifice.
The thickets blocking your path are anything
that keeps you from that, any fear that you
may be broken into bits like a glass bottle.

This road demands courage and stamina,
yet it's full of footprints!

Who are these companions?
They are rungs in your ladder. Use them!
With company you quicken your ascent.
You may be happy enough going along,
but with others you'll get farther, and faster.

Someone who goes cheerfully by himself to the customs
house to pay his traveler's tax will go even more
lightheartedly when friends are with him.

Every prophet sought out companions.
A wall standing alone is useless, but put three or
four walls together, and they'll support a roof
and keep grain dry and safe.

When ink joins with a pen, then the
blank paper can say something.
Rushes and reeds must be woven to be useful as a mat.
If they weren't interlaced; the wind would blow them away.

Like that, God paired up creatures,
and gave them friendship.

This is how the fowler and the bird were arguing
about hermitic living and Islam.

It's a prolonged debate.
Husam shorten their controversy.
Make the Mathnawi more nimble and less lumbering.
Agile sounds are more appealing to the heart's ear.

(Rumi 2004)

I've been teaching Hakomi since 1996. Recently, nearing the end
of the fifth and final day of one Hakomi training session, I faced an
unusual challenge. We were at the end of the penultimate session of
the whole training. It had been a gently powerful five days with this
group: people from many parts of the world who'd been coming
together in this way for almost three years. This last half hour was
usually a time for integration and completion, for the sharing of
experiences of the healing and learning that had been happening
in the small groups.

   As the participants were making their way back into the large
circle, I noticed that one of the women (I'll call her Beth) was
unable to contain and manage a flood of tears. She'd been pretty
emotional throughout the day, and one of our teachers had spent
time with her while most of the people in the group were engaged
in exercises. However, now here she was still flooded and miserable.

As I brought the group back together for completion and goodbyes, I acknowledged Beth and asked her: "Would it feel good to have someone's hand on you?" She immediately reached for and held onto the hand of the woman sitting beside her.

"Do you want to say something about what is happening?" I asked.

"I don't want to speak now because I only have negative things to say and everyone else will be sharing positive experiences," she replied.

"If we don't use words like negative and positive, how else can you describe what is happening to you?"

There was another flood of tears. "Disappointment!" she said. I waited for the wave of tears to subside a little, and when it did, she added, "Once again, apparently, I am never going to get my needs met."

I knew we were going to have only about 15 minutes at most, so I needed to proceed cautiously. I've learned from Hakomi that the details of our personal stories, especially the ones that are triggered over and over as emotional reactions, are less significant than the themes they carry and the beliefs they express. Here, I suspected, was an old theme emerging again, going back to childhood experiences and playing out unconsciously a model of reality.

Our Hakomi training sessions create a small safe community out of a group of people who come together as strangers but bond in such a way that they feel safe to explore issues of relationship and emotional intimacy. Often, what is called up for people are old themes that go back to their family of origin: themes of abandonment or exclusion or of not belonging, of feeling not good enough or frustrated or fearful. How we saw ourselves in relation to our parents and siblings has become a kind of template for what to expect from relationships in general, and from membership in a family-like community in particular.

I gently asked Beth if this was a familiar feeling, perhaps based on an old recurring theme. She admitted that it was, that ever since childhood, repeatedly, she had experienced the pain and disappointment of not feeling accepted for who she was.

At this point I was so glad I hadn't been tempted to ask anything about what had happened on this particular day or during this week—this would have gotten us both lost in details that were only triggers. And I was also glad I'd not tried to even suggest that we would try to help her not to feel disappointed. In fact, I realized that Beth's tears and the sharing of what she called her negative feelings needed to be acknowledged, accepted, and welcomed into the group. I told her this. I told her that it was really okay with me that she felt how she did and that she was bringing those feelings into the group. I was glad she hadn't left (another old pattern of coping) and that she'd had the courage to tell us exactly how she felt.

Tentatively she looked up at me, and then slowly around the group. I knew she was checking us out and that she could actually see now that the others were feeling only concern for her and were calm, present, and loving. A moment of breakthrough, what we call in Hakomi a missing experience: in this case, the experience of being totally accepted by a group of loved ones. No one was questioning her, judging her, or demanding she be different; nor was anyone trying to cheer her up, distract her, or even comfort her with anything other than loving presence.

This moment of interface between an old reality that has been triggered (with the accompanying emotional suffering) and a different experience that is actually being recognized in conscious awareness as something new and nourishing: this is the alchemical moment of healing and transformation that Hakomi makes possible. When someone realizes that something unexpected is happening that is not a repeat of old pain and suffering, in spite of some similar ingredients, the whole world opens up in a new way. Some new kind of nourishment becomes possible. The world is a different place.

Since our emotional suffering is usually a result of how we experienced ruptures in our relationships, healing is possible when new relationship experiences happen for us in conscious awareness. Neuroscience is learning that it is experience that changes the brain. Hakomi has developed a relational context-based method for use in group therapeutic and learning settings to promote this kind of emotional healing and repair.

We spent about 15 minutes attending to Beth in this way, and then the last 15 minutes with other participants sharing their own experiences of the training session, mostly expressions of gratitude to the other participants.

Before she left, Beth came over to me and gave me a big hug. "I never realized how painful it was for me in my family that I never felt accepted for who I was," she told me. "I needed to have these experiences this week to help me discover this old pain and how I have kept repeating that experience in my life. Usually I would just leave a situation like this—I'd run away—which of course would just reinforce my sense of isolation. I'm so glad I stayed. Thank you, thank you!" And she turned to hug others in the room, her face soft and radiant, new hope shining in her expression. It was another beautiful Hakomi moment.

MY PATH TO HAKOMI

My path to Hakomi goes back to 1991 while teaching yoga at Hollyhock, a Canadian retreat center. A few months before, I had been given a book by Ron Kurtz, the creator of Hakomi. It was called *Body-Centered Psychotherapy: The Hakomi Method*. I was so impressed that I decided to take a workshop with him at this retreat center where I was also teaching.

In one of the first exercises I was paired with another woman and was supporting her, as instructed, to tune into herself with mindful awareness. Ron Kurtz came along and, without saying anything, placed one of my palms gently against the side of her face. Instantly, she began to weep. She touched into something emotional and meaningful, and her process unfolded spontaneously from that point.

I thought Ron was being so intuitive to position my hand like that. It turned out to be the perfect gesture to assist her to deepen. Later I learned that Ron had seen what he called an indicator: her head was slightly tilted to one side, as if looking for support. Since she was in mindfulness, the touch of my hand registered as the support she was unconsciously seeking. Her response was to be deeply touched, feeling a mixture of sadness, longing, and relief.

By the end of that first day, I was hooked. I told close friends that I had found the name of what I do. This was presumptuous of course, as I was to discover in the years to come. I had so much to learn. But something about this approach resonated deeply enough with me that this meeting turned out to be one of the most significant crossroads in my life.

I remember passing Ron in the garden at Hollyhock one day during the retreat. He stopped me briefly, leaned conspiratorially toward me, and said, in hushed tones, "When two sages meet in the path, they wink like thieves!" It was the beginning of a 20-year partnership and friendship that certainly changed the direction of my life.

I have felt throughout most of my life a deep commitment to the path of yoga, both as a student and teacher. Years later, I discovered that yoga had been an important influence and inspiration for Ron in the development of his unique approach to psychotherapy, as was science, Taoism, Buddhism, and the Feldenkrais Method. These last two had especially informed my approach to yoga and to my other work in helping people to find creative ways of dealing with stress. Stress management, and what I called relaxation therapy or bodymind therapy, had been as close as I'd come to working as a psychotherapist.

About the same time as meeting Ron and discovering the Hakomi method, I had begun work on a master's degree in counseling psychology with the intention of focusing on the therapeutic benefits of yoga, especially for psychological stress and emotional issues. My thesis turned into an exploration of body-centered approaches to psychotherapy with a particular focus on yoga and the Hakomi method.

During the 1990s I was also working at the Phoenix Center for Alcohol and Drug Addiction in Kamloops, B.C. For several years I was a counselor and clinical supervisor of outpatient services. We were funded to provide counseling for persons whose lives had been affected by anyone's substance abuse, a large percentage of the local population, as I discovered.

The issues we dealt with at the Phoenix center included active substance abuse, recovery, codependency, post-traumatic stress disorder, family of origin issues, anger management, relationship issues, parenting issues, all kinds of emotional and physical stress, chronic pain and illness related to trauma, and every kind of psychological theme you could imagine. It was an amazing training ground for all of us who worked there. Hakomi came into my life at just the right time.

During that meeting at Hollyhock, Ron invited me to train with him in Oregon. I jumped at the chance. After two years of training, I was invited to assist him as a teacher in a three-year training program. We also soon began to co-lead workshops together. At the time, Ron was developing what he called the practice of loving presence.

The idea for loving presence came from an experience Ron had while teaching in Germany. In the midst of a demo session with a young man in Hakomi training, Ron became confused with the translation. He lost track of the content of what the man was saying, and his attention was completely drawn instead to the man himself, to his courage and beauty of spirit. Ron recognized that this shift of his attention—away from the person's story to simply being moved and inspired by the person—was somehow changing his way of being present; it was nourishing him in a deep way. Ron was sure that if the man were to look at him, this shift in his own state of mind and demeanor would be apparent to the man; so he asked the man to look at him. The man was so touched by seeing the look of love on Ron's face that his process moved quickly to a healing completion. Not because of what Ron was doing or saying, but simply because of how Ron was being—totally present in a kind and loving way.

The realization for Ron of the importance of loving presence was a turning point for him in the development of the Hakomi method. The idea of the therapist being nourished by the client, by the very act of being present with someone, seemed to be a radical idea. And yet, this state of mind in the therapist clearly had a dramatically healing effect on the client.

What if it is our very presence as one human to another that is the main healing ingredient? What if the best way to shift into this healing presence is to allow ourselves as therapists to be nourished, touched, and inspired by the inner beauty and humanity of the client? What if the research is right and the "personhood" of the therapist (Mahoney 1991, p.271) and the relationship between therapist and client (Hubble, Duncan, and Miller 1999) are significantly more important than any of the therapeutic techniques or methods used? What if, in fact, the essential ingredient in any therapeutic relationship is love? (Lewis, Amini, and Lennon 2001).

Working with the kinds of clients that I was seeing at the addiction center was proof enough for me of the power of presence as I found myself repeatedly in the face of life situations over which neither my client nor I had any control. And yet, simply spending time together week after week seemed to be healing for us both.

MORE ABOUT THE METHOD

Of course, there are techniques in Hakomi that are very effective. The method that we now call "assisted self-discovery" uses simple experiments performed in mindfulness to assist clients to become conscious of their implicit beliefs and habits that have been organizing their experience. Some of these cause unnecessary suffering and most of them limit life in some way, simply because they are outside of conscious awareness. In Hakomi we are interested in helping clients discover more sources of nourishing life experiences by exploring alternatives to their habitual behaviors, by changing their reactions to responses, and by helping them to become more creative and less automatic.

In one Hakomi training session, a participant I'll call Lee came back to the circle after a small group exercise of listening in mindfulness to nourishing statements offered by others in the group. In the debriefing she complained that she never believed anyone when they told her something positive. She said she mistrusted everyone and felt suspicious of their motives, so was never able to take in the nourishment of a compliment. I had noticed a certain non-verbal indicator as she was speaking (she held her head a little turned to one side) so I invited her to try a little experiment in the large group. She was willing.

I asked her, "Is there anyone in the group who you believe could say something positive to you and be sincere?"

"My best friend is here," she replied. "I know she means it when she says she's glad I'm her friend."

"Great!" I replied. "Let's have her tell you that while you listen in mindfulness and just tune in to whatever happens inside you."

Lee's friend waited until Lee was ready and then told her, "I'm glad you're my friend."

Lee frowned and said: "I even feel myself mistrusting her. I can't even take that in and feel good."

"There's a second part to this experiment," I told Lee. "Do you notice that you hold your head turned a little to one side as you listen to her? This seems characteristic of you. Let's have your friend say the same statement, but first, just as an experiment, turn to face her directly and let's see what happens this time."

Lee faced her friend mindfully and said she was ready.

Her friend repeated her affirmation of friendship. This time, tears immediately welled up in Lee's eyes, and her features softened as she looked at her friend. Then she stood up, walked over to her friend, and hugged her. "Wow!" she said afterward, "it can't be that simple!"

Sometimes it is that simple. We carry our virtual reality, with our implicit beliefs and pre-organized perceptions and reactions, in our body, our posture, and our tension patterns. Unless these unconscious habits can come into awareness and can change, we stay in the same old virtual reality. Nothing new is possible.

One of my favorite *Peanuts* cartoons has Charlie Brown standing slumped over. "When you're depressed," he says, "it's important to stand like this. The worst thing you can do when you're depressed is stand tall. If you're going to get any joy out of being depressed, you have to stand like this!"

Learning, as Fritz Perls used to say, is the discovery of the possible. Hakomi is an approach to therapy as a learning process. We help clients learn about themselves and others and about what's possible, and this learning becomes transformative and healing.

MINDFULNESS AND HAKOMI

The very use of mindfulness is, in and of itself, potentially life-changing. When someone goes from ordinary states of mind to mindful awareness, life is seen anew. The present moment, just as it is, becomes apparent, teased apart from all the similar but different past life experiences that tend to shape our perceptions and feelings and reactions. Daniel Siegel (2007) talks about the way our past experiences tend to flood the brain and suffocate the new experiences that might otherwise be possible in any moment.

Mindful awareness can interrupt this "top down" (Siegel 2007, p.144) flooding and open us up to present moment experience just as it is. As Moshe Feldenkrais (1981) used to say, we cannot do what we want until we know what we are already doing.

Stu came to see me in my office to deal with grief after the death of his father. Sometimes psychotherapy helps someone with unnecessary suffering caused by implicit beliefs and unconscious habits. Sometimes the pain is a natural response to life, and all that is needed is a kind of unburdening, a sharing of the feelings. This is true of grief, and with Stu we spent most of the session in this way. When he felt complete, we still had a little time left. Stu told me that he had chronic lower back pain and since he knew I was a yoga teacher, he wondered if I could suggest an exercise that would help. I invited Stu to stand up. In his standing posture I had already noticed a certain indicator, which was a way he had of lifting his sternum and inflating his chest.

I placed my index finger on his sternum and asked him to tune in to his lower back mindfully. "Let's do a little experiment," I said. "Very slowly and mindfully, lower this point [sternum] just slightly and notice what, if anything, happens in your lower back." He did so, and exclaimed, "The pain stops! Wow! Thank you!" He was about to leave, but I stopped him and said, "Wait just a minute. Let's do another small experiment."

Stu was curious and willing. I asked him to close his eyes, and to move mindfully a few times between his old and new posture, lifting and lowering his sternum just slightly. Then, while in his new posture, I asked him to imagine standing face to face with someone. "Is there any situation," I asked him, "where this would not feel okay?" "Wow," he replied. "I wouldn't feel safe standing this way with anyone! I feel really vulnerable."

"Okay," I said, "one more little experiment. From this new posture, very, very slowly and mindfully move back into your old posture, lifting your chest. Notice anything that happens when you do that. What pops into your mind—a memory perhaps? Image? Thoughts? Let's just see what associations there are with this movement."

As Stu made that small change slowly, he said, "I feel like I'm 12 years old! I'm being bullied and doing this movement to try to look bigger and tougher. Wow, this is sure an old strategy that I don't need any more!"

Several more insights came to mind as Stu played with that pattern for a minute or so. He completed by saying that he now realized that his lower back pain was trying to help him pay attention to something he was doing unnecessarily. How he was standing in relation to the world was a continuation of his old reality. As he opened his eyes and looked at me, he concluded, "I might just have to experiment with feeling vulnerable for a while. But it will be worth it!"

HAKOMI IN MY PERSONAL LIFE

From time to time something happens in my life, usually in a relationship, that triggers a reaction I know to be connected with something old. I know it because the emotions seem out of proportion to what is actually happening. My rational mind can look clearly at the current situation and make sense of it, but somehow my emotional brain is having a whole different experience.

With Hakomi I've learned to respond differently to times like this, to those emotional reactions triggered by something present but informed by something old, usually something outside of consciousness. So when I can feel this kind of emotional reaction, and hear how my thoughts are turning this into a story, I use a Hakomi approach to interrupt myself. The witnessing part of my mind which has developed from mindfulness practice remains a little outside the reaction. It's the part of my mind that can say, wow, look at the story you're telling yourself, look at how painful it feels when you think those thoughts, look at the experience of suffering you're creating.

This awareness is the beginning of a significant shift. The next step is a real key to Hakomi. I don't try to change what's happening. I don't try to make myself feel better by distracting myself or by telling myself an opposite story—not just yet. What I do now is turn this witnessing attention to what I'm thinking, to listen to my thoughts and how they are connected with my emotions. And then I turn my attention in the same way, with as much kindness and curiosity as possible, to my bodily experience without trying to change this either. I want to be with it to fully experience it with mindful awareness. This is a skill that develops from the practice of Hakomi and what I now call applied mindfulness: the Hakomi Way. It is what Pema Chodron (2009) describes as the Buddhist practice in the face of neurosis or *shenpa*—that is, to notice what's happening, to interrupt it, to turn attention to one's own present-moment bodily experience, and finally, to do something different.

So I might notice, as I did recently, a feeling that at first seemed connected with betrayal, triggered by a seemingly minor situation that my rational mind understood. But the crushing pain in my chest and sense of despair were far beyond what seemed appropriate for the current events happening in my life. This caught me off guard.

From Hakomi, along with my background in yoga and meditation, I'd developed enough of a witness to be able to notice how much these intense feelings seemed out of proportion to the real-life situation. So I became very curious. I gave myself time to just be with what I was thinking so that I could see the beliefs and generalizations I was making.

I could hear the voices in my head having an irrational conversation, and having a melodramatic monologue that was generating tightness in my chest.

I then turned my attention to this tightness and saw how it was connected with a whole bodily pattern of tension. I knew that if I kept my attention on this tension, congruent ideas and memories, or perhaps old beliefs would probably surface. Associations from the past could arise just by staying with this tension and pain.

Of course, my mind kept returning to my unreasonable thoughts and storyline. These are the basis of the trance that pulls us into a whole cycle of unnecessary suffering. But trying to stop them and change how I'm feeling in the midst of it is impossible. What Hakomi has shown me is how to stay with the experience, to study it, to engage with it, and participate in it with curiosity and friendliness toward myself. To keep an experimental attitude toward it. I've learned that by staying with it and by not fighting what's happening, not only does the change happen more easily and spontaneously, but there also is the possibility of having an important insight about myself and a healing of some old wound.

So what I uncovered by simply paying attention to the tension, especially the pain around my heart, was a kind of grief around a very painful past relationship. I connected with the disappointment I'd felt then, and the loss, which was natural, but along with the grief went a feeling of shame and humiliation about being too trusting. This was the feeling that was causing me unnecessary suffering. The loss of confidence and trust in myself was making the loss of relationship almost unbearable.

Our brains are designed to remember, implicitly, the most painful lessons we've learned from life and to be on the lookout for any signs that they might be happening again. It's an important survival strategy. Unfortunately it means that we sometimes (often) overreact to anything that looks similar or even hints at the possibility of a recurrence. Then we go into a reaction as if the old experience is happening all over again. As long as we keep focusing on the current situation, rather than staying with the feelings, we miss the opportunity to let go of the old ideas and beliefs that are either outdated or just wrong, and that are causing us most of the pain. In my case, it was an idea about being "an idiot" to let myself be so deceived and dishonored, a voice telling me I should have seen it coming, I should have known better, and there was a fear about not being able to trust my sense of reality. No wonder the pain was so intense.

This Hakomi practice doesn't stop the experience or make the pain go away. But it shifts it considerably. It leads more quickly to the discovery of why I'm really hurting, so I don't continue to blame it on someone or something outside me without checking out if that is real. And it leads more directly to the discovery of what I need. This often includes sharing with someone else who can simply be a compassionate companion to my process and who can offer a safe, reassuring, comforting presence while I move through the painful feelings and tease out the past from the present, the imagined from the real, the child from the adult, and the chaff from the grain.

Inevitably, I've found, this Hakomi way of studying my emotional reactions brings me to a new awareness of myself, and a new perception of reality. When I stay with my embodied experience, I've found that it changes and transforms almost magically in a positive way.

YOGA

Early in my personal path I had found the value of mindful awareness with yoga and meditation practices. I had seen how habitual we are in our bodies, and that how we do things is how we do things. This is what I used to tell my yoga students. Someone who was a workaholic usually came to yoga classes driven to accomplish. Someone distracted and insecure approached yoga practice in that same way: worrying and self-conscious.

Tension patterns—in the shoulders, for example—show up in the way a person tends to move into and hold the postures, and not just in the standing posture. We might do different activities but we organize them with the same habits and attitudes that organize most of our life experiences. And this tends to happen, for the most part, outside of conscious awareness. By doing new things the same old way, we are simply reinforcing the old patterns and nothing significant really changes.

I had also learned as a yoga practitioner and teacher that we might resist change for reasons beyond the force of habit alone. Even when our habitual patterns come into consciousness, they can persist. Even when more effective alternatives to how we use our bodies are offered and explored, people often leave yoga classes while quickly reorganizing their bodies back into their familiar postures with all their old tension patterns. I have seen people who go to yoga classes for years but still hang on to some of their most characteristic postural distortions such as tight shoulders, locked knees, the head jutted forward, or the chest pulled in. Why?

Teaching and practicing Hakomi has helped me understand that the postural habits and body tension patterns that are most resistant to change are usually the ones with implicit beliefs and unconscious meanings attached. When we explore in mindful awareness a pattern of tension that holds our posture in a certain way, perhaps one that expresses our idea of who we are, or who we need to be to be safe in the world, simply bringing this pattern into consciousness may not lead directly to a change in the direction of relaxation. But it is usually the first step.

The next step in using Hakomi with this kind of pattern may involve studying the connection between the body pattern and the memories associated with it that reveal the pattern to be an adaptation to past events or a historical situation. This was the case with Stu.

In Hakomi, we are not interested in memories as a record of what actually happened, but rather as information about how we experienced what happened, what we thought it meant, or what we learned to expect from others or from life. We know enough about the mind now, and about memory, to give up any delusion about the accuracy of our memories. Our way of remembering our past, however, holds important clues about how we organize present experience, about implicit beliefs, about how we make meaning of things, and about how we have learned to cope in order to survive.

THE HAKOMI PROCESS

Once we have helped someone to investigate thoroughly and study a pattern we have discovered (physical or emotional), the next step in Hakomi might be to experiment with alternatives. We might, for example, assist the person to observe what happens when someone "takes over" the pattern, which might be bodily tension, a gesture, or a habit of posture.

In Hakomi we often work with assistants who are available for these kinds of experiments. In fact the method is a powerful way of working in a group and, although it can be adapted for one-to-one therapy situations, it works even more effectively as an approach to group therapy. Because the style of this approach is collaborative, the spirit of it is best experienced with peers assisting on the journey of self-discovery. One person's discoveries and healing experiences are shared with others.

In Hakomi we might help someone to study the way her mind creates internal conflict or stress with something like an internal voice. We can have another person "take over" that voice and allow the person to listen to it outside of her own mind for a change. This invites a shift in her relationship to this mental activity, creating some distance between her witnessing mind and the voice or part that is causing the stress or suffering. We might do this, for example, when we hear the person say something like "I can't trust anyone."

We could have someone (usually assistants, but the therapist in a one-to-one setting could also do it) take over the voice and say to the person, "Don't trust anyone." When this is used as an experiment in mindfulness, this taking over might create enough space to allow the person to retrieve an image or memory that helps her to make sense of this voice as an adaptation to past circumstances or as a kind of protection. We could also offer to take over a bodily reaction as a voice, as in the case of a person saying "I don't feel anything" where we could have someone else say: "Don't feel anything."

The key to this kind of taking over is that the person must understand that this is an experiment in mindfulness, that someone is taking over something the person has been doing unconsciously to themselves, and that by having someone else take it over, they might make an important discovery about how this seemingly negative pattern or voice is attempting to serve in some way. They may simply discover that this pattern was an adaptation to a situation from the past, which is no longer relevant in the present.

My addicted clients in recovery used to quote something from their 12-step groups: if we always do what we've always done, we'll always get what we've always got. By continuing to organize our lives in an "as if" reality, we perpetuate the reality we are still coping with it as if it is still happening. If I'm organized around the idea that I can't trust anyone, I won't trust anyone even when there are trustworthy people around me. This is how we carry our past into our present and perpetuate unnecessary suffering. The missing experience is not unavailable. It's missing because of our own beliefs, habits, adaptations, and perceptions that keep us from experiencing something nourishing even when such an experience would be possible. We live in a virtual reality that is not a true experience of the present moment as it is.

This part of the Hakomi method that involves taking over is a powerful way of doing several things. First, it helps the person shift more and more into their witness, their ability to use mindful awareness for self-study. This is fundamental to Hakomi and can be life-changing. Second, it allows for a space around a previously unconscious and habitual way in which the person organizes experience. In this space, what usually shows up is one or more associations that help to make sense of it.

Once the person sees what their mind is up to, in terms of interpreting and reacting to life, and connects this with associations such as memories, assumptions, expectations, emotions, pre-conceptions, or implicit beliefs, it gradually becomes clear that there is more than one possible way to respond to a given situation. On automatic, there's no choice. Consciousness, we like to point out, brings choice; choice brings freedom.

This possibility of freedom has become, for me, one of the most important by-products of practicing Hakomi.

As a yoga practitioner, my teachers kept pointing out that the practice was a path to liberation: liberation from what has been called the "unbearable automaticity of being" (Bargh and Chartrand 1999, p.462). I began to realize that, just as bodily tension patterns and postural distortions imprisoned people in chronic discomfort or pain, so too do our psychological and emotional beliefs and habits imprison us in repeated experiences of what Buddhists call unnecessary suffering.

Years ago, a teacher at Naropa University watching Ron told him that Hakomi looked like applied Buddhism. When Buddhists encounter Hakomi, they notice similarities. Both are concerned with unnecessary suffering. Both recognize the value of practicing mindfulness. Both address the way we suffer because of how we see and react to life. Both are concerned with cultivating wisdom (as opposed to ignorance and delusion) and compassion (as an alternative to selfishness and insensitivity to others).

Yoga, Buddhism, and meditation have become, along with Hakomi, a way for me to live my life. The way they complement each other has helped me to integrate them into my personal life and relationships, as well as into how I teach and practice therapy.

Through my yoga, meditation practice, and Hakomi, I began to realize that both wisdom and compassion rely on a new view of reality, a view which took me back to the original teachings of yoga: the truth of intrinsic oneness, or wholeness, that everything is connected, that we are part of a greater whole and that nothing is separate. This is implied in the Sanskrit word *yoga* which is often translated as meaning unity, unity of body, mind and spirit. It could just as easily be translated as oneness.

Science is beginning to confirm what the yogis have taught for hundreds of years: that there is one energy field, and everyone and everything is part of it (Laszlo 2007). In *Social Intelligence*, Daniel Goleman (2006) points out that the source of conflict is always "us and them" thinking. And this is also the greatest obstacle to the natural compassion that can arise spontaneously when we attune to another. When one person suffers, we all suffer. The Buddhist path of the bodhisattva has become a way I define my own path, and what, as a Hakomi teacher, I invite others to explore. This rests on the belief that since we are all connected and interdependent, we cannot limit our search for happiness, and for an end to unnecessary suffering, to ourselves; we must reach out to others, or at least respond wholeheartedly when called.

PEACEMAKING

What has become most satisfying for me in teaching Hakomi to groups all over the world has been seeing a group of individuals come together and become very quickly a community. It is clear to me that being together in a Hakomi way invites us out of our delusion of separateness, without the need to philosophize about it, and into an experience of feeling part of, and at home with, other human beings like ourselves. This surprising bonus of being in Hakomi training is, in my view, the most important contribution that Hakomi makes in all the places in the world where I've had the pleasure of teaching.

One year, in Japan, the organizers suggested that I offer a weekend workshop and not call it Hakomi. They had the idea that as long as people assumed the training was about learning a psychotherapy method, many people who would otherwise enjoy it might not come. So they suggested I could call it whatever I liked, thinking that the retitled program could have a wider appeal.

I knew right away that I wanted to call this workshop Peacemaking. The entire weekend consisted of typical Hakomi exercises, mostly in pairs or small groups. Never was it presented as a way to do psychotherapy, but rather as an invitation to be mindfully aware of oneself and others. The participants invariably reported being surprised at how quickly they felt safe in the group and ultimately part of a harmoniously evolving community, even at the end of day one. This experience of group safety—the possibility of sangha—has become a primary focus for teaching Hakomi as something more than just another psychotherapy method.

HAKOMI GROUPS

This method of assisted self-discovery based on mindfulness and the practice of loving presence often has a transformative effect on people. I've seen it in the many parts of the world where I've worked: the response is invariably the same. There is something wonderful about seeing beauty and inspiration, instead of looking for pathology, or what needs fixing. This way of perceiving creates a unique experience. Seeing what's right, seeing strengths and resources, along with seeing where there's a need for insight and support and comfort—it is about seeing another as a reflection of oneself and seeing the greater we beyond the I.

Daniel Siegel calls the science of this "the neurobiology of we." He talks about how the triangle of wellbeing must include relationship along with body and mind. In *The Neurobiology of "We"*

(2008), he says that wellness cannot ignore any of these three. Integration is the linkage of separate differentiated parts into a functioning whole.

Hakomi groups, supporting each other in this practice of assisted self-discovery, begin to morph from a collection of individuals into a community. The feedback we get from participants is that they've never before felt so safe so quickly in a group of strangers. From this feeling of safety, people open up to each other and share their deepest places. They listen to each other and feel the openhearted compassion that arises spontaneously when old attitudes and perspectives are not in the way. They feel the natural sense of acceptance and belonging for which we all crave. They fall in love.

This experience of group safety—the possibility of *sangha*—has become a primary focus for teaching Hakomi as something more than just another psychotherapy method. It expresses the potential for harmony, peace, and mutual respect that seems so lacking in our world today. It seems to offer hope for new ways of bringing people together in more conscious and compassionate ways of relating.

In *Tricycle* magazine, summer 2008: Thich Nhat Hanh wrote:

> Two thousand five hundred years ago, Shakyamuni Buddha proclaimed that the next Buddha will be named Maitreya, the "Buddha of Love." I think Maitreya Buddha may be a community and not just an individual. A good community is needed to help us resist the unwholesome ways of our time. Mindful living protects us and helps us go in the direction of peace. With the support of friends in the practice, peace has a chance.

Georgia Marvin is one of our senior trainers in Canada. She heads up the training sessions in Mexico and is a guest trainer in many other parts of the world. She and her husband work with individuals and couples and lead Hakomi trainings in Vancouver.

Georgia writes:

> When clients come into any therapeutic setting, whether individual sessions or group work, we are asking them, implied or overtly, to be vulnerable and that is a fear-provoking situation.

As a therapist and teacher, I must therefore understand my own fears. I have an obligation to risk being vulnerable myself; I must know what it takes to feel my fear and take a risk anyway.

THE HAKOMI WAY

I'm moving beyond seeing Hakomi as just a way of doing psychotherapy, although it is that and more. I see the method that I now call "applied mindfulness: the Hakomi Way" as something that applies to many more settings than psychotherapy, including education, parenting, support groups, personal growth, and organizational team-building.

This way of applying mindfulness is one of the most effective elements of the Hakomi method. It involves the willingness to interrupt oneself and to notice and reflect, in the moment, on one's embodied mind experience. Every reaction we have involves bodily tension, feelings, and thoughts, most of which are organized by our past experiences and the meaning we made of them.

We cannot change our reactions into more appropriate responses without attention to our bodily experience. How does our breathing change? Where are we feeling tension? What impulses arise for what actions, and which of these feel contained or blocked? How do we perceive the current situation and how does it remind us of something familiar? Is what is happening a surprise or what we expected? How do our unconscious expectations set us up for repeated experiences? What else might be possible? Can I experiment with something new and find a way to change something stressful into something that is actually nourishing?

THE MISSING EXPERIENCE

In Hakomi we talk of what we call the missing experience. The way we organize present experience is based on our past: on how we experienced situations and events, how we perceived them, how we made meaning of them, how we took them personally, and how we learned to adapt. Now, as adults, most of these adaptations are on automatic, and produce reactions to anything even remotely similar.

My friend Paul Brenner, M.D., and I have developed a way of helping people see their coping strategies in a new light and we've described it in a book called *Seeing Your Life through New Eyes* (2004). Using three questions and a triangle formation to map someone's historical narrative, we found a way to assist others to make sense of their lives, to see both the gifts and the hurt as part of how they were shaped by life to be the person they are.

We all learned to cope with hurt and unmet needs in childhood and we have made many unconscious decisions about ourselves and about relationship based on what happened in our earliest relationships, especially with our parents. In some cases, the way we learned to cope as children was perhaps the only choice we had. Now, as adults, those very coping strategies may be causing us unnecessary suffering. At the very least, they limit the possibilities of happiness and nourishing relationships.

What we mean by the missing experience in Hakomi is certainly related to our history, or at least to the way we experienced it. But what we are missing now is a result of the beliefs and habits that organize our experience. What are we missing that is actually available, if only we were able to believe in it, or believe we deserved it, or could open to the possibility of it? Our past has set us up to recreate those hurtful experiences as self-fulfilling prophecies because of how we act (react), and express ourselves.

For example, a person might tell her story over and over and never really take in the nourishment of being listened to, perhaps because she tells it in a way that causes the listener to tune out, or become distracted, or bored. Or perhaps because she never actually notices that someone is listening.

Another person might be convinced that he cannot express anger without being rejected. Perhaps he expresses it only with others who are so afraid of anger that rejection is their only response. Or perhaps he contains it and only lets it be expressed inwardly, either in acts of self-destruction, or as a kind of passive aggressiveness, which might also lead others to reject him.

What we have learned to expect from our history becomes our repeated experience—it becomes our life. Just as in the movie

Groundhog Day (Ramis 1993), we are trapped in an endless cycle of the same old experiences until we finally wake up to the possibility of something new. This waking up is the point of Hakomi, just as it is in Buddhism. Hakomi trainer and Zen priest, Flint Sparks, calls this "growing up and waking up" (www.flintsparks.org).

So the effects of Hakomi in my life have been enormous and pervasive. As a Hakomi trainer I've had the opportunity to invite people from many different cultures to share in an experience of community and harmony, along with assisting each other in a personal journey of self-discovery. I've found that there are more similarities as human beings than differences that create the illusion of separateness. I've convinced myself of the truth of the teachings of yoga: that we are all interconnected and part of a non-dual reality. I've seen the wisdom of the yoga greeting namaste, which expresses the idea that, in spirit, you and I are one.

Through both yoga and Hakomi, I've found the essence of healing to be what I call remembering wholeness. If healing is the verb of wholeness, as I like to point out, then healing can be thought of as wholeness happening. And this journey of remembering wholeness is not a solitary journey. We each hold important pieces of the mystery for those who come together for healing. We cannot do it alone.

The word Hakomi comes from the ancient Hopi language and signifies a kind of "who are you?" question, or "how do you stand in relation these many realms?" I have learned that this "in relation to" is the most important ingredient. Martin Buber (1958, p.25) said that "all real living is meeting." In Hakomi we learn to meet each other in the most authentic, natural, and loving human way possible. And this reminds each of us who we really are and where we belong, that we are all a part of the fabric of life, as Rumi reminds us in "Of being woven" (Rumi 2004). It is this possibility that lets Hakomi make a contribution to the psychological and spiritual healing of individuals, families, communities, and—in my vision—the world.

REFERENCES

Bargh, J.A. and Chartrand, T.L., 1999. "The unbearable automaticity of being." *American Psychologist, 54*, 462–479.

Brenner, P., and Martin D., 2004. *Seeing Your Life through New Eyes.* San Francisco, CA: Council Oak Books.

Chodron, P., 2009. *Getting Unstuck* [audio CD]. Louisville, CO: SoundsTrue.

Feldenkrais, M., 1981. *The Elusive Obvious.* Cupertino, CA: Meta Publications.

Goleman, D., 2006. *Social Intelligence: The New Science of Human Relationships.* New York: Random House.

Hanh, T.N., 2008. *Tricycle 17*, 4.

Hubble, M.A., Duncan B.L. and Miller S.D., 1999. *The Heart and Soul of Change: What Works in Therapy.* Washington, DC: American Psychological Association.

Kurtz, R.S., 1990. *Body-Centered Psychotherapy: The Hakomi Method: The Integrated Use of Mindfulness, Nonviolence and the Body.* Mendocino, CA: LifeRhythm.

Laszlo, E., 2007. *Science and the Akashic Field: An Integral Theory of Everything.* Rochester, VT: Inner Traditions.

Lewis, T., Amine, F. and Lennon, R., 2001. *A General Theory of Love.* New York: Vintage Books.

Mahoney M.J., 1991. *Human Change Processes: The Scientific Foundations of Psychotherapy.* New York: Basic Books.

Ramis, H. (dir.), 1993. *Groundhog Day.* Columbia Pictures.

Rumi, J., 2004. "Of being woven." In C. Barks with J. Moyne (trans.) *The Essential Rumi* (New Expanded Edition). New York: HarperCollins.

Siegel, D.J., 2007. *The Mindful Brain: Reflection and Attunement in the Cultivation of Well-Being.* Los Angeles, CA: MindYourBrain Inc.

Siegel, D.J., 2008. *The Neurobiology of "We": How Relationships, the Mind, and the Brain Interact to Shape Who We Are* [audiobook]. Louisville, CO: SoundsTrue.

CHAPTER TEN

CONTINUUM
AT THE EDGE
Amber Elizabeth Gray

THE LUNAR BREATH SAVES LIVES

Done correctly, it is barely audible. Inhaling through the nose, with
mouth closed; exhale with mouth closed. The exhale is sent with
intention through the torso cavities, like a wave. The internal sound
is the sound of ocean, of tide withdrawing. The image that was
first given to me when I learned this breath was of the moonlight
sparkling across the ocean's surface, dancing, moving. It's that
movement that is the sound. This breath honors our legacy as
creatures derived from the seas of millions of years ago.

After the January 12, 2010, Haiti earthquake, I did more
Lunar breaths than I could count. At first, I did them inaudibly—
correctly—as I sat, one by one, with over 400 people, and listened
to their stories. My work was to provide psychological first aid to as
many Haitians as possible, in groups and individually. The individual
sessions were the hardest. People shared more information, more
details. Hearts breaking, shattering, while lives unraveled in
35 seconds of hellish, violent movement and destruction.

I did the Lunar breath because Emilie Conrad, originator and mother of Continuum (and of all Continuum teachers), teaches that the Lunar breath cools the system. Reduces shock, stress, and trauma. And because, when I first met her, that's all she would allow me to do.

I called Emilie in November 1998 because a teacher in the field of somatic traumatology told me I needed to know her, and her work. I was preparing for my first trip to Haiti to launch my thesis research. The cold call surprised Emilie, and in her unflinchingly clear and direct style of communication, she said, "I don't know how I can help you. My connections to Haiti were a long time ago."

She mentioned the woman that she had started one of Haiti's most illustrious dance troupes with (Odette Weiner). The troupe, Ballet Bacalou, still danced.

I only learned this when I arrived to Port-au-Prince on New Year's Eve 1998, with my husband, and we took a taxi to the hotel that a friend of a friend, who spent her childhood in Haiti, recommended we stay at. We were staying with her friend, Odette Weiner, whose hotel was the same hotel Maya Deren, Katherine Dunham, and Emilie Conrad had spent time in, many years before.

I danced daily with Ballet Bacalou. I listened to Odette describe with glee visible in her now old and tired body, Emilie's dance, the Spider. She asked tentatively about Emilie. They had fallen out of touch almost immediately after Emilie left Haiti.

I called Emilie again, and she and Odette re-established contact. Odette has since died, Ballet Bacalou is no longer together, and Odette and Emilie were sadly unable to meet, as planned, due to Odette's declining health. But my connection to Emilie and to Continuum—a body of work she developed in the loving, suffering laboratory of her body—was born.

Emilie Conrad created Continuum because her body was too familiar with suffering. This glorious, divine movement practice arose from a body where breath was painful, and memories even more so. Her work, I believe, is revolutionary, and will be part of the future of healing and humanity. What she has birthed through endless practice and commitment is, not unlike the cosmology of Vodou that has partly inspired our work, a full body, global, way of being. Not living, not doing: being. The practice itself becomes us, and those of us who teach, or carry, this work do not simply give classes or apply it to work with private clients. We study it inside the complex and fluid laboratories of our own bodies.

When I first met Emilie in early summer of 2000 I had begun studying Continuum with a wonderful teacher, Gael Ohlgren, who was then based in Boulder, and was already captivated. I drove to Santa Fe for a week's retreat, and the first breath we began with were the "Hu"s. The "Hu"s might best be described as opposite of the Lunar—fiery, staccato, short and hot. They fuel deadened weight, density, frozen matter into movement.

Having just returned from three weeks in Kosovo, I was exhausted and depleted. The people I worked with in Kosovo were new to humanitarian work, and eager to become trauma experts. The entire time there was one long inhale, no exhale. Inhaling fear, misery, suffering, cold, death, depleted uranium, and blood. No attention to security, to our own wellness, to the details that keep individuals and groups safe in these post-conflict situations. So I ended up being that role, and it wore me down. I returned to the United States with 20 percent of my usual breathing capacity, and my husband had to drive me to the ER several times before I was able to begin working and moving again.

My first Continuum workshop with Emilie was toward the end of my healing. I loved the "Hu"s, and began to feel myself move in familiar ways—wild, ecstatic, almost spasmodic undulations. I felt myself going beyond the limits of my body (a pattern that only Continuum has helped me to begin to unwind). By the end of day one, Emilie, who watches everyone closely with the same owl-like intensity and accuracy of a mambo, came over to me and insisted I not do any more "Hu"s. "Stop doing the 'Hu's right now! Those are not helpful for you. You have way too much stress in your body; you are carrying too much heat." Then she demonstrated the Lunars, which bored me to tears, but which I dutifully did when everyone else was huing.

Now I understand. After my never-ending silent Lunars in post-earthquake Haiti, I began to make them audible. I taught them to classes, groups, and individuals I was working with. I did them loudly when the group was sharing a collective distress too immense for even the whole of our collectiveness to bear. People who had not slept since the earthquake now slept. And they found me the next day to share with and weep with in gratitude. People who were panicking at every aftershock found calm. Increased concentration. Less fear. More response time. More hope.

The Lunar breath saves lives, because it affirms life.

THE WORK: BONE (CONNECTING TO ROOT)

I will describe what Continuum is, so that you have as a reference point in your bones, the deep root place of movement and matter, to connect to while you read. Continuum is a movement practice created by Emilie Conrad. It inspires and supports vitality, fluidity, creativity, and restores our core or integral birthright movement to our bodies. Having studied and danced ethnic (and in particular, Haitian and Caribbean) dance for many years, Emilie grew deeply curious about the "intelligence" beneath the undulate or wave-like movement that is core to Haitian traditional and sacred dance. She lived in Haiti from 1955 to 1960. Her explorations of the intelligence of this movement are part of what gave birth to Continuum as a movement and healing practice. This work has been developed over a period of more than 50 years. For more depth about Continuum, read Emilie's beautiful book, *Life on Land* (2007).

What does Continuum look like? I often tell first-timers who come for private sessions that if you were to peer through a window into a Continuum class, you might see people lying, apparently still, on the floor, almost cocoon-like. You might also see people in inverted postures, on the floor, dangling from chairs, or playing off the walls, to explore some glorious movement impulse that the many different breaths and sounds we make inspire. Someone may be moving snake- or bird-like in the air, standing, or on the floor, or on all fours. The whole point of Continuum as a movement practice is to invite, encourage, and invoke movements that we know through our long histories of evolution and individual development, or that we have not yet imagined, and return these to our daily movement repertoire. This does not mean we will begin to undulate our spines in the grocery store; but we will find more fluid and resilient support for the daily movements of living we have to engage in—whether it's sitting typing at a computer, driving long hours in a car or truck, or packing and stacking boxes. The word that I often hear, after a beginners' course in Continuum is freedom. "I have found freedom in my body."

I am lying on my favorite beach in Haiti. I have just lost my job there, due to the usual contractual fickleness of the development world. My husband and I, planning on a five-year stay in Haiti, had sold our house and had only a storage unit left in Boulder. We were a mess, no jobs, no home, and no idea what was next.

I watch a young boy asleep under a palm tree. The light in Haiti is unusual—artist light. He is sleeping while light and shadow dance around him. Beautiful, yielded rest. I try to mimic his body posture, breath, state. I still feel miserable.

I get up, unable to rest or yield. I start fitfully moving around. UN troops are everywhere, and they begin to eye me strangely. My husband tries to calm me down; it doesn't work. I storm out to the parking lot where the troops are preparing tanks and helicopters to head back to Port-au-Prince. I am freaking out. Writhing, thrashing, screaming. This is my home, and I am being torn away. I feel like I am being ripped from a uterine soft lining. I had, only a few months before, begun my initiation process with one of Haiti's oldest, wisest, and most beloved mambos. I was bereft at the likely prospect of leaving to return to the United States.

A month later, I am home in Boulder with a herniated disc and in so much pain that I can't even walk uphill. I miss ManChoun, my teacher and mother in Haiti. She is already 95; her time is short. I mourn the time we are not together, when I cannot learn from her.

I stay with a dear friend who is perhaps one of the most knowledgeable healers and movers in Boulder. I am nestled in a sweet, cozy, warm room in a wonderful mountain home amidst Colorado's majestic pines. It is winter. I still cannot find the peace and solace I usually relish in this environment.

I awake from a dream on January 6, 2005. A voice has awakened me. She said, "ManChoun, Emilie, are your teachers. Call Emilie now. Go to mystery school."

I had been invited to Emilie's mystery school a year before but was unable to go. I called the studio—mystery school had begun that same day. January 6 is also a big ceremonial day at ManChoun's *Lakou Jissou* (community or gathering place). I was not at either place. I was adrift in a sea of back pain, loneliness, and directionless.

I reached Emilie a few weeks later. "I want to be a teacher."

Again, characteristically direct and clear: "A teacher? In Haiti? That's crazy. You can't be a teacher in Haiti—you can't support yourself doing this work there." For months, I felt like Emilie was fighting me. Now I know she wasn't. This was part of my initiation into the world of teaching and carrying Continuum as a body of work.

I was adrift, and she knew that. I needed to find ground, and in her words years later when I became a teacher, she needed to see that my movement style and the way in which I inhabit my body (i.e. muscle tension and effort, fluidity and range of movement, etc.) had changed. I went from overly efforted, muscular movement to visible fluid movement—the change in density that is necessary to become a teacher. I was lighter, freer, and more motile. I can initiate movement from my fluid body, which is the source of healing and connection. The big, glorious, ecstatic movements were no longer the desired outcome they once were for me. It was the ability to find stillness and fluidity in the breath- and sound-inspired micro movements and undulates of Continuum, to connect to the earth in my body, and to find groundedness from an internal reference point. No longer lost, no matter where I land or what is going on around me.

This is how I first became intimate with Continuum. While my work with survivors of war, torture, and political violence intensified, and I began to once again work more directly in complex humanitarian emergencies, Continuum remained a side practice. It was what I taught that didn't have to do with trauma. And it was what I did for self-care.

A primary premise of Continuum is that we, as beings or creatures, originated in the murky and vastly potential depths of the ocean. Continuum acknowledges our developmental trajectory, phylogenetically and ontologenetically, as originating somewhat mystically from the same space that holds the cosmos; on a more physical plane, it has roots in the origin of species born of the oceans. An important concept of this practice is bio-intelligence—which I have come to know as one of the deepest intelligences available to us. Intelligence is not only a matter of the mind; it permeates our bodies at all levels—cellular, neurological, and most important in Continuum's world, through the fluid body. Our knowing is not just a cognitive perspective, idea, analysis or belief, the aspects of knowing so often lauded in our high-speed, technology-happy modern world. We are intelligent at more primal levels, and this knowing, which may be linked to the intuition or felt sense that others have written about in this book, is a skill we have crafted and developed over our long evolutionary history. It's a skill we might celebrate more, and even cultivate toward mastery.

As an example, it has been widely stated that prior to the tsunami that devastated many coastal areas of Sri Lanka, Indonesia, India, and Thailand, animals and gypsy peoples headed for higher ground. Others, who perhaps might be described as under the influence of the more bipedal, modern, Western-influenced mind, walked curiously out toward the retreating waters—and later, they paid a tragic price.

As a practice in Continuum, we work with breath (which fires, contains, and liberates our movement), sound (frequency medicine, in a sense), and movement itself. The movement is not fixed, postured, posed, or choreographed—in essence, it is called up when the practitioner and practitioners' body become temperate or neutral, quiet and still enough to listen, by the frequency of sound and breath. Sound and breath are the invitations to respond (open attention), and we respond with the movement, below movement, below even impulse for movement. It is the deepest stirrings of our movement, of our stillness, of our bodies, and of our knowing. In Continuum, practitioners will at some point discover this truth.

Continuum forced me to slow down. I no longer returned from assignments completely burned out. When I came home from Rwanda in 1994, I was very tense. A year later, because I did not attend to this tension, I had a back spasm that grounded me for a week. Seeking help, a friend and bodyworker with extraordinary sensitivity in her hands paused our session to ask: "Rwanda is still in here. What did you bring home from that war?" I had not yet made the connection.

In 2007, I returned from an assignment in Darfur in a state of grace. I felt healthy, grounded, and clear. I was grateful for the starriest skies I have ever seen, but was moved and concerned by the horrors of that place; but I wasn't deeply distraught or scarred, despite my having been moments away from an ambush that killed the chauffeur of another NGO. I remember learning of the ambush when the Program Director interrupted a training module on resiliency practice for humanitarian workers, which I was providing for almost 50 staff of a large NGO. As I observed the group react to the news, I felt my body tense. My deep belly suddenly filled with firework-like activity, hot and staccato. Unsettling. My legs felt nauseous, and I felt their usually grounded strength ebbing into the floor. I was afraid.

The teacher's voice kept telling me not to let it show—I was in charge here. Then I remembered our conversation the day before about reaction and response, and I remembered my own teaching voice telling students "the only way to learn body-based work is to experience it in your own body." So, I shared: "Before I check in and see how you are all doing, and because I want to use this moment as both an opportunity to support you and to demonstrate critical incident support, I am going to tell you exactly what is going on in my body: my legs feel weak. I know this because they are trembling a little. I feel as if they would not be able to run if I need to right now, and that scares me. My belly is nervous and agitated: I feel like there are fireworks going off inside." For a moment, I had a thought in my head that said, "You are in Darfur. It's dangerous. You can be killed. Then you would never go home." As I shared, I breathed Lunar breaths. Tiny, inaudible ones, between phrases.

The feeling in the room shifted. There was a rustle of movement and energy, and then everyone began sharing: what was going on in their bodies. We used this time to do somatic check-ins, and in that moment, I decided to ask the group if they wanted me to add a half-day to the already three days of training, and teach them body-based, self-care skills. The yes was unanimous.

For the rest of the afternoon and evening, when I had to fall asleep in my room without opening the window for security to the starriest skies, I did Lunars. I began to write down regularly changes and effects—before and after—baseline and change. I stayed calm. I slept. It's hard to describe in words the sense of the internal feeling of Lunars, in contrast to the outer environment. Somehow, for me, they seem to melt away division. Soften the lines between the world and me. Perhaps this is somehow related to the Buddha's understanding of the relationship between separation and suffering.

THE WORK: BREATH (MERGING WHERE SPIRIT MEETS FLESH)

One of the first times I taught Continuum was in West Darfur, as part of resiliency practice training. It was the morning of the half-day added on. I taught until the moment the convoy fetched me for my flight back to Khartoum.

I introduced the Lunar breath as a calming, cooling, and relaxing breath—something helpful to do when stress levels rises. We had spent the first day thoroughly covering the causes, signs, and effects of stress, along with some standard coping skills. Here is how I taught the Lunar:

"Sit on your chair, closer to the edge than you might usually. It's best for your spine to sit yourself so that your spine is neither too taught nor rigid, nor too collapsed. Your spine supports you—so let's allow the chair to support our spines. The easiest way for me to do this is to find the bones in the bottom of my butt, and poise them close to the edge of the chair.

"Now take a few normal breaths. Notice your inhale, exhale and see if there's a little pause at the end of the breath. That's a rest. If you find that pause—that's great! You're resting!

"Now I am going to demonstrate the Lunar breath. Watch, and listen. First, here's an explanation of what I'm doing: I am inhaling through my nostrils. My mouth is closed. I am exhaling with my mouth closed too. Don't worry—even with your mouth closed—you will exhale! Your body knows how to do this.

"Listen to the sound I make on the exhale. Normally, we don't make it this loud—I am doing this so you can hear. Have you ever heard the sound of the water retreating from the shore when the tide pulls itself back? The sound of ocean surf from a distance. It can even resemble the sound of wind swirling around a house if you've never seen or heard the ocean.

"I am sending the breath of my exhale downward through all the spaces in my torso. I like to imagine ocean waves lapping up against and around my organs. I can actually feel the air rushing gently downward. That's what you're hearing."

After I demonstrated, we practiced together, and then I listened to the group practice. Sometimes I go from person to person, listening—I did not do this here for cultural reasons. It would not have been appropriate for me to stick my head so close to many of the men's faces.

We practiced a sequence of five. Usually, we do not count or choreograph how many breaths we do in Continuum—but in working with survivors of many types of extreme traumas, and especially in working in insecure, low resource, and dangerous environments, containment is absolutely necessary. Counting a specific number of breaths—and even doing them together—affords that containment, and creates a sense of control in situations where this is essential to survival and sanity.

We also worked with the basic, contemplative, Samatha Vipassana breath, a simple yoga routine I developed called centering yoga, some energizing movement activities, and some stretches to release muscular tension. We also did a fair amount of work with spinal curls or C curves, which are essentially flexion and extension of the spine. This movement in Continuum is a recapitulation of our fetal positioning and development, and in Emilie's words it is an "opportunity to erase history." I would add that this takes place without the levels of processing and sometimes dramatic re-storying that are so often considered essential in other therapeutic practices. The absence of the spoken word in Continuum makes it a non-verbal process, which distinguishes it from many somatic trauma therapies.

In the past, I relished and reveled in Continuum courses whenever I went, but didn't take Continuum with me—I created a separation between my Continuum world and my work or other life. After Darfur, I began to "sneak" Continuum into my workshops and courses worldwide. And I became much more conscious of practicing it for me—something that I had not done in my early years with the work.

On planes when trying to fall asleep against major time changes, when stressing about travel, teaching, or people's suffering, I was becoming more acquainted with Lunars, and "eee"s, which are in their simplest form, an "eee" sound. This sound lateralizes and spreads tissue, creating more space. I also began to use a lot of "o"s, which I sometimes teach to those new to Continuum or in other countries where I am uncertain as to how more "unusual" sounds will be received. An easy way to teach "o"s is to describe them like "ohms without the mmmm" which organizes and recalls overextended or wiry energy back to the core or center of the body. "O"s are powerful containment for people suffering from anxiety disorders (especially post-traumatic stress disorder) and those who are frequently stressed in a high-energy mode due to dangerous, insecure, or stressful situations.

Another application of this began to creep into my work with organizations and larger systems. About ten years ago, I began to teach more and more about secondary trauma, self-care, stress management, and similar concepts at the organizational level, (i.e. assisting organizations to develop protective and nurturing systems for their staff and employees). This arose naturally out of my work with individuals.

These workshops, called *Tending the Helper's Fire* (Brown 2000), take a systems approach to self-care—except the self is the organization, a body in its own right. Now commonly called staff support, the work at organizational level is modeled on a primary premise of Continuum: closed systems cannot change. It's only with open, fluid movement, and consciousness that any lasting change is possible.

THE WORK: BODY (INTO THE FIELD)

My perspective, strongly influenced by Continuum, is this: we are all connected, and events do not occur in a vacuum. We are bound by natural laws to acknowledge our common roots, and the interconnectivity of all things.

This perspective is reflected in my courses and workshops on organizational approaches to staff wellbeing. Taking Continuum out into the larger world necessitates that I adjust the teaching to that context. An example is the best way to clarify what this really looks like.

I have worked with management and organizational levels of staff care in Indonesia, Sudan, Haiti, Norway, and Chad. This means that the "softer" practice of taking care of people, and honoring their rhythms and needs as workers, staff, colleagues, or teammates, must meet the "harder" science of productivity, staff retention, outcomes, security, and so forth. The simplest way to apply the principles of Continuum in this context is to open up communication, as this is precisely what Continuum does on a bodily (cellular, fluid, tissue, neurological) level.

In Sudan and Indonesia, I worked with groups who were often comprised of supervisors and supervisees. There is an inherent risk in sharing information, even in the context of a workshop activity, with someone who has the power to direct, evaluate, or fire you. Aside from teaching the Lunar breath as a relaxation practice, which also helps in easing the power differential in the room, we worked on creating systems that would support managers within humanitarian aid organizations to provide feedback to staff who appeared to be suffering the consequences of long-term exposure to stress, danger, and the likelihood of life-threatening situations. As a part of the same system, managers can receive feedback from their staff. At these workshops, I ask each participant to create a plan with their team (including people they supervise and their supervisers). We then talk openly about the dangers of open communication and information-sharing without a very clear and explicitly agreed upon understanding of the limits of how this information can be used. While it may seem kind and caring to create a system wherein a manager has the right to say: "I notice you look tired this week; are you sleeping ok?" or: "How are things at home; it seems like you've been coming in late a lot more often," the challenge is that coming in late or a decrease in performance caused by tiredness can be reasons that a worker gets written up for poor performance. There are also some bosses who might use personal information against employees.

For example, what if a person is sleeping later because they are drinking more (a very common coping mechanism amongst humanitarian workers) in response to the stresses of their work? There are obvious potential negative repercussions, especially in a culture and context where drinking is against the law.

Accordingly, as part of the workshop and the establishment of self-care systems, we open communication much in the same way we prepare and open the body in Continuum. In Continuum, we work in layers—the actual sound-and-breath "menus" we create are repeated at least three, if not more times, sometimes targeting different areas of the body, as each time deeper layers of tissue are invited into the fluid system response. It's the same principle in organizational work: we begin by talking about less harmful, more simple-to-solve problems at work. By the end of the workshop, we conduct problem-solving activities for challenging, real-life problems, in teams where everyone has equal power. These activities are timed, so that no one person can dominate. Everyone is invited to participate, and a scribe documents each person's participation. Various breath or body-based methods are taught to de-escalate tensions and contentions that may arise. This changes the *field*; the synergistic, unified, and combined presence of each person present (this includes anyone/place/time they are carrying, consciously or unconsciously, into the moment and into the group). A simpler way to say this is that it is the practice of our interconnectivity, and our natural brilliant complexity, playing out in the work we are doing together.

Another application of this principle has to do with the marriage of Continuum with the ceremonial practice of Vodou as taught to me by ManChoun. In initiating me as a Sevito (servant to the spirits), she taught me facilitation skills that are present every time I conduct a three-hour Continuum "dive" evening; teaching a beginners' Continuum class; working with clients in an individual or group setting, or teaching a self-care workshop for managers.

I also teach a depth retreat I call ceremonial Continuum, which is a healing five-day course for survivors of trauma. There are two foundations to this retreat: Continuum as a practice with the potential to "erase history," through its opening of the fluid systems of communication and the release of bound, trapped energy and memory in the tissue; and the ceremonial rituals and rhythms of Haiti. In my many years of observing, dancing and facilitating ceremony in Haiti, I have found a cyclical sequence of rhythmic principles that are present in every ceremony, which I call continuurhythms:

Gestation: the invitation to birth, rebirth, life. It's the process of formulating, of energy evolving, growing, innovating, preparing for birth. It is the preparation. All ceremonies necessitate a long preparation process, sometimes days, and all tissue work demands preparation so that layering of Continuum Movement, sound and breath sequences can liberate the blockages and ensuing reductions in communication. This fosters and enhances complexity.

Invocation: the invitation to engage with spirit, mystery, the field. This is when the horizontal, human realm and the vertical, spirit realm are beginning to meet. The intersection of these two realms is a potent space—the center; where true healing occurs. In restorative processes, this is where we begin to understand our intentions—to recognize limitations or blockages in our bodies, our movement, and our minds. We are opening to change.

Salutation: spirit arrives, and we are guided. This is where we show our respect and honor for the mystery. "Owning" in our own bodies. In healing work, this is where we seek to be present to whatever arises, and to own the accompanying emotions.

Excitation: energy increasing and the ensuing opening of energetic blockages. Movement changes occur here; as we move through each layer, we find more innovation, less familiar patterns, more possibility, and more energy in each movement. We may also encounter tensions, pains, constraints, restrictions, and patterns that no longer serve us. Slowing into open attention, the response assists us to move through these.

Elation: freedom and liberation from our usual constriction and limitations whether physical, mental, emotional, or spiritual. Being "broken wide open" so that we may release, grieve, process, and let go. We may find ourselves engaged in dynamic, liberated movements—moving in brand new ways, with the curiosity and openness of a newborn.

Prostration: the deepest surrender. Rest. Being held in the arms of beloved, bowing to the mystery and to the unknown. Paying our deepest respects to spirit, the mystery, and the field.

Gestation: Dying into rebirth. The cycle continues.

In the retreat, we work with each of these rhythms or energies of the ceremonial and healing process through a menu of breath, sound, and movement sequences similar to those described earlier. Depending on the intention and composition of the group, each rhythm is explored and moved by a "menu" that is created for this particular retreat, much as Mambo facilitates a ceremony based on the interplay of ancient structure and current spontaneity (i.e. what's showing up in the present moment). These rhythms are not named in the actual practice of Vodou; they are observations of the principles that are enacted in the subtly to wildly ascending and descending, escalating and de-escalating, crescendo and decrescendo rhythms of ceremony, which are the rhythms of interconnectivity; birth, life, and death.

In a sense, this application of Continuum might be a coming home of a powerful and innovative work that has some of its roots in Haiti's ancient traditions. These rhythms, I believe, are the rhythms of life, which we are all a part of, and which comprise our organismic and collective complexity. A shamanistic principle—that to know something we must become it—is core to this work, whether it's applied in our own bodies, in workshops, in airplanes, in disaster zones, or in war zones. Emilie Conrad discovered this because she recognized the integrity of the fluid body in the definition of our true nature, in our capacity to process information and act responsively and creatively to life's most challenging situations, and to the restorative or healing process. Fluid movement is coherent and therefore rhythmic. It connects our internal landscape like waterways and oceans connect the earth, and like water as an element connects us to the sky and to further galaxies. Water resonates with all of time, space, history, and our collective journeying and story.

This is what the ancients have always known and perhaps science will one day prove. Emilie, who bore this work because her body gave her no choice, and, I believe, because she recognized the essence of fluid movement as it has always existed in her encounters with the ancient principles of healing in Haiti, has accomplished something few ever do: the ongoing innovation and modernization of ancient wisdom. Emile continues to teach the evolution of her discovery in response to the unique challenges of these times.

As I write, there are three fires burning around my hometown of Santa Fe. The air is unclean—it's painful to breathe. The dryness penetrates at bone level and the heat is stifling. My evening "dives" are filling more than usual with people coming to reconnect and rediscover their watery natures—to imagine cool, refreshing, rejuvenating water. It's essential for us here, as it is for us everywhere. The angry wars and the fires of injustice that have fuelled the recent revolutions that have occurred throughout the Middle East, the vast changes in the earths relationship to us—shifts in earth, water, fire, air—tornadoes, tsunamis, earthquakes, droughts, floods—we have no choice but to reconnect internally and to one another, and to earth, and to the wisdom of our history. Our survival and "thrival" depend on our capacity to adjust with responsiveness and insight, not reactivity and fear, to these vast changes. Our world is increasingly complex, and the problems we face as a collective are increasingly complex. Continuum serves the natural complexity of our human species by teaching us to cultivate the awareness, rhythm, slower pace, thoughtfulness, mindfulness, and soulfulness, the spontaneous awakenings that will support more meaningful insights into our world's solutions.

REFERENCES

Brown, K., 2000. Tending the helper's fire: a body-centered approach to the prevention and amelioration of vicarious traumatization in caregivers. Unpublished thesis. Boulder, CO: Naropa University.

Conrad, E., 2007. *Life on Land: The Story of Continuum, the World-Renowned Self Discovery and Movement Method*. Berkeley, CA: North Atlantic Books.

THE CONTRIBUTORS

Charles Eigen is a psychotherapist and bodywork/movement practitioner based in Milwaukee, Wisconsin. He has trained in a variety of approaches to psychotherapy, bodywork, and meditation. He is a Certified Therapist in Internal Family Systems Therapy, Certified Advanced Rolfer® and Rolf Movement® Teacher, and a Certified Workshop Leader for the Progoff *Intensive Journal*® Method. He leads groups in therapy and personal growth, and works with individuals in person and by phone and Skype. He can be reached at charleseigen@gmail.com.

Joe Goodbread, Ph.D. practices and teaches process work in Portland, Oregon and throughout the world. He is a founder of the Process Work Institute in Portland, where he has served as president and as a member of the board of directors. His latest book, *Befriending Conflict: How to Make Conflict Safer, More Productive and More Fun*, is a guide to using inner work to prepare for conflict, and to processing the disturbing states of consciousness that often stand in our way in difficult interpersonal interactions. He has also published three other books and many articles. He is currently researching the connections among extreme states of consciousness, interpersonal conflict, and social issues. joe@befriendingconflict.com.

Amber Elizabeth Gray is a longtime practitioner of body-centered arts and sciences, a licensed mental health professional, and an advocate of human rights. She is an authorized Continuum Movement teacher and an award-winning dance-movement therapist. She is also a Sevito in the Fran Ginee tradition of Vodou. Amber has worked for many years with survivors of human-rights abuses, war, natural disaster, and humanitarian response teams. Amber's teaching combines Continuum Movement, dance-movement therapy, somatic psychology, current trauma, and neuropsychological research, life impressions bodywork, ritual, and creative arts.

She is director of Restorative Resources Training and Consulting, and is the refugee mental health coordinator for New Mexico. She is a frequent speaker on body-based and creative arts therapies with survivors of war, violence and torture, and she has been adjunct faculty at Naropa University, Southwestern College and New York University's trauma studies program. She is a board member of the American Dance Therapy Association. She teaches Continuum Movement regularly in her home base of Santa Fe, New Mexico, as well as for Continuum Australia.

For more information on Amber's work in Santa Fe, Australia and globally: www.restorativeresources.net; restorativeresources@ gmail.com; +1-505-603-7021. For more information about Continuum Movement: www.continuummovement.org.

Susan Gregory is a gestalt therapist in private practice in New York City. She also teaches singing and the Gindler approach to breath and bodywork. A former president of the New York Institute for Gestalt Therapy, Susan teaches therapists around the world. Her professional articles have been published in national and international peer-reviewed journals. Before becoming a therapist, Susan was a professional singer, which included a stint as principal artist with the New York City Opera. www.GestaltSing.com.

Harvey Honig, Ph.D. Originally a Lutheran minister, Honig was introduced to Carl Jung's work at the Oberlin School of Theology in 1963. He was one of the four original trainees in June Singer's analyst training program, and in 1979 he completed his Ph.D. in clinical psychology at Loyola University and received his Jungian diplomate. He has a private practice in Madison, Wisconsin, where he also works with therapists of other disciplines and orientations, and as a staff member of several clinics. He recently received a lifetime achievement award from the Chicago Society of Jungian

Analysts. harvey.honig@gmail.com, www.psychmadison.com, and www.jungchicago.org.

Joan Klagsbrun, Ph.D. is a licensed psychologist in private practice who works with adults and couples. She is also an adjunct graduate faculty member of Lesley University's Department of Counseling Psychology. She met Eugene Gendlin in 1976 and was immediately taken with Focusing, both as a philosophy and a mind/body practice. She has gone on to teach Focusing internationally to psychotherapists, counselors, physicians, nurses, clergy, coaches, and graduate students at Lesley. For the past decade, she has trained Focusing-oriented psychotherapy as both a method for working with clients, and a process of self-care and supervision. She was recently a principal investigator in a study (Klagsbrun, Lennox and Summers 2010) on how Focusing affects mood and resilience in women with breast cancer. She has published several journal articles and a CD, and is featured in two DVDs on Focusing and Focusing-oriented psychotherapy. She was a founding board member of the Focusing Institute. joanklag@mac.com. More information about Focusing at www.Focusing.org and www.focusingnewengland.com.

Donna Martin is a therapist and international trainer in Ron Kurtz's Hakomi method of assisted self-discovery, which is now known as applied mindfulness: the Hakomi way. From 1990 until Kurtz's passing in 2011, she worked closely with him, and shortly before his death, Kurtz named Donna and six others as his key legacy holders. Donna has taught Hakomi in the United States, Canada, Japan, England, Ireland, Mexico, and South America. Her books include *Remembering Wholeness; Seeing Your Life Through New Eyes* (with Paul Brenner, M.D.); and *Simply Being* (with Marlena Field). She has taught yoga, meditation, and stress management since 1970. www.hakomi.ca and www.donnamartin.net.

Susan McConnell, M.A., C.H.T. is a senior trainer for the Center for Self Leadership and a teacher of Internal Family Systems Therapy in the United States and Europe. Her involvement with the center since 1995 includes developing the training curricula, training IFS training staff, and designing and leading somatic psychotherapy retreats and seminars. In her private practice in Chicago, Susan specializes in recovering the wholeness of body, mind, and spirit, drawing from her bodywork and movement experience and her Buddhist practice. susanmccon@gmail.com and www. embodiedself.net. Information about IFS at www.selfleadership.org.

Richard Schaub, Ph.D. is a licensed psychotherapist and co-director of the New York Psychosynthesis Institute and the Huntington Meditation and Imagery Center. He has trained hundreds of professionals internationally in the clinical applications of meditation, imagery, and transpersonal psychology. His work has been featured in Oprah's *O Magazine*, and he is the co-author of three books on psychospiritual development: *The End of Fear: A Spiritual Path for Realists*; *Dante's Path: A Practical Approach to Achieving Inner Wisdom*; and, *Healing Addictions: The Vulnerability Model of Recovery*. www.huntingtonmeditation.com and www.huntingtonmeditation. com.

Judith Tamar Stone, M.A., C.H.T. is the founder of Voice Dialogue Connection. She is an internationally renowned psychotherapist, consultant, and senior Voice Dialogue facilitator, and the creator of the Body Dialogue Process. She offers a variety of Voice Dialogue experiences for individuals and professionals, and she is the author of the *Body Walk Meditation* CD; *Selves in a Box*, an interactive therapeutic card deck; and the book *The Body: A Path to Presence*. She lives in Boulder, Colorado. www.voicedialogueconnection.com and jtamar@voicedialogueconnection.com.

Carolyn Kelley Williams is a Certified Journal Consultant for the Progoff *Intensive Journal* program. She regularly presents *Intensive Journal* workshops throughout much of the United States. For more than three decades, she was the managing editor of three international scientific publications. She is also a novelist, published poet and stained glass artist. carolynkelleywilliams@comcast. net. Information about the *Intensive Journal* programs at www. intensivejournal.org.

SUBJECT INDEX

AUTHOR INDEX